State Punishment

International Library of Philosophy

Edited by Tim Crane and Jonathan Wolff,
University College London

The history of the International Library of Philosophy can be traced back to the 1920s, when C.K. Ogden launched the series with G.E. Moore's *Philosophical Papers* and soon after published Ludwig Wittgenstein's *Tractatus Logico-Philosophicus*. Since its auspicious start, it has published the finest work in philosophy under the successive editorships of A.J. Ayer, Bernard Williams and Ted Honderich. Now jointly edited by Tim Crane and Jonathan Wolff, the I.L.P. will continue to publish work at the forefront of philosophical research.

State Punishment

Political Principles and Community Values

Nicola Lacey

Fellow and Tutor in Law
New College, Oxford

London and New York

First published 1988
in the International Library of Philosophy
under the editorship of Ted Honderich
by Routledge
11 New Fetter Lane, London EC4P 4EE
29 West 35th Street, New York, NY 10001

Paperback edition published 1994
in the International Library of Philosophy
under the editorship of Tim Crane and Jonathan Wolff

Typeset in Times by Columns of Reading

Printed and bound in Great Britain by
T.J. Press (Padstow) Ltd, Padstow, Cornwall

British Library Cataloguing in Publication Data
A catalogue record for this book is available from the
British Library.

Library of Congress Cataloging in Publication Data
A catalogue record for this book has been requested.

ISBN 0–415–10938–8

for my mother
with thanks for many years of
encouragement and support

CONTENTS

PREFACE

This is a book about the justification of state punishment. Any writer starting out on this task must feel some need to explain to her readers why she has the presumption to inflict on the unsuspecting world yet another book on a subject to which so many books and articles, let alone years of academic effort, have already been devoted. The obvious justification – that of exciting new ideas – seems excluded by the feeling (which I have certainly had at many points in the research) that just about everything short of the totally ludicrous (and occasionally including it) has already been said about what does or might justify the infliction of punitive sanctions on offenders. In terms of goals, aims and reasons, it is genuinely hard to say anything which is new. Rather, what I hope to provide in this book is a different way of looking at the problem of punishment and a fresh approach to the methodology of theorising about that issue, which in turn leads to a recasting of the traditional arguments in a new light.

The book defends two main general arguments. The first is that the problem of punishment can only satisfactorily be addressed within the context of an integrated political philosophy: in other words, that the best possible arguments for punishment can only be developed and defended through an examination of other major questions of political philosophy, and that punishment cannot be treated as a discrete, isolated political and moral problem. This basic thesis has, of course, made the book hard to write, because its logic entails the need for a general treatise on political philosophy as part of the enterprise of considering whether and on what basis punishment can be justified. The compromise has been to select the major questions of political philosophy which I judge to be most intimately related to the question of punishment and to try to draw out their implications for that issue.

The second major argument has to do with some of the often unexamined political and philosophical assumptions underlying the traditional theories of punishment. It is my contention that some of the most pervasive and intractable problems encountered by apparently very different theorists of punishment in the twentieth century have to do with their arguments being set within a particular type of liberal framework. I have tried to expose the basis of this framework and the political principles from which it proceeds, to criticise these assumptions and principles, and to develop a somewhat different set of arguments for punishment based on a different set of political principles. Thus through an examination of the traditional theories of punishment, some related questions of political philosophy, and the underlying assumptions of much contemporary theorising, I have worked towards an argument for punishment which incorporates many of the traditional elements in a pluralistic account, and which proceeds explicitly from a background communitarian political theory. In this gradual progression, I hope to have produced a book which is accessible and comprehensible to students confronting the issues for the first time, yet which holds at least something of interest for those already familiar with the debate.

Throughout the text, except where the context renders it unsuitable, the words 'she', 'her' and 'hers' appear rather than the more usual 'he', 'him' and 'his'; they should be read as referring to both genders. Happily, feminist scholarship is beginning to break the silence and to end the invisibility of women in political theory. This book cannot claim to count as a piece of feminist work, but by means of this simple device it can at least avoid contributing to the invidious and still predominant impression given by books on political philosophy that the world which claims its attention is inhabited solely by men. When most male writers have adopted the practice of alternating between pronouns of different genders, or avoiding 'she' and 'he' altogether, I shall be happy to do the same.

In writing this book, I have incurred more debts of gratitude than I can reasonably acknowledge here, but I should like to offer special thanks to several people who have helped and supported me with exceptional generosity. First and foremost, my thanks are due to Ted Honderich, who encouraged me to write the book, discussed it with me at several stages and gave me detailed and constructive comments on a draft. I am also enormously grateful to Hugh Collins, Joseph Raz and Mary Stokes, who read the final draft, and to Andrew Ashworth, Antony Duff, Liz Frazer, Michael Freeman, John Gardner, Hyman Gross, Dawn Oliver, Jeremy Waldron and Celia Wells, who commented on particular chapters. The comments and criticisms of these friends and colleagues helped make this a much better book than it would otherwise have been. I also benefited from the views of participants at various meetings and seminars over the last few years, to whom I have given papers which represented earlier drafts of several chapters: these include seminars at the Universities of Warwick and Glasgow, University College London, and the Oxford Centre for Criminological Research; the Society of Public Teachers of Law conference, 1986; and a meeting of the All Souls moral philosophy discussion group. James Griffin, Roger Hood and William Twining all helped in tracing references. I have learnt a great deal from the students whom I have been lucky enough to teach both at Oxford and at University College London. My very warm thanks are due to all of these people. I have also been fortunate, as are all writers in this area, to have had the stimulus and insight provided by the work of Professor H.L.A. Hart, whose ideas have influenced the development of every part of this book.

Last, but by no means least, I want to thank David Soskice, with whom I have had useful discussions of many of the ideas in the book, and who undertook with generous cheerfulness the difficult task of living with me while I was writing it. It remains only to offer it to the reader, along with all its flaws for which I alone am responsible, and with the somewhat diffident attitude which seems appropriate to any mere lawyer who has the temerity to stray onto philosophical terrain.

NICOLA LACEY
OXFORD, 1987

CHAPTER 1

PRELIMINARIES

INTRODUCTION

The many problems raised by the issue of punishment, and especially that of state punishment, have concerned and puzzled generations of philosophers, lawyers, politicians and others. Yet today, even in the face of the existence of extensive and ever-stronger institutions of punishment in almost every state, we are seemingly as far from any consensus about the fundamental question of what justifies the continued existence of those institutions as we have ever been.[1] Indeed, the only question on which anything approaching a consensus exists is that of the impossibility, impracticality or undesirability of abolishing these institutions about whose underlying rationale we are so unclear. And even this consensus is illusory, for there are as many different views about the reasons why the abolition of punishment would be difficult, dangerous or simply wrong as there are views about what justifies it in the first place.

This book addresses the questions of moral and political philosophy raised by the issue of state punishment. In what circumstances may and should the state exercise its powers over individuals or groups in the name of punishment, and how much power is the state justified in using? But it is important to realise that punishment raises a wide variety of questions, ranging over many disciplines. And although the issue of justifying the place of punishment within a society is fundamental, that question cannot be finally determined, especially if a consequentialist or consequence-sensitive view of justification is adopted,[2] without the learning and understanding provided by those other disciplines. Questions and answers thrown up by areas of study such as law, economics, psychiatric medicine, criminology, psychology and social theory constantly bear upon questions which have to be tackled in the enterprise of justification; insensitivity to these connected areas is bound to render our justifying arguments at best, incomplete; at worst, totally inadequate.

Two brief examples should suffice to make the point. First, take the familiar theory which asserts that punishment is justified by its economical deterrence of crime,[3] confronted by empirical data supplied by the social sciences, which strongly suggests (perhaps 'proves' is too strong a word) that punishment has no significant general deterrent effect. Such data, whilst it does not affect the integrity of the theory, has radical implications for the amount of punishment which the theory could justify. Secondly, consider the brute question of the economic costs of punishment, bearing in mind the point that our justification of punishment will be but one part of an integrated political philosophy. These costs are likely to be high, since commodities such as due process and humane and secure conditions of incarceration are extremely expensive. And they will have to be balanced with and possibly traded off against the costs of pursuing other values within the political system – health services and education, for example – before the question of what the justifying argument actually justifies in a particular society can be finally resolved. These and many other possible examples show that the enterprise is more complex than it at first appears. For if, as I assume, the object of theoretical reflection is not only to increase understanding but also, ultimately, to inform political change, we must constantly bear in mind the implications of the theoretical arguments when applied in the real world.

State punishment is not only an issue which concerns a wide variety of disciplines, it is also one which <u>directly concerns every</u> <u>member of society: we are all potential subjects of punishment,</u> and many are in addition potential or actual actors in the institution of punishment, as lawyers, probation officers, warders, prison visitors and police officers among many other roles. Furthermore, punishment is not only the ultimate threat which enforces the criminal law, it is also indirectly concerned in supporting almost every aspect of legal regulation. Taxation and compulsory education, for example, are ultimately backed up by sanctions, although they are not in the first instance examples of penal law. Civil law is finally backed by the sanction of punishment for contempt of court: and indeed <u>the whole</u> <u>existence of the legal system seems to be, in practice, if not in</u> <u>theory, inextricably bound up with the existence of sanctions of</u> one kind or another. Thus it is impossible to consider the question of the justification of punishment in isolation from questions about the justification for the existence of the legal system as a whole: a fact which complicates our question yet further.

[handwritten margin note: punishment and the legal system are so linked that you cannot talk about one without mentioning the other.]

Finally, our attitude to state punishment is likely to be influenced by the existence of analagous practices both in the state and the non-state spheres. Of the latter, although the most obvious examples are those of the teacher or parent punishing a disobedient child, formal and informal practices of punishment are possible within the context of any relationship in which there exists a disparity of power or an acknowledgment of authority, even if that power or authority exists only in certain circumstances or for certain purposes.[4] Both the complexity of the question of state punishment and its added dimension prevent me from dealing directly with non-state punishment: but it is nonetheless vital to keep in mind in exploring our principal question both the analogous practices and the reactive attitudes which support them, as well as the important differences which exist, notably in terms of the way in which the relationship between punisher and punished affects the rationale of the punishment itself.

Conversely, it is also important to notice some analogies between punishment as a form of state action and certain other forms of coercive state intervention in human lives, for example, the practices of quarantine and the compulsory civil preventive detention of mentaly ill people.[5] These analogies are sometimes used in arguments justifying certain practices of punishment, and they will have to be kept in mind in the course of what follows. But what it is of interest to note at this stage is merely the point that even these analogous practices are themselves backed up by sanctions, by the threat of compulsion in the event of disobedience; the threat of coercion is pervasive in any legal context. Yet punishment itself is not only the threat and the sanction which backs up the law, it is also itself a product of law and enforced by law. No wonder, then, that the notion of sanction is definitional in many influential descriptive legal theories.[6] The arguments about the analytic connection of law and sanction will have to be carefully examined at an early stage, in order to determine just what it is which we have to justify; if there is a logical connection, a conclusive justification for law itself will also mean justifying punishment. We shall also have to examine the nature of political obligation; if citizens have no moral obligation to obey the law, the task of producing a moral justification for punishment seems likely to be more complex than if such an obligation exists. Thus a number of interrelated theoretical questions have to be answered if we are to provide a full set of arguments for punishment.

DEFINING PUNISHMENT

It is generally assumed that a necessary preliminary to producing a justification of punishment is the development of a concise definition of state punishment, as a starting point. Why do we need to start with a definition: what is its function? Certainly, it can promote clarity, particularly in the early stages of the argument, and it helps to be sure about just what it is which we are exploring justificatory arguments about: exactly what is being referred to each of the countless times the word 'punishment' appears. Furthermore, in considering the arguments of other writers, we have to be alive to the possibility that some of their differences are to be explained by the fact that their starting points differ: that they are not talking about the justification of the same practices. Nevertheless, the enterprise of definition is fraught with conceptual and methodological problems which go to the very heart of theorising about punishment. We have to tread an uneasy path between two dangerous extremes. On the one hand, if our initial definition is too narrow or specific, we shall have built in assumptions which ought to be argued for openly. If we begin thus by begging important questions, any justification we ultimately come up with will be subject to grave objections. What is more, we may have failed to consider the possibility of justifying a somewhat different set of practices because of the blinkers imposed by our definition. It is all too easy to allow definition to serve a covert normative function, to represent just those practices which we want to justify. To the extent that we do so, we risk treating the justifiability of the described practices as a fixed intuition, not subject to substantial modification in a process of reflective equilibrium.[7] In this way we either render the task of justification unnecessarily difficult, or else the values behind our allegiance to those specific practices identified by the definition will not be revealed or tested, and our whole enterprise will be more akin to a testing of political or moral principles against the measuring rod of the described practices than to the converse, which it purports to be. This may seem an extreme characterisation of the situation, but it is, I believe, an accurate picture of some theories of punishment which start out from a relatively precise definition which is not modified in the course of the argument.[8]

At the other extreme, if we start out from a widely inclusive definition, or even forego any definition at all, it is not clear what place we leave for theorising specifically about punishment. If we start, as I do, from the position that the theory of punishment is but one part of a general political philosophy, how are we to avoid writing a lengthy treatise on the justification of the state and its interventions in human life through all exercises of its considerable power? We may acknowledge that the proper methodology would be to start from general political principles and work 'downwards' to a theory of punishment, asking ourselves what consequences in terms of law-enforcement and official response to disobedience to the law a particular theory of the state would have. But the method will have to be somewhat modified, not only for reasons of space and time, but also because there are particular facts, difficulties and arguments which have a special bearing on the question of punishment. Moreover, within actual and conceivable punitive institutions, namely criminal justice systems, actions and decisions are made within the framework of special sets of guiding rules and principles, and are thus to some extent (just how far will be an important question for us to consider) insulated from the general flow of practical moral reasoning in a society. At the fundamental level of generality, we may fuse all our normative questions about state action into one; but at levels of greater specificity we must not lose the extra dimension of particular issues such as punishment. It is their relatively distinctive nature which makes it worthwhile to consider in some degree of isolation all the questions which political philosophers have traditionally so considered (for example, curbs on freedom of expression, prohibitions of racial discrimination and so on). So, our definition must tread a middle path which neither precludes significant arguments nor destroys the very point of the enterprise from the start. In other words, we must not confuse the enterprise of producing a definition with that of developing a theory: the definition must act as a starting point which describes the practices which will be not only argued for and against, but also their extent and nature argued *about*. It precedes and sets relatively flexible terms of reference for the substantive argument.[9]

Two other preliminary points must also be mentioned. First, there is the question of how far we should or can be guided by usage in producing our definition. Since the aim of the enterprise is to clarify and influence the thinking of people who already have their own ideas about both what punishment is and what justifies its use, it is clearly desirable to conform a definition to that which a possible audience has already adopted as closely as possible. However, this will not be conclusive if those preconceived ideas violate one of the requirements of compromise outlined above, and it will not be possible where the audience I am appealing to in fact vary in the definitions of punishment which they have adopted, the conceptions of that practice which they hold. The widespread and well known disagreement as to whether punishment of the innocent is a moral or merely a logical impropriety should be a sufficient pointer to the limitations of usage as a guide to definition.[10]

However, and secondly, the difficulties inherent in the enterprise of definition can be mitigated if we bear in mind some important arguments developed in the context of legal theory by H.L.A. Hart.[11] In the first place, we must recognise that language is inherently 'open-textured': most words have both a core of settled meaning, and a penumbra of non-focal meaning over which there will be disagreement. This is certainly true of punishment, and it would be naive to expect even a detailed definition (comprised itself of open-textured language) to conclude all questions about the meaning of the word. Secondly, it may be useful to employ what has come to be known as a 'central case technique'. This recognises that the features chosen as definitional are those which are most significant from the point of view of the theorist, and that what they identify are the 'central' or paradigm instances of punishment. The criteria of importance or significance will have to do with the nature of the theoretical inquiry and the theorist's appreciation of the understanding of the concept shared by people in a particular society or type of society. The technique emphasises that there may be 'deviant' or 'non-central' cases which share some of the features of the central case and which need at some stages to be included within the ambit of our theoretical inquiry.[12] Thus the technique allows us to identify the deviant cases by reference to the central ones, and to recognise them as penumbral cases of the same phenomenon. On this view, for example, deliberate or mistaken punishment of an innocent person might properly be called punishment, since it shows sufficient of the central features of the general practice: but we may nevertheless regard it as a deviant case and go on to argue further about whether and in what circumstances it may be justified.

At the most basic level, what all this adds up to is the need for a definition which does not obviously favour one of the familiar 'theories of punishment'; neither a retributive, backward-looking, nor a utilitarian (in the widest sense of the term), forward-looking justification of punishment. Let us begin with the definition most widely adopted by writers on the subject, which could be put thus:

> Punishment is the state's imposition of unpleasant consequences on an offender for her offence.

Does this formulation meet the criteria we have set out? In several respects it falls short of them. First of all, there is the question, raised in Quinton's well-known article,[13] of whether this traditional definition of punishment is inherently retributive; the words 'for an offence' seem either to imply some retributive, backward-looking intent or to be redundant. On the other hand, it could be said that even Honderich's revision,[14] prompted by this point, which omits the words 'for an offence', does not entirely escape a weakened version of the same point: the very idea that punishment is of offenders seems to draw on a retributive notion, whilst causing problems for utilitarian theories which do not embody that limitation as a matter of principle. Here we reach the kernel of insight in Quinton's argument, which is the inescapable fact that our notion of punishment, even undefined, already contains a backward-looking or responsive element.

Secondly, there are certain ambiguities in the definition which will need either defence or clarification before we can accept the formulation. Is an offender to be regarded as someone who has breached moral rules, legal rules, or both? If we are talking of legal infractions, must they be committed deliberately or at least recklessly, and by the agent herself, or are cases of negligence, strict (no-fault) or vicarious liability properly classified as 'offences'? Similarly, if the words 'for an offence' are to be maintained in the formulation, some account of their place must be given which does not concede the argument to the retributivists before the debate has begun. Finally, are 'unpleasant consequences' to be defined by reference to the preferences of the particular offender, the average or reasonable person, or what? Let us begin our own deliberations with a much wider formulation, in the context of which we can examine and revise each component in turn:

legal punishment is
1 the principled infliction by a state-constituted institution,
2 of what are generally regarded as unpleasant consequences,

3 on individuals or groups publicly adjudicated to have
 breached the law,
4 as a response to that breach of the law, or with the motive of
 enforcing the law, and not intended solely as a means of
 compensation.

The first part of the definition underlines the fact that we are
concerned primarily with regular practices, institutions of punishment, as opposed to ad hoc exercises of state power in a
particular context. Institutions or practices, in this sense, are
simply activities regularly governed by rules or customs, ema-
nating from an authority or, in some cases, from a set of ranked
authorities or some non-state body to which the state has
delegated some of its power for certain purposes. Later, we shall
have to take up the vexed question of the relationship between
the justification of the institution of punishment and that of
particular inflictions of punishment. But for the purposes of the
definition, it is important to stress the existence of the institution
as the context in which individual decisions to punish are made.
This part of the definition also makes it clear that we are
concerned principally with punishment inflicted by the state.

The second part of the definition is not ambiguous as between
what might be called the objective and subjective views of
unpleasant consequences. On this view, it would not count as
punishment to make an ardent egalitarian a hereditary peer (let
us assume that it was not possible to divest oneself of such a
smear) in circumstances in which many people would regard this
as an honour rather than a degradation. Nor would it be a
paradigm case of punishment (although it might well be a
sensible course of action in a different context of argument) to
give a poor offender (however much she objected on grounds of
its likelihood of ruining her life, as some 'pools' winners have
claimed) a large fortune, although, as we have seen, such non-
focal cases do not have to be totally excluded from our
consideration because of our adoption of the central case
technique, which allows us to identify them as penumbral cases of
punishment because some significant characteristics of punishment
are present. The idea often appealed to on this 'objective' conception of unpleasant consequences is that of the reasonable person –
familiar enough to all lawyers and probably not unfamiliar even
to non-legal passengers on the Clapham omnibus – which enshrines a judgment about social norms. In this particular context,
however, its implications are probably not very different from
alternative standards based on what the average person, or most

people, would consider unpleasant. Although this does constrain what can count as punishment, it is probably not as restrictive as it may at first appear, for it would cover a combination of pleasant and unpleasant consequences (for example, education and training in the course of incarceration) so long as the unpleasant feature was an integral part, and so long as the total package would nevertheless be regarded as unpleasant or undesirable – something to be avoided – by the reasonable or average woman or man. Of course, there will be many states of affairs on which there exists insufficient agreement to support a judgment of unpleasantness on this conception; but it seems unlikely that in a society not unlike our own there would not be consensus on a sufficient range of consequences as unpleasant to generate an adequate number of punitive measures. The normative and practical arguments for such a restriction are clear enough (imagine the widespread jealousy and sense of unfairness which peerage for bank robbers would promote), but within the scope of the definition the main arguments for it are firstly that it accords with the conceptions of the vast majority of experts and lay people alike – it has usage on its side; and secondly, since the infliction of such consequences will be harder to justify than the infliction of consequences generally regarded as pleasant, we can at least be satisfied that we are not making the task of justification illicitly easy. Of course, the definition *is* neutral as to whether the *particular* offender in any case would regard the consequences as unpleasant: it would be quite within the definition (although probably rather useless) to punish an ardent egalitarian peer by divesting her of her burdensome peerage, despite the fact that she might be very glad of such a sanction.

The third part of the definition makes no assumptions about whether the individuals or groups in question have broken the law voluntarily, intentionally, recklessly, or otherwise; these questions, and also those about the proper methods of adjudi-cation of guilt and sentence, would be left up to the content of the substantive law – although naturally I shall have something to say about some of these particular questions of justification later on. Similarly, the issue of vicarious liability remains open to consideration in the substantive context; it would seem to violate the requirements of compromise outlined above to marginalise such practices at the definitional stage. But the most striking feature of this third part as it stands is that it leaves open the possibility of counting punishment of the innocent, not just in the sense of the unintentional offender, but also the wrong person – someone who was in no way involved in producing the 'actus reus' of the offence,[15] whether by mistake or design, as a central case of punishment. What are the arguments for and against this at the definitional stage? The arguments from usage are not conclusive: we *do* talk of 'punishment of the innocent', but we certainly think of it as a marginal or atypical case. In cases of mistaken decisions, when they occasionally come to light, we are perhaps more inclined to label them simply 'mistakes', rather than mistaken punishment. With reference to our earlier argument, the definition as it stands has the advantage of begging no questions and making no prior assumptions about these issues, but possibly at the risk of blunting our perception of the distinctive features of the special issue which is our primary concern. Bearing in mind our discussion of the central case technique, and particularly the important point that non-focal cases are not necessarily those which cannot be justified (they may call for different justifying arguments, just as it may turn out that some central cases of punishment simply cannot be justified, at least in particular circumstances) we must ask ourselves whether these cases are sufficiently different from cases of unpleasant treatment following correct adjudication to be removed from the ambit of the definition which seeks to elucidate the features central to the phenomenon we are concerned with. After some hesitation, and recognising that this in no way closes (or even begins) the argument about the justification of these practices, I choose to rework the definition to exclude them from its ambit. Thus it should now read:

> on individuals or groups publicly (i.e. according to publicly recognised standards) and correctly (i.e. without error or deliberate deviation from the principles and facts as known to the adjudicator) judged to have breached the law.[16]

The final part of the definition tries to be neutral as between retributive and utilitarian implication: it is an attempt to replace the words 'for an offence', capturing what is acceptably neutral in them, and what is at the core of our views about the nature of punishment as a practice. It is not just that we happen to punish only offenders. The punishment is intimately connected with the occurence of the offence: it is a response which could be said to be made with the aim of 'enforcing the law'. I believe that this is part of our conception of punishment, and that this formulation constitutes an acceptable starting point from which to assess the merits of both forward- and backward-looking theories of punishment. As such, it is vulnerable to attack from both sides:

the retributivist will object that the ideas of enforcement and response are inherently consequence-oriented: the utilitarian will say that the ideas of response and enforcement smack of retribution. This seems to me to be a strength rather than a weakness, for the ambiguity flows from the fact that the definition captures the essence of both a 'core of desert'[17] and the relevance of consequences, thus suggesting that both main traditions in the justification of punishment have, as one would expect, their own particular illuminating potential.

Finally, the definition emphasises that although there may well be some overlap between the practices of punishment and compensation in practice, the two are conceptually distinct; the functions and concerns of punishment are peculiar to it, as are those of compensation. Full compensation will be defined as the provision to the victim (collective or individual) of a harm of some material or other good with the principal aim of attempting to negate the effect of the harm by putting the victim in the position in which they would have been had the harm not occurred, or in a position which is not materially different from that position. Partial compensation would be the provision of some good with the aim of bringing the victim some of the way towards full reparation. In the many cases in which total equivalence is impossible (such as where some personal injury or affront is in question), compensation may take on a symbolic form, and the distinction between full and partial compensation becomes blurred. Thus whilst many actual punishments may incidentally compensate the victim of the offence (as in the case of restitution orders) or indeed society as a whole seen as a collective victim of the offence (as in the case of community service orders), a 'punishment' inflicted with that sole aim would not count as a central case of punishment. In so far as the definition makes any positive gesture towards explicating this distinction, it does so in terms of the notion of 'enforcement' – but, once again, this seems to me to be too complex an issue to be susceptible of disposal at the definitional stage. The question of the distinction between civil and criminal law will have to be addressed in a later chapter.[18]

Our final formulation of the definition of punishment, then, which will guide, although not entirely constrain, the ambit of our inquiry, will be stated thus:

> *legal punishment* is the principled infliction by a state-
> constituted institution of what are generally regarded as

unpleasant consequences upon individuals or groups adjudicated, in accordance with publicly and legally recognised criteria and procedures, correctly applied, to have breached the law, as a response to that breach, as an enforcement of the law and where that response is not inflicted solely as a means of providing compensation for the harm caused by the offence.

THE NEED FOR JUSTIFICATION AND THE NATURE OF THE QUESTION

Having selected our definition of punishment, our next preliminary question is why it should be thought necessary to provide justifying arguments for punishment so defined. The reasons are, of course, primarily moral ones, and this confronts us with a further complexity which cannot be tackled in this book. This is the question of the status and nature of moral reasons and reasoning themselves: what does it mean to provide moral arguments for one position or another? Are we arguing about moral standards which, in principle, have truth value? Are moral arguments, on the other hand, simply arguments about people's opinions? Or is the truth somewhere between these two extremes? These second order ethical questions cannot be addressed in this book, although it is probable that much of the argument will turn out to be inconsistent with either of the extreme views. In other words, some view of the nature and worthwhileness of moral argument will be implicit in what follows.

In addition to this large problem, there is the question of the extent to which our views about the moral arguments for punishment should be expected to be connected with our moral views in general. It has been claimed by Lessnoff,[19] for example, that being a retributivist in punishment 'implies nothing about the general criterion of morally good or bad action'. I am prepared to concede that this may be true of a certain form of retributivism, but as a general assumption it seems highly suspect; punishment may have special features introducing particular considerations in justifying argument, but this needs explanation and defence, not just assertion. Indeed, as an assumption, it seems more likely that our thinking about punishment *is* connected with and indeed proceeds from our general thinking about what is right and wrong. Here, then, as in the political context, I want to emphasise the connection between our moral reasoning, thinking and attitudes in general and in the particular sphere of punishment.

The most obvious reason for a need to justify punishment is that it involves, on almost any view of morality, prima facie moral wrongs: inflicting unpleasant consequences (objectively or subjectively understood) and doing so irrespective of the will or consent of the person being punished. It has been suggested[20] by J.L. Mackie that first-order moral theories may be divided into those which are right-based, those which are duty-based and those which are goal-based. On any of these views, it is not difficult to see what is prima facie objectionable about punishment. On a right-based view, it violates some very basic rights of the subject of punishment, personal integrity and liberty being the most obvious. On a duty-oriented approach, the inflicter of punishment would be seen as violating duties of restraint and non-interference with others. On a goal-based position, the immediately obvious consequence of punishment is the infliction of pain or disadvantage, consequences to be avoided in the absence of compensating goods on almost any conceivable goal-based moral theory.

It is clear, then, why moral arguments for punishment are thought to be necessary by moral philosophers of all complexions. It sometimes seems to be suggested by strong retributivist theory, however, that punishment is a 'good in itself', quite apart from any good side effects or consequences it may produce, and this is sometimes taken as a claim that punishment in fact *needs* no justification. But this view seems wrong, for the simple reason that the retributivist claims the inherent moral goodness of punishment only after producing a set of arguments which rebut (or purport to rebut) the prima facie moral case against it: arguments typically based on the restoring of a moral equilibrium, or the vindication of rights. Presumably these arguments would be redundant if retributivists really thought that punishment needed no justification. The claim to the contrary is rather, I would argue, an implicit assertion by the consequentialist that only her goal-based view of morality really counts as a moral theory, or, less radically, that only consequence-oriented arguments can serve to justify punishment. The first argument is beyond the scope of this book: the second debate is its subject matter.

Thus far we have dealt with the need for a debate on the justification of punishment within moral philosophy. However, the fact that we are concerned with state punishment adds another dimension to the argument; why should *the state*, rather than the victims of crime or private bodies such as vigilante groups, punish? Although we are still in the realms of moral argument, this does raise a new set of moral problems, traditionally dealt with as problems of political philosophy. Punishment now becomes not a prima facie moral wrong committed by an individual, but a prima facie morally wrongful exercise by state officials of state power. As such, it raises a wide range of questions about the proper relationship between the state and its citizens: the limits of state action, not only in terms of what punishment it may justifiably inflict, but also in terms of what kinds of actions it may justifiably sanction in the first place. Of course, this idea that any state intervention has to be supported by justifying reasons is generally associated with classical liberalism,[21] but it is basically at the root of all political philosophy, and it would be quite wrong to assume that, for instance, socialist theories are not equally concerned with arguments for principles about the limits of as well as the reasons for state action, even if they are less stringent or restrictive principles. The arguments which justify any form of state action must be bound up ultimately with the reasons for having the state in the first place, and anybody who believes that there is any value in political philosophy cannot accept that any form of state action is self-justifying, especially where that action is to some extent directed at the maintenance and stability of the state itself. A commitment to political philosophy is a commitment to the idea that the existence of the state calls for moral justification, and that its form requires moral argument: as one possible activity of the state, punishment is thus a problem of any complete political philosophy.

In conclusion, our primary task is to establish whether there are reasons for having institutions of punishment and for inflicting punishment in particular instances, which outweigh the reasons which militate against them. This is an exercise in moral argument and, as I hope to show, in political philosophy, in so far as these are distinct. The exercise will involve us ultimately in sketching a framework within which ideal institutions of punishment might be developed, and in tackling questions of constitutional theory internal to political philosophy: which organ of the state is properly held responsible for the running of the institutions? How many resources should be allocated to them? Above all, it is vital to bear in mind that the justification of punishment is incurably relative; it is relative to the justification of the content of the standards in response to the breach of which it is inflicted; it is ultimately relative to the justification of the existence of the state itself; and it is relative, in a somewhat different sense, to the type of society in which it functions. The practical implications of justifying arguments for punishment are dependent on complex and changing social facts; for example, in a poor society the costs of punishment would be far more influential in determining the conclusions to which the justifying argument would lead, for the price of any morally acceptable practice of punishment might be too great, for instance if its continuance meant giving up an adequate supply and distribution of food. There is no one neat, polished, final justification for punishment: there are only arguments for and against it, which apply differently not only within different political systems but also according to the social and economic conditions holding in different societies in which the institutions exist. A set of justifying arguments for punishment *in theory* is no guarantee that punishment can in fact be introduced and carried on in a morally acceptable way in any particular society.

During the course of this book, the problem will be explored in three stages. First, I shall try to explain why no adequate justification of punishment has as yet been offered. This will involve a discussion of the more important of the traditional theories, a critique of those theories, and the raising of some new questions. The second stage will be to explore certain salient background questions of political philosophy so as to build up a more thorough appreciation of the issues raised by punishment. Finally, I shall raise some questions about the nature of the political framework within which most theories of punishment have been developed, and offer an account of what I take to be the strongest arguments that can be put for punishment on a somewhat different set of political and philosophical assumptions.

CHAPTER 2

THE TRADITIONAL JUSTIFICATIONS

This chapter will deal with the traditional justifying arguments which have been put forward in defence of institutions and acts of punishment. The literature on this subject is vast, and in order to prevent this chapter running to several hundred pages I shall adopt the following method. I shall give an account of three models of justifying argument which I take to encapsulate the essentials of the various traditions. These will consist of backward-looking or desert based justifications; forward-looking or consequentialist justifications; and mixed theories which incorporate both backward and forward-looking elements. Each of these models will be evaluated in terms of the answers which they generate to three central questions: why ought the state to punish individuals or groups; how much punishment ought to be inflicted by the state; and whom ought the state to punish and for what kinds of action? The aim of the chapter will be to argue that no completely convincing justification of the practice of punishment has as yet been put forward.

BACKWARD-LOOKING JUSTIFICATIONS

The central case of an exclusively backward-looking justification is that of classical retributivism in its strong form. I take this theory to be making the claim that the state has both a right and a duty to punish, in the sense of inflicting unpleasant consequences upon an offender in response to her offence to the extent that, and by reason of the fact that, she deserves that punishment.[1] Desert thus operates as both a necessary and a sufficient condition for justified punishment. Theories which present desert as a necessary but not a sufficient condition will be considered as mixed theories. Thus the key notion employed by backward-looking theories is that of desert. Some writers treat desert as an axiomatic or self-evident moral principle, assuming that it needs no further explanation. Others, however, (the present writer included), whilst acknowledging the place of desert in our moral intuitions and reactive attitudes, find the concept puzzling when they attempt further to analyse its normative appeal, at least in the context of punishment. Indeed, it has been argued that the apparent irreducibility of the notion gives rise to suspicions that the claim that X ought to be punished beause she deserves to be punished merely amounts to the claim that X ought to be punished because she ought to be punished.[2] If the intuition is not shared, it seems impossible to push the argument further – so this is hardly a helpful contribution to the complex debate about the justifiability of punishment. Thus many writers have acknowledged the necessity of further unpacking the notion of desert, and we need to examine some of these attempts in order fairly to evaluate the adequacy of backward-looking justifications of punishment.

The lex talionis

Perhaps the crudest yet the most fundamental attempt is represented by the ancient lex talionis: an eye for an eye, a life for a life, and so on. This principle, if it merits the name, certainly has the attraction of simplicity: unfortunately this is all that can be said for it. Two devastating objections eliminate it from the list of possible candidates as adequate explications of the desert principle. Most obviously, in terms of the question of how much punishment should be inflicted, it supplies clear practical guidance as to the proper measure only in a selective number of cases. The penalty for murder or mutilation may seem clear, but what punishment ought to be inflicted for fraud, perjury or blackmail? The indeterminacy of the principle in these cases ought to make us wary of the status of its apparent clarity in others. And any subtler reinterpretation, such as the argument that murderers simply lose their right not to be killed, or thieves theirs not to be stolen from, hardly generates a morally adequate or even clear set of prescriptions for a criminal justice system. Secondly, and more importantly, this principle fails to capture one of the greatest strengths of the retributivist tradition: that is, its accommodation of a strong principle of responsibility generating limitations on who may properly be punished. It is generally claimed that no punishment is deserved unless the offence is committed by an agent who is responsible in the sense of having a certain degree of knowledge of relevant circumstances and capacity for control of her actions. The significance and meaning of the principle of responsibility will be explored in Chapter 3:

for the moment it is sufficient to recall that our moral responses appear to differ enormously according to whether a killing is intentional or accidental; a wounding deliberate or negligent. This commonly acknowledged moral distinction between responsibility based merely on causation – strict liability – and that based on 'mental elements' such as intent or recklessness – is ignored by the lex talionis, which directs the same response in each case. Added to the fact that the lex talionis offers no real arguments about why we should punish in the first place, these defects make it clear that we shall have to look further afield for an adequate explanation of the principle of desert central to the retributivist tradition.

The culpability principle
A more promising account explicates the idea of desert in terms of culpability, using this notion not only to identify the justifying reasons for punishment and those who may properly be punished, but also to fix the proper measure of punishment, in terms of a relationship of commensurability or proportionality between the offence and the punishment inflicted.[3] Culpability is generally explained as a function of the gravity of the harm caused (such as death, injury or damage to property) combined with the degree of responsibility (intent, recklessness, negligence or mere inadvertence) of the actor. But the notion of culpability also enshrines, as indeed it must if it is to count as a justifying argument for punishment, a moral judgment about the wrongfulness of the behaviour in question. Culpability, in other words, is equated with blameworthiness, and blameworthiness is equated in turn with punishment-worthiness. This does seem to reflect an important aspect of our entrenched habits and attitudes of praising and blaming, and in a more accurate way than does the lex talionis. However, as a normative theory of punishment, this approach too has its difficulties. Some of these, which I shall call internal criticisms, take the form of problems thrown up by the argument from culpability taken on its own terms: if we were to accept the principle, what would its implications be? Others, which I shall call external criticisms, cast doubt more fundamentally on the adequacy of the principle itself: does it offer an adequate explication of the content and normative force of arguments from desert? Both kinds of difficulty will have to be addressed in order to give a fair appraisal of the culpability principle.

Let us begin our appraisal with some internal criticisms of the culpability principle. The first cluster of problems has principally to do with the question of who ought to be punished. A difficulty seems to be thrown up by the fact that not all offenders against familiar systems of criminal law are clearly morally blameworthy. This is both because there are often thought to be sufficient reasons for criminally proscribing what is essentially morally neutral behaviour (such as driving on the right hand side of the road, or selling liquor at ten o'clock in the morning), and because it is sometimes thought necessary to sanction negligent or even accidental behaviour in the interests of public health or safety. Furthermore, even where some measure of responsibility is a condition for criminal liability, it is not clear that this entails moral blameworthiness in a full sense. For example, there may be a background explanation of the behaviour of the reckless injurer or the intending thief which exculpates her morally yet which, for policy or practical reasons, does not excuse her behaviour according to the criminal law. Thus in actual criminal justice systems it is not safe to assume that every offender is morally blameworthy and therefore deserving of punishment in the given sense, and we are in need of more convincing positive arguments as to why prohibitions generally acknowledged to be of social importance, such as those based on negligence liability, should be excluded from the criminal law.

This difficulty can be mitigated by producing arguments to show that citizens have a prima facie moral obligation to obey the criminal law. We shall have to consider in later chapters[4] whether these arguments can effectively dispose of the difficulty presented by cases of strict or vicarious liability as well as of that of morally neutral laws, but what is clear is that they do not rest entirely on the culpability principle or any other purported principle of desert. The picture is also complicated by the fact that the culpability principle could only hold good in the case of just laws or at least of laws insufficiently unjust to displace any assumed prima facie obligation to obey them – although of course this is not a difficulty encountered exclusively by desert theories of punishment. It is worth noting, however, that a logical conclusion of the blameworthiness/punishment-worthiness equation is the relevance of motive not only to sentence but also to the issue of conviction under the criminal law, given that certain kinds of altruistic motive do seem to be capable of displacing a judgment of moral blameworthiness for responsibly breaking even a just law.

Conversely, it is true in the case of most criminal justice

systems of the type which is our focus that it is not thought appropriate to proscribe many instances of what is generally acknowledged to be immoral behaviour through the criminal law. Some adherence at least to the spirit of Mill's famous principle of liberty,[5] to the effect that wrongs ought only to be criminally regulated where they result in harms to others, and that where behaviour (such as private sexual behaviour) is totally 'self-regarding' it should be left free from coercive state intervention, is to be traced in many legal systems, along with positivistic attitudes towards some degree of separation between law and morality.[6] Thus adoption of the culpability principle of punishment alone would lead to institutions of punishment considerably more extensive in this respect than the ones which we currently think of as being legitimate.

Again, the difficulty can be mitigated by means of a supplementation of the culpability principle along the following lines. It might be argued that what is in question is the issue of state punishment: the state assumes responsibility for the administration and enforcement of the criminal law only: it has the right and the duty to punish for breaches of the criminal law, but not for other, perhaps equally deserving, wrongs. This right presumably inheres, if anywhere, in the individuals or groups most closely affected by the wrong in question. This argument gives us the distinction which we need, but it raises more questions than it answers. First of all, the argument is, once again, not an argument from culpability alone: other elements need to be introduced to explain why it is that one person, group or body has the responsibility for punishing certain types of wrong and not others. Secondly, the argument begs yet another, more fundamental one: upon what principles are we to decide which wrongs should and should not be proscribed by the criminal law? Again, this does not seem to be an argument which can be satisfactorily concluded by appeal to principles of desert alone. None of this is fatal to the culpability theory of punishment, but it does point in the direction of a need for its augmentation or supplementation.

Another difficulty internal to the culpability version of the argument from desert appears at first to be a practical one, but on closer examination the practical problem can be seen to mask a more fundamental problem of principle. The practical issue is that of determining just what type and measure of punishment is in (moral) fact proportionate to the offence committed by the offender. The difficulty of principle underlying this problem is that the two elements are actually incommensurable; there are no acceptable common units of measurement in terms of which we can assess the relationship of equivalence. In deciding just what punishment a murderer or robber deserves, we seem to be thrown back on the unacceptable lex talionis, or on some conventionally established scale of penalties, or forced to admit that this is a matter for the untrammelled discretion of the legislator or sentencer, perhaps for her determination on consequentialist lines. In either case, the force of the appeal to consensus, convention or consequences needs further explication and sullies the purity of the culpability principle.

In the face of these difficulties some writers have modified the culpability thesis and have put forward instead the claim that the principle generates only a conception of comparative as opposed to absolute deserts.[7] The idea is that at least culpability can tell us that a murderer deserves more than a robber, who in turn deserves more than a petty thief. But this does not advance the argument very far. In the first place, even comparative judgments are often very difficult to make with any degree of confidence. How are we to compare the drug trafficker with the armed robber, the careless driver with the shoplifter, the murderer with the industrialist who ignores safety regulations creating a grave risk to life? And secondly, even if we allow that comparative judgments can be made, we are thrown back on arguments from convention or consequences in order to determine the upper and lower limits of the actual scale of punishments, and indeed its general content. Thus, as in the case of the lex talionis, the attractive practical certainty which the culpability principle appears to offer turns out on analysis to be illusory.

Finally, and most importantly, however, serious external criticisms can be made of the culpability principle's account of why it is that we should punish. For it is not clear that the move from a judgment of blameworthiness to one of punishment-worthiness should be made so lightly. Even though our desert-based reactive attitudes may be firmly held, surely we should reflect carefully and seek further reasons before we take the additional step of deliberately acting in a harmful way against a particular individual on the basis of them? A judgment that someone has behaved wrongly does not involve or justify the further judgment that they should be punished. Ultimately, the culpability principle seems to give us no explanation of why we should think it right to punish offenders merely by reason of their past culpable actions. By what means does such an argument, if argument it is, distinguish itself from a principle of vengeance? By what moral alchemy does the prima facie wrong of punishment following on the wrong of the offence create a morally preferable situation? Why should an offence alone generate a moral reason for punitive action? None of these issues is demystified by the culpability principle.

Forfeiture of rights, unfair advantages and the restoration of a moral equilibrium

Given what has been said of the failure of these first two models of desert theory to generate a satisfactory justification of punishment, it makes sense to attempt further to explicate the desert principle within the context of some wider, compatible, background political philosophy. Thus the other attempts I shall consider explore the links between the concept of desert and those of justice, fairness and equality. The concepts of justice and fairness have indeed been central to the desert tradition, and it is thus with these that I shall begin.

The first of the more sophisticated versions of the desert principle which I shall consider may conveniently be labelled the forfeiture of rights view. On this view, the meaning of the claim that an offender deserves to be punished is explained within the context of the existence of a legal system which generates reciprocal political obligations upon citizens to obey its norms.[8] Thus by virtue of a voluntarily committed offence an individual violates her obligations not only to the state but also to all other citizens, and the state is justified in depriving her of her civil rights. The thesis can be put in an extreme and a moderate form. In its extreme form it claims that an offender forfeits all her civil rights by virtue of any voluntarily committed offence. This seems on the face of it to be an implausible claim, generating as it does no limit on the amount or type of justifiable punishment and thus abandoning the proportionality principle central to the retributivist tradition. A more plausible version is that which argues that the offender only forfeits a set of rights equivalent to those which she has violated: once this proportionate set of rights has been forfeited, the offender can re-enter political society on fair terms with the law-abiding.

Thus on the moderate view a full set of political rights is due to a citizen only so long as she meets her political and legal obligations. This argument does generate a clear principle identifying who may be punished, but doubts remain about just what the argument amounts to as a set of positive justifying reasons for punishment. *Why* should an offender forfeit any civil rights? What does the argument add to the blank, mysterious claim that she deserves it? A further refinement argues that a voluntary offence is taken to show that the offender in a sense chose or willed her own punishment, or at least consented to it, where she was responsible for the offence, aware of its normative consequences, and acting within a fair system of rules.[9] The punishment therefore respects the autonomy of the agent, treating her as an end in herself rather than as a means to some diffused social good. Again, this argument has some appeal as a claim about who should be punished, but as an account of why they should be punished it is inadequate: it can hardly be claimed that offenders consent to their disadvantaging punitive treatment in anything like the strong sense of consent which we generally take to be necessary to justify harsh treatment of one person by another. We can easily imagine an offender who meets the conditions of the principle yet who states in committing her offence that she does not consent to any punishment: the only way in which such an offender can be brought within the ambit of the principle is through some form of social contract argument. I shall consider the difficulties with this approach in commenting on the second sophisticated version of the desert principle, which raises a similar issue. Before moving on, however, it is worth raising the question of whether in any case the consent argument for punishment could count as a genuinely desert-based principle. In attempting to unpack that idea, we seem to have moved a considerable distance from our unreconstructed starting point.

The second version may be called the unfair advantage view. Again, we are to imagine a background system of reciprocal political obligations, and we are invited to take the view that the essence of a voluntary offence is the taking by the offender of an unfair advantage: in failing to restrain herself, the offender has had the advantage of fulfilling choices forbidden to others.[10] The purpose and justification of punishment is, in effect, to remove that unfair advantage and to restore the 'moral equilibrium' or relationships of justice which existed prior to the offence. On one extreme version of the view, until punishment is inflicted, all members of society are in some way implicated in the moral disequilibrium created by the crime, which they have failed to redress. It is presumably this type of thought which prompts Kant to say that even on the dissolution of a society all murderers held in the jails ought to be executed.[11] There is perhaps a connection between such views about the value to be attached to the restoration of the moral equilibrium and the argument that punishment 'reaffirms the right' – both in terms of the rightness of the standards breached by the offence[12] and in terms of the pre-existing relationships of justice between the members of political society. Here at last we have not only an argument about who may properly be punished, but also a positive claim about the reasons for that punishment – although reasons which, as I shall argue, are at such a high level of abstraction that their contribution to the demystification of the desert principle is limited.

These two versions of desert theory have the important advantage over those so far considered of locating principles of punishment in their proper context – that is, within a general set of political principles. Indeed, these views are probably best understood within the social contract tradition in political philosophy, which asks us to imagine some hypothetical initial agreement upon a certain system of rules and methods of enforcement which can and must then fairly be administered by means of imposition of the agreed sanctions.[13] But these views are not without their practical and theoretical difficulties. In the first place, neither of them gives very clear practical guidance about the fair measure of punishment in particular cases. What actual punishment would forfeit a set of rights equivalent to those violated by a rapist, a petty thief, a reckless driver? What sanction would be sufficient to remove the unfair advantage gained by the provoked manslaughterer, the tax evader or the burglar? As in the case of the law of the talion and the culpability principle, resort to arguments from conventionally agreed, customary or consequence-based penalty scales seem hard to avoid. Secondly, real difficulties have been raised about the social contract tradition itself; in what sense can a *fictitious* agreement generate obligations for real people? This subject will have to be taken up in detail in later chapters.[14] Furthermore, these views are dependent for their force, as we have already noted, on the existence of a fair set of rules. This is not fatal in itself, but the criteria which dictate that there is indeed a just equilibrium which can be restored are not generated by the forfeiture of rights or unfair advantage principles alone. The views do presuppose an independent account of what counts as an unfair advantage and a just equilibrium.

Finally, it seems legitimate to ask whether the metaphorical ideas of restoring relationships of justice or moral equilibria outweigh the obvious disvalues attached to the suffering and other costs of punishment. Do these theories really ignore such costs completely? If not, what weight do they accord to them? In what real sense does punishment 'restore the right'? Do these theories really remove the mystery attaching to the original, simple desert principle, or are they, too, a form of moral alchemy? Or, in trying to avoid the mystery, do they not collapse into versions of utilitarian or other consequentialist justification? Is the real reason for punishment underlying these theories the need to uphold a just and effective legal system, to prevent private vengeance, to remove feelings of unfairness on the parts of victims? Can any account of punishment which ignores these factors generate a satisfactory justification? And if so many questions crucial to the justification of punishment can only be answered by looking beyond the desert principle, how strong a claim can that principle make to constitute *the* justification of punishment?

Let us turn finally to a version of the desert principle which explores its links with a principle of equality. On this view, to punish someone who deserves a punishment is to act in accordance with a principle of equal treatment: treat like cases alike, and different ones differently.[15] Through her voluntary offence, the offender has singled herself out from other citizens: offenders and non-offenders ought to be treated differently. But this will not do as a theory of desert, let alone as a theory of punishment. First of all, it is too minimal: on this basis alone it might justify treating the offender better than the non-offender, so long as this was done consistently. In addition, the principle generates no answer to the question of how much we ought to punish. Finally, the principle tells us nothing about why an offence makes the offender relevantly different in a way which justifies punitive treatment. Not every type of voluntary differentiating action, even one affecting others, justifies a punitive response. Thus the principle of equal treatment cannot explain the principle of desert, although it may form an important part of that principle.

Retributive theory

We are now in a position to evaluate the question of whether any of the arguments we have considered as possible explications of the idea of desert makes sense of the puzzle of the justification of punishment. This can best be done by means of a summary of the answers generated by those arguments to the three questions originally posed. First of all, why should we punish? It is really in answering this fundamental question that the arguments associated with desert are at their most deficient. Even the more sophisticated versions barely rise above the level of metaphor, and leave us with the suspicion that the idea of desert cannot be distinguished from a principle of vengeance or the unappealing assertion that two wrongs somehow make a right. Within the context of a general set of political principles, arguments such as that from unfair advantage can answer this question, but when such a supplementation is made, it is no longer clear that what we have is a desert theory at all, rather than a consequence-based account. In addition, the possibility of a background system which is not universally just complicates the force of the claim that punishment aims to restore a moral equilibrium. Moreover, why should we necessarily give absolute priority to the demands of this narrow retributive conception of justice as opposed to those of mercy, forgiveness and humanity?

Secondly, how much ought we to punish? This is the question to which the idea of desert promises us a clear and determinate answer, yet on analysis it fails to fulfill that promise. Without supplementation by either conventionally agreed scales of punishment or arguments from consequences, arguments from desert actually tell us very little about what punishments we ought to inflict. Thirdly, many of the arguments closely associated with the retributive tradition do generate a determinate answer to the question of whom we should punish: we should only punish those who have responsibly committed offences. It is perhaps in this area that the tradition really does encompass a principle which will be fundamental to the justification of punishment, and one which is indeed reflected in our differing responses to the accidental, the negligent and the deliberate offence. Yet it is not clear why these arguments need employ the concept of desert: they can be developed perfectly adequately in terms of responsibility, fairness and other arguments from distributive as opposed to retributive justice, as we shall see. And in the absence of any adequate explanation of what the desert principle amounts to, let alone of a desert-based answer to the central question of why we should punish, the responsibility principle in any case only operates as a limiting one which would have to be combined with some other arguments to generate a justification of punishment. In addition, with respect to the broader aspect of the third question, that is, what kinds of actions ought to be punished, the principles we have considered have to be supplemented by a set of general, consistent yet independent political principles in order to give any complete guidance.

Negatively, then, the retributive tradition seems accurately to reflect our considered judgments about excuses, justifications and mitigating principles:[16] it can tell us why not to punish certain categories of person; but it fails to tell us why we should punish any persons, and in what sorts of circumstances. In addition, consistent adherence to the main purported arguments from desert would issue in a criminal justice system in some respects radically more extensive, in others greatly less so, than those generally acknowledged to be acceptable. This last factor is of course not decisive, but we may use our intuitions where they are reflected in the shape of current systems as at least pointers to the need for modification of possible theories.

In view of these difficulties with the chosen models of backward-looking justifying argument, it now seems appropriate to turn to the opposed tradition of consequentialist argument to see whether it can provide a more convincing rationale for institutions and acts of punishment. For if we were really to believe that punishment did nothing other than to restore a moral equilibrium: if it had no other good consequences whatsoever, would we really be prepared to support it as a social practice, whatever our accustomed attitudes and discourses of praising and blaming?

FORWARD-LOOKING JUSTIFICATIONS

The best known of the forward-looking justifications of punishment stem directly or indirectly from classical utilitarian philosophy, perhaps the most influential in this sphere still being the theory of economical general deterrence espoused by Jeremy Bentham.[17] Against the backcloth of the general moral and political principle of the maximisation of aggregate utility, in the sense of pleasure and the avoidance of pain, the threat of punishment is argued to have a generally deterrent effect on potential offenders, such that the saving in pain from reduced crime and additional happiness from increased security, outweighs the pains and costs of punishment. And in order for the threat of punishment to be effective, punishment must (at least sometimes) actually be inflicted in accordance with the threat.[18] Modern utilitarians[19] have variously modified this conception, arguing, for example, that utility should be conceived in terms of desire-satisfaction rather than happiness, or that average rather than aggregate utility should be measured. I shall not concern myself with these modifications in any great detail, for in most cases they do not fundamentally affect the structure of the underlying argument – and it is that structure which poses the most intractable problems for utilitarian theories of punishment.

In addition to the familiar goal of general deterrence, there are many other forms of utility, or sought consequence, which punishment may and has been argued to achieve, many of them compassed by the imaginative Bentham.[20] Deterrence of actual offenders through the experience of punishment, rehabilitation of offenders through treatment during or instead of punitive measures, thus reducing the likelihood of their reoffending in the future, social protection through incapacitation of dangerous offenders or even social nuisances, satisfaction of victims' or public grievances, the upholding of the legal system, reparation and restitution to the victim, moral education of the society at large: all these can be argued to contribute to a utilitarian theory of punishment. I shall examine the peculiar features of each of these species of utility before going on to consider the general arguments for and against forward-looking justifications of punishment. Such an individual consideration has been relatively neglected, but it is, I think, crucial in view of the very different assumptions made by each of the goals about the proper role of the state and the function and scope of the criminal law. It is therefore necessary to pay the price of some measure of repetition in order to examine these salient differences.

General deterrence

The goal of general deterrence shares with other forward-looking aims the feature of, at least in principle, empirical verifiability – a feature not shared by backward-looking principles as traditionally conceived. On this particular goal clear empirical evidence is in fact scarce, due to the difficulty, for obvious reasons, of setting up adequately controlled experiments. But we do have some statistical evidence, as well as the testimony of personal experience and common sense, that the threat of punishment does make some contribution to the reduction of crime via a deterring effect, although the available data suggests that most of the effect flows from the fact of the possibility of punishment rather than from beliefs about its type or amount.[21] Thus the nature of potential offenders' beliefs about the likelihood of apprehension will clearly be crucial to the efficiency of the system.

The next feature of the general deterrence goal is that it only connects the justification for particular acts of punishment, the answer to the general question of *why* we punish, in a very minimal way with what is actually being done to the offender. The offender is merely used as a means to achieving a diffused social goal and no assumptions are made about the effect of the punishment on or its significance for her. It is thus open to the objection generally aimed at utilitarian principles, that they treat individuals as 'means to ends' rather than as 'ends in themselves'. This criticism clearly needs considerably more analysis, which I shall provide when I come to examine general criticisms of forward-looking theories. But it is worth noting that the criticism does apply to general deterrence theory in a particularly striking way – as opposed, say, to the goal of rehabilitation, which does in some sense focus upon the direct effects of the punitive response on the individual offender. The state's role in punishing, on the general deterrence theory, is to reduce certain unwanted and economically reducible forms of behaviour: individuals may be sacrificed to this dominant purpose.

Thirdly, the general deterrent effect is achieved by means of the threat of punishment: all, therefore, that is needed is a general belief in the reality of the threat; in fact the whole system could be a sham, if it were feasible to maintain the pretence over a long period. Of course in practice there will always be a grave risk of unwanted side-effects in terms of people discovering the pretence with the consequence not only of loss of deterrence, but also of loss of respect for the system in general. But in principle, if these risks can be eliminated or even greatly reduced, the sham system would actually be preferable to the real one in terms of overall utility. So in fact the general deterrence theory might justify no punishment at all, or only punishment in a small number of strategic cases.

Fourthly, in answering the question *who* may be punished, the argument which the general deterrence theory generates for punishing the guilty also serves to justify inflicting unpleasant treatment on those who have not in fact committed offences, and indeed who are not believed to have done so. This of course would only count as a deviant or non-focal case of punishment according to our definition, but we must not be led into the trap of employing a 'definitional stop'[22] to disguise the fact that the arguments used by utilitarians to justify punishment actually serve to justify a much wider and apparently less acceptable practice. Again, side-effect arguments such as the extra pain an innocent person will suffer from punishment or the risks to general respect for the system should the victimisation be discovered can be employed at least to show that in most cases the utilitarian will prefer to punish the guilty, but the possibility in principle of victimisations or punishments of those thought likely to offend in the future does appear to raise a substantial moral (rather than a logical) difficulty, and point to a need for modification of the bare utilitarian principle. A similar difficulty arises in the general deterrence answer to the question of *how much* we should punish, in that occasionally draconian penalties might be seen to have an economically deterrent effect. These difficulties will be considered in greater detail in the general section on problems of consequentialist theories.

One other argument has been put forward specifically with respect to general deterrence theories, and that is the argument that the good consequences aimed at by such theories can only be achieved if the person or body inflicting the punishment is not known to be acting on act-utilitarian lines. For, the argument goes, in any particular case it will probably not produce best consequences to punish unless doing so will generate certain kinds of expectation.[23] Basically, these expectations must be that the punishing agent will punish irrespective of best consequences in individual cases, or they will not be sufficiently secure to set up the desired deterrent effect. If individuals are aware that the punishing agent is genuinely act-utilitarian, they have good reason not to form such expectations, and can thus short-circuit the whole utilitarian claim. This raises a general problem for act-, as opposed to rule-utilitarian principles, and will be further considered below. Suffice it to point out for the moment that, yet again, the device of pretence could be used by a utilitarian punishing agent to enable her to generate the consequence-independent expectations necessary to secure a deterrent effect.

Rehabilitation

Rehabilitation is, in principle, capable of at least an indirect measure of empirical validation: and vast amounts of empirical work have been carried on during the twentieth century, particularly during the past thirty years, aimed at establishing or refuting the rehabilitative effect of various forms of treatment programme, ranging from group counselling through employment and training schemes, psychotherapy, administration of drugs to extreme measures such as electric shock therapy and surgery.[24] Yet after years of optimism, experimentation and research, there is very little data available to show that the methods tried have had any impact on reforming offenders, at least as judged through recidivism rates – though some success in terms of reducing neurosis and other mental health problems has been recorded.[25] Various speculations have been made as to why this should be so. Is it the case that human nature is deeply intractable? Or is it simply that coerced treatment or treatment within the essentially punitive environment of the prison is unlikely to be successful? In either case, the prospects of producing data which would support a utilitarian justification for punishment based on individual rehabilitation seem remote.

We have already noted that rehabilitation as a reason for punishment does not have quite the same problems as general deterrence in terms of its use of the offender as a means to a social good. It may well be argued that to attempt to reform an individual is to treat her with great concern and as an end in herself.[26] But this goal does have worrying implications connected with that objection. It is often argued that recidivism is an inadequate test of failure, yet any other measure would appear to have to be based on some vague conception of social or moral health. It is not hard to see the possibly repressive implications of such a conception, never to mention its wide vulnerability to abuse. Are we really entitled to try to change people by punishment? For the utilitarian, of course, it is solely the contribution of reform to overall utility, most obviously in terms of reduced offending, which is relevant. Yet implicit in this goal lurks a very much broader view of the proper role of the state, perhaps more analogous to what we normally conceive as the parental role in punishing a child, where a central goal is to persuade or coerce the person punished to internalise certain standards of behaviour.[27] Doubtless many people would allow that one legitimate function of punishment is to uphold the standards embodied in the criminal law, but the concept of rehabilitation seems dangerously general and manipulable. For it is always possible that an assessment of an offender's rehabilitation will depend on official belief in a degree of socialisation far broader than a mere willingness to conform to the criminal law, and dependent on adherence to standards far subtler, more pervasive and harder to challenge than those enshrined in that law.

Taking these points a little further, it does seem legitimate to ask (and a parallel question arose with respect to general deterrence) whether what the utilitarian reform theory generates can truly be described as a justification of punishment, or whether it in fact justifies a much wider set of practices, some being of a very different nature from our original conception of punishment. In terms of *who* might be punished, would this theory in its unamended state not justify the state in taking preventive action against those deviating from the social conception of moral health and thus adjudged likely to offend in the future, or even against those who are thought to be likely to increase the crime rate by adversely influencing others whilst not actually offending themselves? Could preventive action be taken on the basis of statistical generalisations predicting more frequent offending among members of certain groups within society? So long as the pains and costs of rehabilitation can be outweighed by savings in offences, gains in security and so on, there is nothing in the reform theory to warn us against such practices or to distinguish them from central cases of punishment. Indeed, it is not clear that the rehabilitation theory generates a justification of punishment within the definition set out in our first chapter at all. Since we have accepted an analytic connection between punishment and unpleasant treatment, and there seems to be no reason to believe that all forms of reformative treatment should be unpleasant, even if coerced, it is clear that the principle justifies practices far wider than mere punishments – such as a large donation from public funds to a bank robber to enable her to set up her own business, or, more realistically, the instantiation of educational schemes as the sole 'punitive' response. Again, utilitarianism seems to suffer from the problem of overextensiveness, which moreover applies to the question of the proper measure as well as to the proper distribution of punishment.

Individual deterrence

The individual offender may be deterred by her experience of punishment because of its unpleasant effects, both direct and indirect. Again, there is a dearth of conclusive empirical evidence, but in the case of incarceration, such evidence as there is appears to suggest that the experience of punishment is criminogenic rather than the reverse.[28] However, some forms of sanction, such as the fine, do appear to succeed in producing individual deterrence, although, as with other principles, the difficulty of inferring a causal rather than a merely contingent relationship from the data, and of setting up adequately controlled experiments, makes confident empirical assertions problematic.[29] The other difficulties with individual deterrence as a goal mirror those with general deterrence and rehabilitation. First of all, the practice could be said to be using the offender as a mere pawn in a game aimed at the good of society as a whole. Secondly, there is no inbuilt reason why the principle should justify punishing all or only offenders: repentant offenders ought not to be punished since deterrence is unnecessary: those thought likely to offend in the future should be 'punished' now in order to deter them and prevent the harm. Again, the principle is overextensive to the extent of justifying ill treatment by the state wherever this would result in a maximisation of utility.

Social protection

To aim at social protection can, of course, mean a number of things: here I shall be interpreting it merely as the goal of reducing the total number of offences and thus the risks to the public at large of being the victims of offences, by means of the incapacitory effects of punishment. In the sphere of incapacitation, the empirical evidence does indeed suggest that some forms of punishment, such as incarceration and the removal of driving licences, do prevent (partly because of the fact that some types of offender tend to become less criminally active as they grow older),[30] or at least postpone, the commission of a certain number of offences.[31] The effect should not be exaggerated, however, by ignoring the existence of many offences committed in prison or through violations of incapacitory sentences (such as driving bans) themselves. Thus, on a short-term utilitarian calculation, such punishments are sometimes effective and justified, always depending, of course, on their costs.[32] But the argument only really touches on a limited number of types of punishment, and on a long term view the utilitarian calculation may well go the other way due to criminogenic effects of imprisonment. There is always the possibility of permanent imprisonment, exile, driving bans and so on, but the disutility attached to many such severe measures seems unlikely to be outweighed by their socially protective advantages. And as in the previous two cases, such a principle appears to use the offender with only a minimal amount of respect and concern as a reason for punishment, and to be overextensive in its answers to the questions of who may be punished and how much. There is no reason why such socially protective measures should be limited to offenders, ignoring other potentially dangerous individuals; nor is there any reason or justification for the incapacitation being unpleasant in any respect other than its curtailment of a certain degree of liberty. The social protection argument again justifies something different from and considerably wider than punishment.

Grievance-satisfaction and the maintenance of respect for the legal system

The goals of the satisfaction of victims' and the general public's grievances[33] and maintenance of respect for the legal system are difficult to subject to any form of empirical validation. However, common sense and general experience suggest that these are indeed important functions of the penal system. For the system of criminal law aims not only to present a set of public standards of behaviour, but claims allegiance and aims to enforce those standards. Given our general intuitions with respect to praising, blaming and desert, which we explored in the section on backward-looking justifications of punishment, it is clear that criminal offences give rise not only to direct harms but also to feelings of insecurity, desires for vengeance, feelings of unfairness and so on. At this stage it is possible for the state to step in, and to reaffirm the social commitment to the standards breached: one such means of reaffirmation or vindication is that of punishment of the offender. If it fails to punish, the argument goes, two problems will ensue. First of all, those closest to the victim or the victim herself may be tempted to act privately to avenge the wrong. In addition, general feelings of insecurity may lead groups of individuals to form private police forces or vigilante groups, all of which may lead to a disordered and essentially anarchistic situation. Secondly, even if these more drastic problems do not eventuate, it seems likely that systematic failure on the part of the state to vindicate its laws will gradually lead to a loss of faith in the effectiveness of the legal system as a whole, which may in turn lead to the more radical results. These arguments cohere with Durkheim's thesis that one function of the criminal law and its enforcement is to reinforce the collective moral consciousness of a society,[34] and derive some support from the preoccupation of the press, at least in the UK, with reports of criminal cases, with great emphasis on the sentences handed down in sensational cases.[35] By these means the criminal justice system may fairly be argued to increase a sense of social solidarity or cohesion, and a sense of public security, although questions may be raised about just how crucial and effective punishment is among other means of fulfilling these functions. As with the other goals we have considered, problems arise with this set of reasons for punishment and the distributive principles which it generates, both with respect to the possibility of thus justifying victimisations and pretence punishments, and in the objection that such a rationale fails to treat the offender as an end in herself. Furthermore, problems arise in the context of excessive and perhaps manipulated grievance-desires, which may point to the need for, but not the method of achieving, an 'objective' conception of grievance beyond which the state could not be expected to respond.

Reparation and restitution

As with the goal of social protection, these aims can only justify certain forms of punishment (such as the payment of compensation) and indeed only appear to apply in a straightforward way to the punishment of certain sorts of crimes, typically property offences. In addition, it is not clear that what we have here is truly a principle of punishment: the concepts of reparation or compensation and of punishment, as reflected in our definition, have always been thought to be distinct. Is compensation not something that an offender may be made to give in addition to her punishment? We can certainly accommodate such a rationale within our original definition, but only as a subsidiary and not as a principal goal of punishment. There must be some idea of additional loss, inconvenience or stigma in order to preserve what I have assumed is a genuine distinction between punishment and compensation.[36] That utilitarian arguments alone cannot furnish the tools for drawing such a distinction should alert us once again to the fact that what utilitarian arguments justify is a set of practices far wider than those marked our by our definition of punishment.

Bearing this in mind, it is clear that a utilitarian justification of unpleasant treatment in response to offences could be made out in terms of the restitutionary or reparatory effect of that treatment, especially when this effect may be combined with that of individual deterrence, grievance-satisfaction and so on. Furthermore, this rationale is not subject to such a strong form of the means-to-an-end objection as, for instance, general deterrence, for it does at least connect what is done with the offender to her offence; it does seem fair to regard her as the most appropriate person to be used as the means to the end of compensating her victim. Indeed, this fact, when seen in the light of the grievance-satisfaction argument, also has some bearing on the punishment of the innocent objection. For, although reparation might equally effectively (from the victim's point of view) be provided by the state or some other individual, if it were known that the reparator were not the offender, people's general moral (apparently non-utilitarian) sense would be offended and the punishment would not achieve nearly so much general utility as if the offender were the compensator. However, this move may be countered by pointing out the possibility of a sham in such a case. As before, side effect arguments from the risks of discovery of such a deception, for example, may be used, but the case still appears to pose a problem of principle, if not of practice, for utilitarianism in general. It is thus to arguments about the general inadequacy of consequentialist theories of punishment that we shall now turn our attention.

Utilitarian theory. Why should we punish?: Treating individuals as means rather than ends

This is one of the strongest retributivist criticisms of utilitarianism, and proceeds from ideas fundamental to the moral theory which underlies the retributivist view of punishment.[37] What does the objection amount to? The claim seems to be that it is wrong that punishment should be motivated by a social goal: whatever is done to individuals should be primarily be concerned with them as ends in themselves: should treat them as autonomous moral agents who have chosen their actions: and should respect the choices which they have made. But does this really make sense? As we have seen, certain forms of retributivism claim that infliction of deserved punishment does respect the individual because in some sense she has willed her own punishment by breaking the law. I have argued that this is hollow, for it is simply artificial to claim that any offender has freely chosen to be punished in a sense sufficient to invoke the autonomy argument in the strong form which is needed. Furthermore one can question how much value really ought to be attached to such respect, when the treatment which it issues in may in fact be pointless in the sense of having no compensating good effects.

Moreover, it may be argued that the view of individuals as autonomous moral agents must be modified in order to generate an adequate conception of political society. Can the total integrity of individuals in an imaginary state of nature really be preserved on the transition to political society; is it enough to view that society merely as the sum of the individuals within it, its creation forming no extra or incompatible rights or obligations, as Nozick suggests?[38] Can we even make much sense of the idea of an atomised individual abstracted from society? These questions will be considered in a later chapter; for the moment, we must merely acknowledge that we seem to be caught in a dilemma between two extreme and opposed views. It cannot be right that actions toward individuals, even coercive and disadvantaging ones, can never be justified by their generally good effects with respect to others. The logical conclusion of such a view would be an extreme libertarian critique of systems of taxation and the welfare state which most of us would regard as wholly morally misguided. Yet equally it cannot be the case that actions towards individuals can properly ignore their interests except as components of the pursued common good. The truth must lie somewhere between the extremes. But this characterisation of the objection does, I think, reveal what is central to, and correct in, this retributivist objection to utilitarian theories. This is essentially the Rawlsian point that they ignore the separateness of persons,[39] in the sense that although each individual's interests are counted, what is focussed on is the aggregate of interest-satisfaction or pleasure-creation: whose pleasure is created or whose interests are satisfied is of no concern to aggregative utilitarianism. In other words, the principle lacks an *adequate* distributive aspect, and although diminishing marginal utility will generally favour more rather than less equal distributions, there is still room for what would strongly be felt to be unfair distributions to arise through the pursuit of utilitarian values. Hence, in the context of punishment, problems such as the apparent justification of draconian penalties which have a generally deterrent effect, arise. And a switch to average rather than aggregate utility as our maximand seems unlikely to do more than slightly mitigate this difficulty, given that it too is only indirectly related to the way in which the utility is distributed. Seen in this way, the means-to-an-end argument is closely connected to the victimisation objection, and it is to this that we now turn. The question of whether the alternative approach commits the opposite error of unduly and unrealistically sanctifying the 'separateness of persons' is one to which we shall return.

Who should be punished?: Overextensiveness in punishment of the innocent

It appears that utilitarian theories are incapable in principle of generating a limitation which most people strongly feel to be necessary in answering the question of who may properly be punished: there seems to be no reason in principle why it should be the offender who is used as a means to several of the utilitarian goals. Thus utilitarianism appears to justify practices considerably wider than those represented by our original definition of punishment. It is worth looking at this central problem in some detail.

The problem is not merely that utilitarian theory is willing to countenance the occasional mistaken punishment of innocent defendants for the sake of general benefits to be had from the creation and enforcement of a system of penal law, and perhaps as an unfortunate and inevitable side-effect of it. It is the much more radical and counterintuitive implication that utilitarian theory would in certain circumstances actually require a judge or some other actor in the penal process, such as a prosecutor (for example, by fabricating evidence), or even a legislator (in the framing of procedural or substantive rules) deliberately to engineer the conviction of a defendant about whose guilt she entertained a substantial doubt, in order to maximise utility.[40] And indeed it is not difficult to imagine a case in which the principle of utility might be served by the punishment of an innocent defendant. Especially in circumstances where commission of a particular crime had become damagingly widespread, where there were grave difficulties of detection, and where the mischief caused by the type of offence was serious, there might well be substantial preventive and other social gains to be made by the conviction of someone secretly known or suspected to be a scapegoat. Even if such cases were very rare or practically non-existent, this would raise a problem of principle for utilitarianism, and it is worth bearing in mind that there are precedents in history, and in sensational cases (for example the Dreyfus or Yorkshire Ripper cases) it is apparent that judges and others might come under considerable pressure to allay public alarm and increase respect for the legal system, as well as providing deterrent motivation, by convicting and punishing an innocent defendant. Thus, the wider we cast our utilitarian net in the search for justifying benefits, the more reasons we seem to find in support of this intuitively obnoxious practice.

Is this objection fatal to any theory of punishment based on Benthamite utilitarianism? (We shall postpone consideration of the alternative possibility; that of modifying the background moral theory without entirely abandoning a consequentialist concern). Two possibilities present themselves. The first response sometimes offered replaces argument by mere appeal to definition: punishment, it is said, is something we do to an offender for an offence. Thus punishment of the innocent is simply a contradiction in terms: it is not punishment at all.[41] The simplicity of such a solution is, as we have seen,[42] its only recommendation. Bentham's theory in this case justifies something more than, or different from, punishment. In which case, if we are to rely on his theory, we have to find some way of distinguishing punishment from the wider practices, within the theory itself. By definition, this is something we cannot do. So, we must either abandon the theory, or modify it. We cannot replace theory by definition.

A second, much more promising defence, is that offered by Bentham himself.[43] In characteristically single-minded style, he lists a number of disutilities peculiar to punishment of the innocent as opposed to the guilty, which aim to show that such an act would never, or only exceptionally (and of course, we cannot always rely on our intuitions in exceptional cases, but must be willing to be guided by our considered principles) maximise utility. The list includes the extra suffering caused to the victim by reason of her innocence – her additional frustration and feeling of insecurity, as well as those to her family: the risk of very serious damage to general respect for the legal system should the fraud ever be discovered, plus increased insecurity, apprehension and alarm flowing from the knowledge that one might be punished despite conforming one's behaviour to the law, that a guilty person is still at large, free to re-offend, and that the law is incapable of protecting the law-abiding. We could also mention the pain of sympathy which would be felt for the innocent victim, and, paradoxically, the comfort to the guilty person – which presumably cannot be an evil in itself on utilitarian terms, but may count as one in encouraging her to offend again with impunity.

It is perhaps worth noting at this point that although Bentham's list of the advantages to be gained by punishment (prevention, compensation, incapacitation and so on) is fairly standard, he gave a long and imaginative list of features which might detract from the achievement of those aims. For our purposes, the most interesting of these is the feature of unpopularity: Bentham recognised that the unpopularity of a form of punishment might seriously detract from its good consequences.[44] At first sight this principle appears to be of help in establishing that punishment of the innocent would never be justified by utilitarian arguments, since its unpopularity on discovery can hardly be doubted. But in fact the principle is of rather limited help: for Bentham rightly recognised that if the unpopularity were not itself based on the principle of utility, but on some 'prejudice', the ultimate duty of the legislator was to educate the public in accordance with the dictates of utility.[45] This is of course unrealistic with respect to punishing the innocent, which depends on secrecy for most of its utilitarian effect. But it is illuminating with respect to the potential success of utilitarian defences of other widely supported limitations on punishment such as the excuses, justifications and principles of mitigation enshrined in most systems of criminal law and based on a principle of responsibility, especially in so far as the utilitarian defences of such limitations on punishment are based on the sense of unfairness (one important source of unpopularity) they engender.[46] This does raise an interesting general point. Why should the source of a pleasure or a pain be of concern to a utilitarian? Presumably the thought is that 'prejudices' such as intuitions about fairness, if persisted in, act as barriers to the overall maximisation of utility. If this is the case, the ultimate goal of the utilitarian legislator must be to educate the population out of those intuitions so that even punishment of innocent or nonresponsible offenders can be accomplished without secrecy. But this is defeated in turn by the other attendant disutilities of victimisation identified by Bentham himself. And it does seem that even the most thoroughgoing utilitarian must be content to regard some pleasures and pains as in some sense 'basic' and not subject to re-education.

Leaving aside the unpopularity argument, how successful is Bentham's defence? There seem to be three possible responses to this question. First, one could take the view that Bentham establishes that actual cases of utility-justified victimisations are inconceivable, and thus withdraw this objection to utilitarian theories of punishment. Secondly, one can take the view that such a case is conceivable, even if extremely unlikely, and that this illustrates that utilitarianism fails to accommodate some of our strongest, most fixed intuitions about punishment. One would probably conclude from this that the theory is in need of modification. Thirdly, one can take the position that Bentham shows that in the real world, a case in which victimisation is justified by utility is barely conceivable – but still just conceivable. This need not necessarily lead us to abandon his theory. The reason, after all, for our adopting moral principles is to be guided by them in the real world, and if in those circumstances their counterintuitive results seem most unlikely to occur, why should we abandon the principles? In exceptional cases, we cannot just rely on our intuitions: if we are not willing to be guided by our principles in problem cases, why bother having them at all? If our reaction is roughly this one, we can find further strategies for supporting the argument. One interesting example of such a strategy is Paley's position[47] that punishment of the innocent is akin to dying for one's country (although it appears that he was envisaging only cases of mistaken rather than deliberate victimisation). Alternatively, we can attempt to wear down the strength of our counter-intuitions by pointing out generally accepted cases in which we do already in some sense punish the innocent, such as by imposing strict or vicarious liability or remanding suspects in custody over long periods. Or we can point to other generally accepted social practices which impose analogously grave harms on innocent individuals outside the sphere of punishment, such as quarantine.[48] We should note that these arguments also apply with equal force to utilitarian difficulties in accommodating the defences and excuses tradition-ally thought to form a central part of the criminal law, such as those of insanity, duress, provocation, mistake, and so on. Although fairly convincing arguments can be produced to the effect that it will not usually maximise utility to punish an insane or mistaken defendant (for example, because they cannot be deterred, or because such punishments are unpopular), we can still imagine cases in which such punishments would be justified by utility, and even though these may be rare, the fact that the principle of utility has no means by which to distinguish them from other cases or to show them as being exceptional may alert us to a fundamental weakness in that principle itself. Thus, despite many ingenious strategies designed to preserve the appeal of straightforward utilitarianism, we are left with the feeling that utilitarian theory is indeed failing to capture an important moral dimension of the question of punishment, and this alone should be enough to prompt us to seek to modify the theory rather than attempting merely to modify our intuitions.[49]

How much punishment should be inflicted?: Overextensiveness in the extent of punishment

It is often argued that utilitarianism cannot generate satisfactory limits on the types and amount of punishment which it justifies. With respect to the type of punishment, it is argued, for example, that if the goal is rehabilitation, anything which rehabilitates (including surgery, electro-convulsive therapy and so on) can be justified. In the instance of the amount of punishment, it is argued that utilitarianism might justify the imposition of a threat of the death penalty for trivial crimes such as parking offences, given that the threat would be so effective that the penalty would probably never, or only rarely, have to be used. Many of these arguments ignore two fundamental features of Bentham's argu-ment: its principle of frugality and its implication, because of its claim to be a general moral theory, that the scope of relevant effects for the purposes of the utilitarian calculation is very wide. The utilitarian gains of acts of punishment have to be traded off against the losses, and only the least amount of punishment effective to produce the optimal utilitarian outcome can be justified by the principle. Thus effects such as general alarm or horror at draconian forms of penalty must be taken into account, as well as the fact that such radical measures are probably needless as less radical ones will produce the optimal effect. General public outcry and sense of unfairness would also have a direct bearing on the possible utilitarian justification for draconian measures such as the death penalty to deter parking offences, quite apart from its evident needlessness. These other arguments are necessary in order to rebut an argument sometimes put to the effect that utilitarianism could justify such laws because the threat would then be so effective that compliance would be perfect and the punishment would never be inflicted. But quite apart from this, it is clear that there would be a larger measure of insecurity, alarm about the danger of mistaken conviction, and general feeling of dissatisfaction at the disproportionality of such a threat, never to mention the possibility of its confusing common moral sentiments by blurring moral conventions concerning the gradations of seriousness of different offences, which it may be important to maintain for the sake of overall utility. And so it hardly seems likely that utilitarian theory in fact produces a justification of such prima facie unacceptable practices. We may feel some legitimate disquiet about the practicality or even theoretical propriety of translating all the goals and bad consequences of punishment into the common units of pain and pleasure, but the very idea of a calculus imports the notion of trade-offs and a principle of economy which would rule out at least in practice the kinds of penalty currently under consideration. However, the fact remains that no absolute limitation *in principle* excludes such penalties, and many will see this, too, as a deficiency in the utilitarian structure. Moreover, it must be noted that Benthamite utilitarianism leaves open the question of time-scale: over what period must we keep the probable consequences of punishment in view? At what point in time is the maximised utility to be aimed for? The answers to these questions must be external to the principle of utility itself, and may have an important practical bearing upon individual decisions to punish.

Utilitarianism and the content of the criminal law

Since it claims to be a complete moral and political theory, it is clear that utilitarianism will generate answers to the questions of what kinds of offences may be punished and who may be punished for committing them. But are these answers compatible with our definition of punishment and such fixed intuitions as we have about these questions? It might at first sight appear that utilitarianism provides an unacceptably broad view of the proper reach of the criminal law in society, justifying its intrusive regulation in any case where this would maximise overall happiness – and indeed this does seem to present dangers where some form of activity is valued greatly by a small minority and found moderately distasteful by the majority, for criminal regulation might then be utility-justified even though non-regulation would cause only mild dissatisfaction to the majority whereas regulation gravely harms the minority. This is a consequence of the lack of any strong distributive principle within utilitarian theory. What is more, the utilitarian approach seems incapable of generating some familiar distinctions such as that between punishment and compensation, given that it takes what has been dubbed the 'extrinsic'[50] approach to both, viewing them in instrumental or reductive terms. The former set of difficulties may to some extent be mitigated by such devices as Mill's harm principle,[51] although it is not entirely clear that even this can be insulated from the flow of utilitarian argument given its utilitarian roots.[52] But on the other hand the principle of utility may not seem so dangerously extensive when we focus our attention on the usually limited tolerance to criminal regulation in most societies and the empirical limits on how far legal regulation can be effective. On the question of social tolerance, it is clear that the concept of crime is generally associated with, on the one hand, actions and harms which are regarded as the most threatening to social welfare and cohesion, and on the other, those most susceptible of deterrence by legal means. There is a general belief that where the criminal law spreads itself into areas where the harm involved is not serious and/or where behaviour is unlikely to be affected by the law, this leads to a diminution of respect for the criminal law in general and possibly of its effectiveness. And as an empirical matter, a very over-extensive and repressive criminal law would probably lead directly to a society of unhappy people and indirectly to an undermining of the stability of a legal system too dependent on compulsion and too little supported by consensus and a sense of community. Thus within the principle of utility there can be found certain guidelines to the scope and limitations of the criminal law which could possibly generate a satisfactory answer to the question of what types of activity ought to be criminally regulated.

However, as we have already seen, utilitarianism does not stand up to analysis when we move on to the question of who maybe punished for those types of conduct. Although we may be content to accept that one important purpose of the criminal law and penal system may be to promote utility (in whatever sense), we also take for granted that that goal is generally pursued in a particular way, and that the rules and institutions pursuing that aim are of a particular type.[53] Thus we view as fundamentally important such things as the presumption of innocence, a standard of proof beyond reasonable doubt, an elaborate system of evidential and procedural rules (which are very expensive to administer and adhere to) designed to minimise the chances of wrongful conviction, and a general presumption in the absence of clear indications to the contrary that some element of responsibility on the part of the offender must be proved as a necessary condition of conviction. As counter-examples to these cases one can cite the widespread instances of strict and negligence liability in the criminal law, but it is nevertheless true that such instances are, at least according to the prevailing doctrine of the criminal law,[54] seen as being exceptional at least in the area of serious offences carrying heavy penalties. It is perhaps also true, as Hart has argued,[55] that in the case of strict liability we nevertheless regard a sacrifice of principle as having been made. Now certainly some measure of utilitarian defence can be given to these aspects of current criminal law, through arguments such as the undeterrability of the mistaken or mentally ill offender, or the reactive attitudes of the population as a whole which would regard the absence of such defences and excuses as unfair (although recall the unpopularity argument). Nevertheless, it has to be conceded that utilitarian considerations would not always dictate adherence to such principles. It simply does not seem that the criminal process should be either a totally forward-looking, or a totally aggregative affair: and this judgment is reflected in the constraints and limiting principles acknowledged in current practice, which go beyond those which would be dictated by the goals identified by utility. The criminal trial would look very different – would be a faster, more efficient, cheaper business, if it were based on totally utilitarian considerations. How is a purely utilitarian view to account for such aspects of the system as the deeply embedded distinction between acts and omissions along with the widespread reluctance to punish the latter in the absence of some special relationship? Of course we must not assume that all our practices or intuitions are in fact justifiable, but the extent to which utilitarian principles fail to correspond with generally accepted features of the criminal law should at least give us pause for thought about the adequacy of those principles.

It may be objected to my comments in this section on forward-looking arguments that my pessimistic conclusions are not justified if applied to forward-looking arguments in general, for most of the objections I have considered and found to be justified are aimed only at perhaps the crudest form of forward-looking argument – Bentham's aggregative hedonistic utilitarianism. This is generally discredited as a political and moral philosophy for just the sorts of reasons canvassed here with respect to punishment: the lack of an adequate distributive principle, a lack of respect for persons as separate individuals through illegitimate generalisation of a principle of action only appropriate to individual decision-making within one life where trade-offs are legitimate, the simplistic nature of its ultimate goal, and so on.[56] Most recent political philosophy has rejected such a view, yet almost all of it by the same token has an important forward-looking aspect.[57] Why have I not adopted one of these more sophisticated consequence-sensitive theories as my target?

There are several reasons for this strategy. First of all, at least until very recently, the vast majority of writing on punishment which takes a forward-looking line has been in the Benthamite tradition;[58] indeed one might almost say that theory of punishment has become isolated from the rest of political philosophy, where it belongs, and thus has got stuck at an early nineteenth century stage of development. Since this is the main flavour of the tradition, it seemed necessary at least to reflect this in an expository chapter. Secondly, the refinements of aggregative hedonistic utilitarianism which most obviously present themselves for consideration – namely, utility conceived as desire-satisfaction rather than pleasure and the maximand calculated in terms of average as opposed to aggregate utility – seem unpromising as candidates for resolving the intractable difficulties met by utilitarian theories of punishment. This is because, as we have seen, the major problems which those theories encounter flow from the *structure* of the argument which they present, in particular its distributive implications, and from the unitary theory of value embodied by the notion of utility. A change from pleasure to desire-satisfaction as the utility to be maximised leaves that structure unaffected and still represents a unitary goal, and a switch to average rather than aggregate utility, whilst it may have some implications for the way in which utility will be distributed, is unlikely to generate the stable limiting principles which seem necessary to solve problems such as victimisation. Finally, and most importantly, the rather primitive nature of consequentialist theory of punishment has to be understood in order to comprehend the development, through dissatisfaction with both it and retributivism, of mixed theories of punishment. My ultimate argument will be that an integrated pluralistic account – a more sophisticated consequence-sensitive rationale for punishment – can be given, through a forward-looking view which explicitly incorporates a distributive principle, and which does not necessarily take all preferences equally seriously in terms of the pleasure and pain their satisfaction or frustration generate. This will amount to a theory which is pluralistic in the goods the attainment of which it directs, and one which strikes a proper balance between the legitimate claims of the community and those of its members. In the utilitarian tradition, the developments which come closest to this kind of enterprise are usually labelled 'ideal' utilitarianism, and since I take it that such positions essentially abandon any simple unitary conception of utility, their place in the context of arguments about punishment lies more naturally with the development of the mixed theories than with the utilitarian ones. Indeed, important moves in this direction have already been made in the context of this final type of theory commonly advanced in the literature on punishment, to which we now turn.

MIXED THEORIES OF PUNISHMENT

Given the problems of backward and forward-looking theories in isolation, many writers have sought to produce satisfactory accounts of punishment through hybrid theories which incorporate both types of argument, thus abandoning the attempt to find a single satisfactory principle. There are two basic models of compromise theory: for the first, utilitarian arguments are the fundamental part; for the second, the essence of the theory is a desert principle. The first type of theory essentially proceeds from the intuition that without some good compensating effects we cannot justify having institutions of punishment, but that we need to supplement or restrain the basic utilitarian principle with side-constraints in order to overcome the lack of a convincing principle of distribution in utilitarianism.

Hart's separate questions

The most famous and influential such theory is that proposed by H.L.A. Hart, who begins by distinguishing different questions which must be answered in order to produce a justification of punishment.[59] Having adopted a definition of punishment, Hart argues that three questions arise: first, that of the general justifying aim of punishment – what it is that makes it necessary and right to have institutions of punishment in the first place; secondly, that of the amount of punishment which may justifiably be imposed in any particular case; and thirdly, that of liability to punishment – who may be punished. The second and third questions may be put together under the general heading of distribution. The general justifying aim of punishment, according to Hart, is a utilitarian one, having to do with general deterrence, social protection and the like. It is with these aims in mind that we set up institutions of punishment in the first place, and it is these effects which must justify the institution's existence. In deciding what measure of punishment ought to be imposed in particular cases, this general justifying aim will have some influence, but it is argued that considerations of proportionality and fairness also come in, arguing against, for example, exemplary punishments which might have some utilitarian benefits. However, the reasons which Hart gives for attaching importance to the question of proportionality to the seriousness of the offence at this stage seem to be essentially utilitarian ones: to ignore such considerations might confuse the common moral sense, and would remove the important incentive to the offender to commit a less rather than a more serious offence, or the chosen offence in a less harmful way. However, in answering the question of who may be punished, a principle of 'retribution in distribution' applies strictly: only offenders may be punished, for their offences. This limiting principle is said to be based on considerations of fairness: a basic principle of justice is that in assessing and responding to the actions of individuals, special significance should be attached to voluntary conduct. Thus before we punish someone we ought to be satisfied that they were responsible for their offence in the sense of having had a real opportunity to act otherwise: only at this stage is it fair for the law to step in to pursue its general aim. Again, some of the reasons for the limitation do appear to be essentially utilitarian ones: without a principle of responsibility people would find it difficult to plan their lives, for they would never be able accurately to predict when their actions would bring them within the ambit of criminal regulation, and this would lead to frustration, insecurity, and possibly a general loss of respect for the whole criminal process. But the moral basis of this principle is clearly seen by Hart as being *independent* of its utilitarian recommendations, for it is to act as a constraint on the pursuit of utilitarian goals. And if we can find an independent basis for the limiting principle, it is clear that it resolves the punishment of the innocent problem and issues in a criminal justice system which has a full complement of the defences, excuses and so on which we generally take to be a central moral feature of such systems. Indeed, this solution neatly combines the respective attractions of both utilitarian and retributive theory, evading the charges of pointlessness and mysticism commonly levelled at the latter.

It is not surprising, therefore, that this type of argument has been taken up by many writers, and several variants on the central idea have been expounded. Nino, for example,[60] puts forward a view in which the underlying rationale of punishment is taken to be social protection: without some further limiting principle, however, this would lead to an unfair distribution of burdens and benefits of the penal system in society. We may only fairly pursue this end, according to Nino, where offenders have genuinely consented to the loss of their immunity from punishment. Thus wherever offenders were aware of all the relevant facts and of the normative consequences of their behaviour, where the offence committed was justifiably enacted as an offence (again, note the assumption of some background political principles necessary to answer this last question), and where the offender chose freely to offend, punishment is justifiable. It seems fair enough to ask what Nino would say to a thief who declares at the moment before taking her loot, 'I do not consent to the loss of my immunity from punishment', but the essence of the idea is, I think, a consent-based version of Hart's limiting distributive principle.

Let us pause at this point to consider some difficulties with this very attractive approach to punishment. First of all, the arguments generally presented in support of the principle of distribution are often susceptible of re-interpretation on utilitarian lines. Arguments purportedly based on fairness, but which appeal to the values of predictability, certainty and security indeed look suspiciously utilitarian: and, of course, once such a re-interpretation is undertaken, although we may have achieved a wider view of what count as relevant utilities and disutilities, which is salutary in itself, we shall not have escaped from our initial problem. Alternatively, if we do accept that arguments from fairness are distinctive and separate from the principle of utility, we then have to explain how the two different principles relate to each other: we cannot escape the problems of one theory by simple addition of a separate, unconnected qualification. This may appear to be a rather abstract quibble, but it does in fact have important practical implications. For example, Hart's discussion sometimes appears to assume that the distributive principle should act, ideally, as an absolute limitation on the pursuit of the utilitarian general aim. Yet it seems implausible that we should always be willing to accept fairness as an absolute constraint upon the pursuit of utility, in whatever sense. There do appear to be emergency cases and possibly even less exceptional ones in which we are willing to make some trade-off between justice and utility: for example, in the case of killing (perhaps through punishment) an innocent person in order to save a million lives. Indeed, taking the most obvious example from criminal justice, it is not clear that we would be willing entirely to abandon strict liability, as indeed Hart envisages when he refers to such liability as being imposed with a sense of sacrifice of principle. What Hart fails to tell us is *when* the principle ought to be sacrificed; when it is 'right' to do a wrong in punishing an offender who is not fully responsible for her offence. We need more information about the relative weightings of the various values involved, so that we can apply them to problem cases, as Hart's reference to strict liability implicitly acknowledges but fails to provide. In dealing with the intractable moral problems of comparison and balancing, one obvious solution is to translate each value into commensurable units such as utility; the apparent straightforwardness of such an approach is probably a source of the continuing influence of utilitarianism as a moral theory, in spite of all its problems. It seems that we need a solution lying in between, and a good deal less neat than, either the utilitarian subsumption of different values as aspects of general utility or Hart's adoption of an independent principle as a side-constraint.

Institutions and application

But perhaps we have been too hasty in our criticism of the promising compromise theory: it is worthwhile to pause and reconsider by looking at a somewhat different version. Putting the matter in Benn's formulation,[61] the proposal is essentially that we distinguish two questions: first, why have the institution of punishment; secondly, why apply the rules of the institution in individual cases? On this version, what really seems to be in issue is a move from act- to rule-utilitarianism: the justification of punishment is not to be made out in terms of the utility of individual acts of punishment but of that of the general rules of the institution.[62] Thus John Rawls argued in a famous article[63] that the justification for the institution of punishment was a utilitarian one, but that within the institution individual punishments were justified on an essentially retributive or rule-based argument. Individuals are simply punished as per the utility-justified rules of the institution: we punish individuals 'because they broke the law'. Again, the attractions are obvious: the principle is a simple one, and we only have to pause for a moment's reflection to realise that there are vast difficulties involved in any conception of an act-utilitarian judge, and that most of these are resolved by the rule-utilitarian approach. However, two additional problems arise on this formulation. In the first place, it is not clear that the institution/application distinction is sufficient to its purpose; surely consideration of the justice of the punishment arises not just at the application stage but also at the design or legislative stage? Secondly, what does it mean to claim that a rule or set of rules is justified by its utility? This cannot mean that rule-application always leads to utility-maximisation, for if this were the case the principle would presumably have the same results as act-utilitarianism and therefore similar problems.[64] The claim must either be that rule-application usually leads to utility-maximisation, or, more plausibly, that regular rule-application leads to utility-maximisation when viewed dynamically over a long period, perhaps because we have limited knowledge and foresight and therefore tend to make mistakes when we try to apply an act-utilitarian principle, or because of the extra benefits of consistency and security which consistent rule-application provides.

Nevertheless, even interpreted in this way, certain problems remain. First of all, is this type of solution not uncomfortably close to the definitional stop adopted by Quinton and criticised above?[65] Is Rawls not in fact appealing to the definition of the institution which he is seeking to justify in order to supply part of the justification itself? The argument is that, for instance, *institutions* of victimisation would never be justified by utility; but if we are true utilitarians, what is to prevent us from appealing again to the principle of utility at the level of the individual case? Why should an appeal to the form and definition of the institution stunt the flow of utilitarian reasoning? It seems unlikely that the occasional deviation from the rule when arguments from utility dictate it would really undermine the long-term utilitarian benefits of having the rule at all. Surely some further principle has been covertly (as it has in Hart's case, overtly) introduced? To put the point somewhat differently, if the Rawlsian account is a genuinely utilitarian one, that is, if it is based upon principle concerned directly with the maxmisation of good consequences in the Benthamite sense, we can imagine a process of having constantly to modify those rules and to add exceptions to them as particular applications are found not to maximise utility. This suggests that we shall have to sacrifice some of the original gains in terms of predictability and certainty, and moreover find ourselves back at the act-utilitarian position and still confronted with our original problem. Indeed, it has been argued[66] that in fact act- and rule-utilitarianism do turn out to be extensionally equivalent. If, on the other hand, we stick to our rule even in a case where its application clearly does not maximise utility, we are no longer really utilitarians: we have become concerned with something other than, or additional to, the maximisation of utility. The problem, therefore, is that act-utilitarianism is 'imperialist' in that it purports to be a complete argument in itself to justify both acts and institutions of punishment: it is thus difficult to supplement the principle without abandoning it altogether. If we are successfully to pursue this promising line of thought, we must elicit and explain more fully than has as yet been attempted what the other values involved are, how they may be grafted onto the principle of utility, and how the various values relate and balance at a more fundamental level.

Perhaps we can push these criticisms a little further by slightly recasting them. All these hybrid theories proceed on the assumption that there are genuinely separate questions to be answered: for Rawls, the questions are, why have rules, and why apply those rules? For Hart, they are, why have the rules, to whom should they be applied, and to what extent? But is this assumption valid? It seems to be true, as Rawls acknowledges, that rules themselves contain their own conditions of application. No sensible system has rules and then fails to apply them: prima facie, the reasons for having the rules generate the reasons for applying them in individual cases. This seems to indicate that the principle of distribution, if one is (as it seems to be) needed, must come in at the first stage: *a* principle of distribution is inevitably contained within or at least envisaged by the general justifying aim of the rules. And if the general justifying aim is straightforwardly utilitarian, the project of grafting on a separate distributive principle begins to look deeply problematic, for utilitarianism does *not*, as its critics sometimes claim, lack such a principle. It rather embodies criteria of distribution which are vulnerable to serious objection. It is necessary, then, to identify an alternative general justifying aim which incorporates or is consistent with an acceptable distributive principle, rather than to separate different questions and give different answers to them. Conversely, I think it can be argued that a justification for institutions of punishment must include a justification for their actual use in individual cases, and that the individual question is in some ways primary: can any single infliction of punishment ever be justified? The mere fact that such an infliction is according to rules does not seem to generate any additional justification in itself. In justifying a system of rules, we generally assume that those rules will be applied: therefore the justification which we seek must also justify the application of the rules. For these reasons it is my belief that neither the Rawlsian nor the Hartian distinction really withstands close analysis.[67]

On the other hand, it does seem plausible and likely that a system or institution of punishment could have effects which isolated, unsystematic instances of punishment could not; the generation of stable support to the legal system as a whole is one instance which springs immediately to mind. The systematic nature of law perhaps points in the direction of an account of punishment which also reflects a systematised nature. A certain threshold of regularity and predictability of punishment may well be a necessary condition of achieving punishment's proper goals: but if we are to solve the distributive problem, can we stay in the realms of straightforward utilitarianism? Or must we graduate to a subtler, more complex form of consequence-oriented theory? And in any case, does the rule-utilitarian solution overcome the means-to-an-end objection (if indeed that objection is not limited to the context of an extreme, libertarian, individualistic moral theory); is not the application of the rules in individual cases in any case using the offender as a means of achieving the end which the system of rules is designed to achieve?

None of these criticisms shows any of these theories to be fundamentally misguided. Rather, the argument is that much

more work has to be done in order to explain and justify the
coherence of the different principles involved in the arguments at
a deeper level. This can only be done by means of integration of
the argument with those of general political philosophy, which is
just what has been sadly lacking in much of the tradition of
writings on the justification of punishment. Without this further
argument, the combination of different principles may be thought
to amount to an example of intuitionism, which of course makes
the philosophical task easier, but less illuminating. If I am right in
thinking that it is as counterintuitive to claim that fairness is
always an absolute bar on the pursuit of utility as it is, at the
opposite extreme, to claim that victimisations are justifiable in
the way in which utilitarianism would have us believe, it must be
necessary to explore the basis of independent principles such as
fairness so as to discover how to go about assessing the relative
demands of fairness and utility in particular types of case, either
through some commensurable measure of the values of fairness
and utility or by some other means. We shall also have to
question whether the setting up of the problem in terms of a
combination of the demands of, and an opposition between,
fairness and utility, is the right approach. What I am arguing at
this stage, then, is that the Hartian and Rawlsian solutions are
unfinished ones and that there is more moral and political
philosophy to be done before it can be shown that their solutions
in fact generate a justification of punishment.

Weak retributivism
The second type of mixed theory of punishment may conveniently
be termed weak retributivism. This is the thesis which regards
desert of unpleasant treatment as a necessary but not a sufficient
condition for punishment: an offence provides the state with a
reason, but not a conclusive reason for the infliction of
punishment.[68] This is also sometimes expressed as the principle
that offences give the state a right to punish, but not a duty to do
so. However, having a right to do something is not in itself a
sufficient reason for doing that thing; it can be overriden by other
reasons, most obviously by other right-based arguments. For
example, I may have a right to exact a debt from you because
you have promised to pay the debt on a certain date, yet in
certain circumstances it might not be right for me to enforce the
promise, for example because your circumstances have changed,
and to pay me now would force you to starve, whereas I can
comfortably wait to be paid. Thus this argument allows and

indeed requires that other values and reasons influence the decision to punish: the state has a right to set up institutions which will be put into action only when certain other conditions are fulfilled. It is perhaps useful here to question the propriety of using rights-talk in this area. What exactly is meant by the claim that the state has a right to punish in certain circumstances? Apparently all that is intended is that in those circumstances it would be right for the state to do so. In the purely moral area, it does seem that rights suffer from a certain 'criterionlessness'[69] which renders appeal to them considerably less useful than in the legal sphere where the criteria which create and validate rights can be more clearly stated. Let us therefore proceed in the more straightforward terminology of what it is right or justifiable for the state to do, rather than the terminology of rights, which lends an illusory conclusiveness to the sound of the debate.

This weak retributivist argument is in a sense the converse of Hart's compromise theory: the latter focuses on a utilitarian rationale for the institution of punishment, using the retributivist principle as a constraint upon the pursuit of the utilitarian goal. The weak retributivist view regards treatment in accordance with desert as the central justifying factor, whilst requiring (at least on some versions) a utilitarian justification for the infliction of punishment in individual cases. Utilitarianism thus acts as a limitation on the desert principle. Given the overwhelming difficulty which we encountered earlier in this chapter in trying to give any clear meaning to the notion of desert, we might well conclude straight away that any theory which places that mysterious and metaphorical idea at its core is doomed to obscurity and hence failure. However, for the sake of completeness, I shall consider some difficulties which are specific to those theories which seek to combine the idea of desert with other arguments for punishment.

To return to our original statement of the weak retributivist principle, the idea that desert furnishes the state with a non-conclusive reason to punish raises the question of what types of extra reason must be adduced in order to produce a justification of particular acts of punishment. On some accounts, apparently non-utilitarian factors are appealed to – factors such as fairness and justice. But it is clear that the most obvious candidates are utilitarian reasons such as prevention, deterrence, avoidance of private vengeance and so on. It is important to note that on most weak retributivist views desert operates not only as the central justification but also as a limit on the amount of punishment: the only function of the consequentialist considerations is to add an element which provides the sufficient reason for some punitive action. On this view, consequentialism cannot tell us whom to punish or how much to punish; it merely defeats the argument from the pointlessness of purely retributive punishment. The difficulty here is that these utilitarian arguments do purport to provide not just an explanation of when we may exercise our right or power of punishment, but actually to make it right for us to punish. According to utilitarianism, it is right to punish wherever such an action maximises the aggregate of pleasure over pain. It is thus hard to see how it is that the weak retributive principle fails to become redundant. In addition, it is not clear whether the desert argument is intended to apply to the design of institutions and the utilitarian one to individual acts of punishment, as the complete converse to the Rawlsian view. If this were so, we would be invited to endorse the unattractive vision of a legal system based on a principle of desert, in which individual acts of punishment were left to judicial discretion which should be exercised on the basis of consequentialist reasoning, or else of a system in which the legislator made utilitarian generalisations in framing the rules which were nevertheless primarily based on considerations of desert. Such a system may have some resonance with our own practices, but its status as a prescriptive vision seems highly dubious.

Perhaps it is worth our while to examine a little more closely one of the most persuasive versions of the weak retributivist thesis.[70] This view argues that the voluntary commission of an offence gives the state a prima facie right to punish an offender, who has forfeited her rights by the offence. However, the offender has only forfeited her rights to the extent that she violated the rights of the victim of her offence, and therefore the state may deprive her of her rights only to an extent equivalent or proportionate to her violation of the victim's rights. Furthermore, the state may only do this if to do so would be in the interest of social protection. In other words, one is to look to the question of desert first of all, and then to see if there is a possibility of an act of punishment serving the end of social protection. With respect to the justified amount of punishment, we have already examined the indeterminacy of the idea of a punishment which results in an equivalent deprivation of rights. But here there are further problems, and they are essentially the same as those we identified in the context of Hart's hybrid theory, namely that there is no adequate explanation given of why the two principles appealed to need to be blended and how the blending may be achieved coherently. It is implausible that an action's accordance with parts of each of several moral theories gives that action a moral justification. This is of course in addition to the general problems with the very idea of desert which we considered above.

Thus, to conclude this section on compromise theories of punishment, we may summarise the difficulties which such theories encounter. These theories attempt to resolve the problems encountered by the unitary principles of punishment by dividing the issue into separate questions and applying different principles in answering each. One central division is between questions about the justification of institutions and of individual acts of punishment, and this division appears to be unsatisfactory in that we expect the justification for the institution or rules of punishment to include, or at least point the way to, an answer to the problem of the application of punishment. Furthermore, although Hart's theory is clearly preferable in that it explicitly introduces a separate principle, we need some fuller account of the relationship between the two principles. For rules themselves do generally include at least some reasons for and constraints upon their own application: thus the principle of non-punishment of the innocent, which we incorporated in our definition of punishment, ought to be incorporated in the general justifying aim of the institution of punishment. In order fully to understand the problem which the question of punishment presents to the political philosopher it is useful and even necessary to bear in mind the many different aspects of the problem, but ultimately the philosopher will have to bring the various aspects together again in an integrated justification which, if it incorporates different principles, will have to explain how they are related and how their relative demands are to be balanced if and when they conflict.

CONCLUSIONS

At the end of this reviewing chapter our conclusions are mainly negative: we have discovered no satisfactory justifying theory of punishment, although we have encountered arguments which are persuasive and appear to capture several of our fixed intuitions concerning the subject. So, we do not start the remainder of our enterprise with a blank sheet, but there are many vital gaps to be filled in, perhaps by asking new questions rather than by merely reconsidering the old ones. We found the retributive theories unconvincing as they draw too strong a moral analogy, assuming rather than arguing for the relation between punishment-worthiness and blameworthiness, fail to rebut the charge of pointlessness or to dissociate themselves from a practice of vengeance, raise unresolved questions of underlying political philosophy, and ultimately leave an unacceptable measure of mystery surrounding the question which they purport to illuminate. Traditional utilitarian theories are unconvincing because they suffer from the general defects of aggregative hedonistic utilitarianism, notably that they lack adequate principles of distribution, are subject to certain empirical doubts concerning efficacy, appear to endorse certain intuitively unacceptable forms of subterfuge, and do not accord with settled intuitions concerning the principle of responsibility. Mixed theories are flawed in that they fail to articulate deeper unifying principles, background political principles which could clarify the surface tension between the demands of utility and desert. At this point it seems that we need to withdraw from the traditional debate to consider some general, related issues in legal, political and moral theory, before returning to the issue of punishment to see if the solution seems any nearer in the light of our excursion. The journey so far suggests that we may look for progress along the path of non-aggregative consequence-sensitive theories which actually incorporate a principle of distributive justice capable of overcoming the major objections to forward-looking theories of punishment.

CHAPTER 3

THE RELEVANCE OF RESPONSIBILITY

We now turn to the wider questions of political philosophy which I have argued must be addressed in order properly to consider the justification of punishment. The first such issue which we shall address is that of responsibility, a concept which is appealed to in a wide variety of spheres of discourse. Notably, apart from forming an important part of the linguistic currency of moral philosophers and criminal lawyers, it also helps to shape what we might call common sense judgments about the status to be accorded to people's actions and what our responses to those actions should be. For our purposes, the significance of the concept flows principally from the fact that both retributive and mixed theories of punishment attach a special importance to responsibility as a necessary condition for a justified punitive response. It is therefore of central importance to our enterprise to analyse the concept and to explore its various possible conceptions so as to form a judgment about what place responsibility might have in a reconstructed theory of punishment.

In this chapter I shall describe two main conceptions of responsibility, and I shall be considering the illuminating potential and moral basis of these two conceptions. We must also investigate the possibility that the conception or conceptions of responsibility which should be employed by the criminal law need to relate in a special way to the particular functions which the criminal law is expected to perform. For the problem of responsibility, like that of punishment, is not an isolated moral and political issue. In the first part of the chapter I shall investigate the nature and extent of the connection between conceptions of moral responsibility and the basis of liability in the criminal law. In the second part of the chapter I shall offer normative arguments for a shift in the conception of responsibility usually thought to underpin criminal liability, and I shall trace the connections between this issue and our principal concern of punishment.

MORAL RESPONSIBILITY, FREEDOM AND PUNISHMENT

Arguments about the place of responsibility at the foundation of the moral basis of criminal liability have played a bigger part in theorising about the justification for punishment than have the other related questions which I shall consider in the next three chapters. I shall not here be primarily concerned with a major preoccupation of other writers on punishment, namely the fundamental philosophical issue of whether individuals can ever be said to be responsible for their actions, in the sense of having some measure of free will, or whether all our actions are in fact causally determined. I do not mean by this treatment to deny the normative importance of this debate to the justification of punishment, nor to imply a *traditional* compatibilist position, which argues that the sort of freedom of choice relevant to responsibility conceived as capacity responsibility would survive the truth of determinism,[1] within the debate. I gave this issue only a subsidiary place for two main reasons. The first is that it has already commanded so much attention from philosophers, who have carried on a complex and often very technical debate, to which it is almost impossible to add in any substantial way without devoting a whole book to that subject alone.[2] The second is that it has in some ways less direct bearing on my account of punishment than do the other less noticed questions, because I shall in fact describe and defend a conception of responsibility as a necessary condition for punishment, the existence of which is not intimately related with the existence of free will or the possibility of what is often thought of as genuine choice.

We should perhaps begin, however, with a brief summary of the relevance of the issue of freedom of the will for the traditional theories. In the case of a substantially retributivist position, the existence of freedom of the will is essential to the very core of the desert argument, desert of punishment only being generated by truly voluntary, freely chosen actions. Thus, whilst the truth of determinism would not affect the integrity of the desert principle, it would render it of precious little practical moral significance, since no human actions would ever deserve a punitive response. In the case of utilitarian theories, again, the empirical truth of determinism would of course not affect the principle itself, but it might well affect the outcome of the prescribed process of reasoning, although not in such a radically destructive way as that of reasoning based on desert. For although the discovery that our actions are causally determined would not affect our desire to reduce the incidence of certain sorts of harmful acts, it would alert us to the possibility that those acts might not be able to be deterred or otherwise prevented in the straightforward way which is sometimes (an assumption of already dubious validity) assumed. The result of determinism in affecting the outcome of such justifying argument is, once again, important, in that a theory of punishment which turns out not in fact to justify any substantial measure of punishment would be of little practical value. Moreover, the truth of determinism would have serious implications for Hart's promising mixed theory[3] because of its adoption of a limiting principle of responsibility, or 'retribution in distribution'. For if we never in fact have a genuine opportunity to do otherwise than we do, and if we reject the compatibilist argument that morally significant *freedom* can be conceived merely in terms of the absence of certain kinds of constraint, thus surviving the truth of determinism, that limiting condition could never be met, and punishment could never be justified. It does seem strange, not to say worrying, that some of our most fixed moral judgments about punishment turn out on this view to be dependent for their validity on a complex set of empirical facts, the truth of which is highly controversial and exceptionally difficult to determine. This, I shall argue, is a persuasive (if pragmatic) reason to at least look for a principle of responsibility which could satisfy our intuitions whilst avoiding the vulnerability of Hart's conception.

We need to be aware of one other qualification to the impact of the truth of determinism on the justification of punishment. I have argued that if determinism is true, this would have important consequences for the outcome of at least all of the result-oriented justifying arguments for punishment which have been advanced, and which will be put forward in this book. What makes the issue particularly complicated, however, is the fact that those consequences will vary according to how far we as members of society are actually able to 'take on board' the truth of determinism, in the sense of not only being intellectually convinced of it, but also allowing that conviction to shape our reactive attitudes, principally those to do with the attribution of blame. Within the context of a consequence-sensitive justification of punishment, one which takes the consequences of punishment to form at least part of the reason for its infliction, the extent to which those reactive attitudes have become influenced by acknowledgment of the truth of determinism will radically affect the measure and type of punitive response which the principles actually justify in concrete circumstances. An obvious example would be that within a theory which acknowledged that one of the justifying reasons for punishment was its necessity in order to prevent individual citizens resorting to private vengeance, the continued existence of strong vengeful feelings even in the face of the truth of determinism would clearly contribute importantly to our assessment of what the state's response to an offence should be: the state would have to take those feelings into account in working out the utilitarian calculus in order optimally to pursue the goal in question. More fundamentally, since I shall argue that the most convincing account of punishment has at its core a notion of the desirability of the maintenance of the state and the criminal justice system as a whole, and if widespread self-help and loss of respect for the institutions of that system would be the result of tempering punishment to the strict dictates of determinism, there may still be room for justified punishments which go beyond those limits. All this indeed goes to show just how radical a change the proving of determinism might work in our personal lives as well as within our social institutions, and it explains the persuasiveness of the argument which is often put, that should that proof ever be rendered and truly internalised by all of us, it would ultimately herald the end of institutions of punishment roughly like our own and issue in a system more akin to the treatment model proposed by Wootton[4] and others.[5] But it is nevertheless important to note that such changes would not necessarily proceed from a proof of determinism; there would also have to be a corresponding conviction and change of attitude on the part of ordinary people – a change which many of us find it hard to envisage.

MORAL RESPONSIBILITY AND CRIMINAL LIABILITY

Let us begin by looking afresh at the common-sense rationale of the general concern shown by systems of criminal law with a responsibility or (as it is often called) fault requirement. This, I think, consists in two main elements, there being a significant interplay between the two. On the one hand, there is the fact that, in terms of its social meaning, criminal conviction expresses something which is analogous to (although *not* the same as[6]) a moral judgment. Our discourse both within and about criminal law is replete with the language of fault, culpability, and condemnation – and despite the fact that many people would question the morality of many of the practices of actual criminal processes and the judgments they express, it cannot be denied that they do express, from the 'legal point of view', a normative judgment, a finding of wrongs committed, which is akin to moral judgments in different spheres of discourse. Naturally, the strength of this analogy varies according to the subject matter of the offence in question, and we shall have to return in a later chapter[7] to the question of the proper scope of the criminal law.

The second core element relevant to the fault requirement is the fact that the criminal process inflicts, in the name of justice, serious harms on offenders (and others), most obviously through the practice of punishment and the process of stigmatisation (often deliberately stimulated, in our society, by judicial rhetoric). The practice of punishment as I have defined it[8] also means that the criminal law embodies an inherently coercive technique which threatens personal autonomy. The interplay between these two elements is clear: on the one hand, punishment and stigma are thought to be appropriate at least partly because of the moral blame analogy: on the other, the prima facie wrongfulness of punishment reinforces the view that only cases in which *some* moral analogy can be drawn should be subject to criminal regulation. Hence these features of the criminal process in our society lead quite directly to the view that it is fair only to convict people of criminal offences if, in addition to causing criminal harms, they were in some way *at fault* in doing so: liability for accidental, inadvertent or otherwise non-responsible acts is seen as morally unacceptable. Thus far, leaving aside utilitarian theories of the criminal process which might reject this starting point, consensus is very wide. It is only when we embark on the crucial task of articulating our assumptions about what should count as 'fault', in the sense of what makes an agent accountable, answerable or responsible for the act or consequence which she has done or caused, or otherwise been involved in producing, that clarity begins to fade and deep problems of principle emerge.

The capacity conception

In considering the philosophical basis of the principle of responsibility which should underlie criminal liability, the most obvious place to start is with the capacity conception of moral responsibility, lucidly expounded by H.L.A. Hart as forming, when combined with a principle of fairness, the basis for his limiting principle of distribution in punishment.[9] This conception of responsibility consists in both a cognitive and a volitional element: a person must both understand the nature of her actions, knowing the relevant circumstances and being aware of possible consequences, and have a genuine opportunity to do otherwise than she does – to exercise control over her actions, by means of choice. If she has not had a real opportunity to do otherwise, if she has not genuinely chosen to act as she does, she cannot be said to be truly responsible, and it would be unfair to blame, let alone punish her for her actions. As we have seen,[10] the value of the principle of fairness is fleshed out by Hart in terms of the harms of uncertainty and unpredictability which would be engendered should individuals not be able to plan their lives so as to avoid the intervention of the criminal law, but the argument is based not merely on its utilitarian recommendations, but on an independent principle of justice (reflected in the widely shared intuition that, other than in exceptional circumstances, it is *unfair* to blame people except for actions which proceed from informed choices). Such a view may perhaps best be understood as proceeding from something like the Kantian ideal of respect for persons.[11] We should beware, however, of regarding Hart's account of responsibility as a fully-fledged account of moral blameworthiness: it is not, but is offered rather as an account of the fair conditions under which the utilitarian goals of the criminal justice system may be pursued. Such is the strength of Hart's account that the most influential commentators on British criminal law[12] generally assume the capacity conception to underlie the *mens rea* or responsibility requirement in that law, and proceed accordingly with a working presupposition of the possibility of freely chosen actions, or of a compatibilist account of the relevance of determinism to responsibility.

The difficulty with both the moral and political thesis offered by Hart and its potential as a rationalisation of the criminal law is quite simply that our intuitions on the subject are complex and often inconsistent. This problem can perhaps best be illustrated by drawing from English criminal law an example which both reflects that complexity and identifies practical and philosophical difficulties with the capacity conception. Most systems of criminal law admit as grounds of responsibility not only intention and recklessness, in the sense of awareness of a risk and a decision to go ahead regardless, but also negligence – a failure to meet an objectively determined standard of behaviour.[13] And this fact about our system of criminal law seems to reflect a settled moral judgment, to the effect that whilst wrongful actions done negligently may not be so culpable as those performed intentionally or recklessly, they are nevertheless culpable to some degree and justify, in the context of criminal law, an attribution of responsibility and some punitive response. Hart argues that,[14] with the modification that the law should inquire into the defendant's capacity and real opportunity to have reached the required (usually 'reasonable') standard of care or behaviour (thus absolving from liability defendants such as the mentally sub-normal, who may not have been able to reach the required standard however much they have tried), negligence liability can be accommodated as a genuine form of responsibility-liability on the basis that the defendant is responsible for having failed to adopt that social standard of behaviour, the reasonably careful attitude demanded by the law. But can it be said that she is in any direct sense responsible *for* the harms which she negligently causes? The abandonment of the requirement of one of the traditional forms of 'mental element' such as intention seems to have attenuated the link between the wrongful action and the responsibility requirement. In a sense, once a negligent attitude is, even 'responsibly', adopted, the harm ultimately caused becomes fortuitous: all that the defendant is directly responsible *for* in the capacity sense is her failure to meet a reasonable standard in her actions. For example, the consequences of the actions of a negligent driver will depend on a number of extraneous circumstances, such as traffic conditions and the standard of care and skill exercised by other drivers: once she sets out on her journey in a careless or absent-minded frame of mind, whether or not she commits a serious criminal offence will be largely a matter of luck. This is not to say, of course, that no adequate link between negligence as a 'fault element' and the ensuing wrongful action can be established for the purposes of an adequate theory of attribution.[15] This can certainly be done by abandoning the traditional emphasis on the fault element as consisting in aware, subjective mental states contemporaneous with the 'criminal' act. Indeed, Hart suggests this when he argues that the notion of 'mens' should be extended 'beyond the "cognitive" element of knowledge or foresight, so as to include the capacities and powers of normal persons, to think about and control their conduct.'[16]

However, the example does, I think, raise a further difficult set of questions for the capacity conception, to which I shall now turn. Let us imagine, for a moment, a system different from our own, in which criminal negligence, in accordance with the capacity conception of responsibility, could only be established by way of proof that the defendant had a genuine opportunity, a capacity to meet the reasonable standard of behaviour or awareness required by the law. A moment's reflection shows that this practice would be fraught with difficulty, for it raises deep problems about whether and in what sense agents can be said freely and responsibly to choose their attitudes, or even to have the capacity to do so. We seem to be drawn into an infinite regress of questions about the formation of interlinked attitudes and dispositions and the possibilities of their having been formed differently which would be impractical, unrealistic and futile, given that, as I shall argue, the salient factor for the purposes of a punitive social response seems rather to be primarily the sheer *fact* of an antisocial, dangerous or indifferent attitude at the time of the offence. Our response may well be conditional upon the existence of normal capacities in a very broad sense, but any attempt to specify those capacities with any degree of precision seems doomed to failure, thus casting doubt on the feasibility of making their existence the subject of legal inquiry. And the difficulty applies not only to cases of negligence, it is merely rendered more evident in that case because of the attenuation of the link between ultimate criminal act and adoption of the relevant attitude, which inevitably casts the net of questions raised by the capacity conception backwards in time in all cases. Indeed, this very difficulty can be seen at the root of the law's tendency to *assume* normal capacity (hence the presumption of sanity in English criminal law) and to define its non-existence in practicable ways through the development of specific defences such as duress, provocation, automatism and self-defence.[17]

The character conception
In the light of these difficulties with the attractive capacity conception, it is tempting to throw up one's hands in despair, surrender to intuitionism and accept that no coherent theory of the attribution of responsibility can be constructed, and that all the criminal law can do is to attempt to reflect our diverse and perhaps contradictory intuitions about what counts as fault sufficient to ground criminal liability. But there is an alternative conception of responsibility which we should consider before we adopt such an attitude, and that is the Humean conception of responsibility, recently reassessed by Michael Bayles.[18] According to this conception, ascriptions of responsibility are based

upon judgments about the *character* of the agent: actions for which we hold a person fully responsible are those in which her usual character is centrally expressed. Thus, to give some examples from the criminal law, actions performed as a result of provocation, duress or temporary mental incapacity will be regarded as non- or partially responsible. The finding of a mental element such as intention or recklessness on the character model provides an important piece of evidence from which the existence of character responsibility may be inferred, given that single acts do not always indicate settled dispositions. Whilst this model seems to give an adequate rationale for some of the most familiar excuses, it also serves to point up some possible reasons for the law's ambivalence concerning others. Actions performed by a person suffering from a long term mental incapacity, whilst they call for a different reactive response in terms of traditional conceptions of blameworthiness, still appear to call for some controlling intervention on the part of the state. For since the action cannot be said to be a mere aberration on the part of the accused, the risks of repetition may be high. Hence, in our current criminal law, although the insanity defence absolves the defendant from any theoretical *criminal* liability, it does not remove her from the ambit of legal intervention of a radical kind.[19] This observation may be said to conflate illicitly criminal and non-criminal state intervention; my discussion of just what, if indeed anything, is distinctive about criminal regulation must be deferred until a later chapter,[20] although I shall return to the character conception's handling of the issue of insanity below. But here it is legitimate to note the potential of the character conception for rationalising and emphasising common issues of justification raised by any coercive intervention by the state, even though this particular example lacks one of the formal features of our definition of punishment. Similarly, although more controversially, a person who claims that her offence was committed because she was labouring under a mistake of fact may be regarded in a different light according to whether the mistake is one which the jury thinks any reasonable person might have made or not: if not, perhaps this is a person who systematically, characteristically makes unreasonable mistakes, causing danger to the interests of others – someone whose behaviour manifests a genuine practical indifference to the interests protected by the criminal law. The link with a possible rationale for negligence liability is obvious.

The rejoinder of the supporter of the traditional theory of

responsibility to these suggestions is clear enough. In her sense, we are not responsible for our characters, and to base our legal conception of responsibility on such a footing would smack of illicitly blaming people for what they are, which they cannot help, rather than for what they do, which we assume that they often can – a practice often roundly condemned in treatises on criminal justice and indeed in judicial rhetoric. What are we to say of the generally irascible, thoughtless or stupid person who seems to run a systematically higher chance of committing actions criminally negligently than a person born with or socialised into a different set of characteristics and dispositions? After all, however dispositions are constructed, most of us would agree that many of their features are either totally or practically impossible to change and moreover not voluntarily acquired. Indeed, the objection flows from the way in which the character conception severs the link between voluntariness and responsibility, as is well illustrated by our earlier discussion of the implications of the conception for mentally disordered offenders. But we should not reject the character conception out of hand simply on the basis that it is not the capacity conception. For the fact that most actual systems of criminal law do not fully accord with the capacity conception has, I think, to do with the link between the concept of responsibility and that of the proper functions of the criminal law. This issue must be discussed fully at a later stage,[21] but we shall have to anticipate some of the arguments of that chapter in order to conclude our discussion of responsibility. For the most obvious merit of the character conception is that it serves to highlight the importantly practical orientation of the criminal law as a form of social control. This is, at least in part, that it seeks to reduce, by means of prohibition, conviction and punishment, certain unwanted forms of behaviour, as well as to mitigate the social effects of unprevented crime and to uphold, perhaps symbolically, certain framework social values. This importantly functionalist, foward-looking appoach of the criminal law is reflected in its frequent departures in practice from the traditional theory of responsibility and in its focus on harms caused and threatened (as in cases such as strict liability and the inchoate offences of attempt, incitement and conspiracy[22]). But it would be wrong to conclude that this model does not also have moral recommendations: it does not simply allow individual defendants to be sacrificed on the altar of general deterrence or public protection whatever the basis and antecedents of their actus reus may be. Instead of inquiring directly into a state of mind accompanying the actus reus, it asks a wider set of questions about the defendant herself and the extent to which the actus reus was a truly representative example of her behaviour. This reflects the reactive attitudes we express when we excuse someone's bad behaviour on the basis that it was 'out of character' or 'not like her' – reactive attitudes every bit as strong as those adduced by the traditional theory in support of its conception of responsibility, and similarly linked to the value attached to fairness: it is unfair to hold people responsible for actions which are out of character, but only fair to hold them so for actions in which their settled dispositions are centrally expressed. On the traditional theory, it may well be true that we are not to blame for our characters. But the criminal law has to deal with us as we are, and given its task of helping to create the conditions for tolerable social existence, it is not open to it to excuse people for unavoidable characteristics which make them dangerous to the community, at least to the extent of removing them from the ambit of criminal regulation completely. This may appear to be a morally repugnant conclusion, but it can perhaps be seen in proportion with the help of some reflection on the extent to which luck and other unavoidable factors inevitably affect people's life chances in almost every area.[23] We must remind ourselves once again that an ascription of responsibility for the purposes of criminal justice is *not* identical with an assertion of purely moral blameworthiness.

RECONSTRUCTING RESPONSIBILITY

We have now considered our two competing conceptions of responsibility, both of which seem to have peculiar moral recommendations and to find some, albeit uneven, support in actual institutions of criminal justice. In this section, I shall try to lay the foundations for my ultimate argument that a modified version of the character conception constitutes the appropriate basis for criminal liability. To do so, we shall have to return for a while to the traditional theories of punishment and the background conception of the criminal process. Let us begin by asking ourselves afresh just what is the nature and significance of the question of responsibility according to each of the major traditions in theorising about punishment. On the retributivist view, the 'diagnosis' of responsibility for the criminal action is both a necessary and a sufficient condition for the justifiability of punishment. The orientation being entirely backward-looking, although the judgment of responsibility gives guidance about the proper punitive response in the sense that desert indicates not only that punishment is justified but also how much punishment may be inflicted, this guidance has no reference whatsoever to any question about consequences (at least in an ordinary sense) sought to be attained. On the utilitarian view, the question of responsibility arises primarily in terms of its evidential value in showing the usefulness, for example through possibility of deterrence, of punishment. Hart's mixed theory departs from that of the retributivist in that the judgment of responsibility operates as a necessary but not a sufficient condition of punishment, but there is an important analogy in that the judgment of responsibility itself is seen as being separate and distinct from any forward-looking question about what ought to be done with the offender. The finding of responsibility operates only as a threshold and does not contribute to the sentencing decision (except in a somewhat indeterminate way in the area of upper limits) in any direct, practical sense. This separation of course flows from Hart's division of questions of general justifying aim and of distribution. In Chapter 2, I suggested that an adequate solution to the problem of distribution would have to incorporate a distributive principle within the general justifying aim (conceived in non-utilitarian terms), and I questioned the methodology of dividing up questions about punishment in such a radical way. This seems to suggest, in thinking about responsibility, that we need a conception of responsibility which flows from our general view about the proper functions of the criminal process, and which is moreover relevant to questions both of conviction and of sentence, according with the continuity between those two questions, arising at different points in one process. This is one important factor to be borne in mind in reconstructing the notion of responsibility.

The tendency to divide problems up into several aspects, and to rationalise each aspect in terms of different and apparently opposed normative concepts arises, as one would expect, in relation to general theories of the criminal process as well. Indeed, I have already adverted to our dichotomised approach to criminal justice; on the one hand we can conceive the criminal process as a set of practices geared to the reflection of quasi-moral judgments of blameworthiness or culpability: on another, we can conceive of it in an essentially instrumental practice geared towards goals such as the reduction of criminal harms or the promotion of (at least a sense of) security in society. Each of these conceptions is, of course, a caricature, but I think most people will recognise them and, moreover, be reluctant entirely to abandon either aspect in constructing a normative theory of the process. Indeed, the starting point for our discussion was the acknowledgment of the role of the conception of responsibility or 'fault element' in the definition of criminal offences in reconciling these two aspects, just as in Hart's theory of punishment it is used to reconcile retributive and consequentialist insights.

I want to use this brief allusion to the functions of the criminal process to make two main points. In the first place, here, too, the way forward seems to lie in rejecting this dichotomised vision of the criminal process and to try to reconceive it in an integrated way, so that its goals and functions themselves contain at least the seeds of the proper limitations on their pursuit. Ends and means, goals and their distributive impact would still be distinguishable and important questions, but they would be addressed in terms which did not proceed from opposing values and conceptions of the criminal process. Secondly, this allusion to the functions of the criminal process should also remind us of one particular aspect of the important disanalogy between the ascription of criminal guilt and the attribution of moral blame. In the case of a criminal conviction, an important part of the enterprise, as well as judging and 'condemning', is its contribution to certain goals, or, as I should prefer to say, its serving of certain functions through its own peculiar techniques. As judicial rhetoric often shows, this is a central part of both the purpose and meaning of a criminal conviction. Now it may often be the case that in attributing moral blame, we hope to alter the agent's behaviour or attitudes, or social behaviour in general, but this could hardly be said to be a central part of the enterprise: such ends seem to be contingently rather than logically related to the practice. It may be objected that I am making a mistake in conflating questions about the goals and nature of the institution as a whole, and the meaning of individual applications of its rules, but such a distinction is, of course, just what I have argued needs to be weakened or reinterpreted. The nature and justifying purpose of an institution will have implications for the justification and affect the meaning of the individual applications of the rules and principles which make up the institution as a whole.[24] It might also be objected that I am illegitimately conflating the distinct questions of conviction and sentence, the former expressing a backward-looking judgment, the latter concerned with forward-looking goals. Again, this would be to surrender to the dichotomised vision which I have argued is fatal to a true understanding both of the nature of the criminal process properly conceived and the justification of punishment. The salient point to be made by reference to the disanalogy between moral blame and criminal conviction is that, as I have already argued, the function of the theory of attribution, the principle of responsibility, is *not* to mirror moral blameworthiness, but rather to represent a more limited constraint, internal to the functions of the system, on the practice of conviction and punishment.

These background points relate directly to the strengths and plausibility of the character conception of responsibility in the context of attributing criminal fault. In general moral discourse, although I have argued that the character conception has some place, it may not count as a sufficient condition for moral blameworthiness (I shall not attempt to conclude this question since it is not important to my main argument). But in the context of criminal justice, the character conception has great plausibility, for several reasons. In the first place, in the criminal justice context we can, I think, see strong reasons for allowing the law to deal with, classify and respond to us *as we are*, on the basis that any full instantiation of the capacity conception through a universal requirement of *mens rea* in its strong sense would prejudice to an unacceptable degree the law's pursuit of its proper goals such as deterrence and public protection. It may be impossible to expect the law to exclude all the effects of bad luck: the law does indeed have to deal with us as we are, and given its primary task of helping to create the conditions for tolerable social existence, it is not open to it to excuse individuals for actions resulting from unavoidable characteristics which make them dangerous to others, at least to the extent of removing them from the ambit of criminal regulation completely. In many cases, the law will have no practical option other than to focus on the dispositions and attitudes which a particular piece of behaviour manifests, because the distinction between freely chosen and determined attitudes, and that between mutable and immutable dispositions, are not realistically possible to investigate in a legal forum. We must not be naive about the subtlety with which the law is capable of reflecting fine moral judgments and distinctions. Conversely, and more positively, it does seem that all citizens can legitimately demand of a criminal justice system that it respond punitively only to actions which are in a real sense *their own* and which manifest a real hostility to or rejection of the norms of the criminal law. I shall return to this issue below.

Secondly, a great attraction of the character conception seems to be its ability to cohere with, its apparent relevance to, both backward- and forward-looking aspects of the criminal process. As we have seen, the values underlying the limitations imposed by the capacity conception oppose themselves to the pursuit of the goals of the process: the character conception, on the other hand, fits well with the criminal law's purposive functions such as its contribution to social protection both in terms of its 'taking us as we are', and in that it is centrally concerned with the extent to which the behaviour manifests settled attitudes and dispositions, thus linking in turn with judgments of the likelihood of repetition of the type of behaviour. Because this conception is concerned with the degree to which an action reflects the settled personality traits of the agent, the question of responsibility becomes intimately (although contingently) linked with practical conclusions about what sort of response is justified and appropriate. Thus character responsibility would not act as a mere threshold, a necessary condition for conviction, a side constraint on the pursuit of policy objectives: it would act instead as an integral part of the substantive justification for the punitive response, and as an important guide to the form which that response should take. Its consequence-sensitive orientation distinguishes it from the retributive model, and it avoids the two-stage procedure of treating the questions of conviction and sentence as subject to entirely different modes of reasoning characteristic of the mixed theories. Conversely, the attribution of character responsibility is not exclusively forward-looking, as is illustrated by its application to the case of the intentional killer whose circumstances strongly suggest that the crime will not be repeated, yet where the intention and any element of premeditation may in themselves justify a judgment that she was responsible in the character sense. Thus the character conception incorporates a genuinely backward-looking element as well as cohering with the forward-looking concerns of the criminal process. As such, it seems prima facie suited to forming the basis for an integrated, pluralistic, consequence-sensitive theory of punishment which appears to represent the most promising direction in which to work at this stage of the argument.

RESPONSIBILITY, DISPOSITION AND AUTONOMY

So far, I think enough has been said to show that the Humean character conception of responsibility is worthy of our serious consideration as the proper basis for the fair attribution of criminal fault. But in order to establish its adequacy more firmly, some additional positive arguments must be given, and certain obvious objections confronted. Let me begin with these objections. One clear difficulty, already adverted to, is that a straightforward application of the character conception would seem to hold the permanently mentally incapacitated (such as the insane) defendant criminally responsible: the blank category of 'undesirable character traits' does not seem to provide us with tools for distinguishing between the bad and the mad, to put it crudely. The most obviously unacceptable feature of this consequence is that it would include insane offenders within the stigmatisation process in just the same way as sane offenders. On the other hand, the character conception does apparently serve to explain why it is that it is thought to be fair to inflict a controlling social response on such offenders irrespective of the lack of capacity-responsibility. Two rejoinders to this argument immediately present themselves. On the one hand, we might argue that we are capable of making and indeed do make distinctions between different kinds of undesirable character trait in terms of our moral assessment of a criminal conviction: it may well be that the distinction between a finding of 'guilty but insane' and 'not guilty by reason of insanity' is not as socially significant as the capacity conception would imply. Alternatively, we could marry the character and capacity conceptions at a very general level in order to argue that the existence of normal capacity, in a cruder sense such as the non-existence of generally recognised forms of insanity, is a necessary condition for embarking on the process of making judgments of criminal responsibility in the first place. Attractive though this second solution is, it must be rejected, since its logical conclusion would be a return to the capacity conception itself, along with its attendant difficulties, including vulnerability to the truth of determinism. For why should insanity be singled out as the negatively defining feature of normal capacities: what about low intelligence, irascibility and so on? The first response seems to be somewhat pragmatic, but further reflection shows, I think, that it is in fact more persuasive than it at first appears. To see why, we need to remind ourselves once again of the merely contingent (even if usual) link between criminal guilt and moral blameworthiness, and the role of the responsibility requirement as ensuring not moral blame but fairness of punitive social response. What the example of insanity shows is that adherence to a character conception of responsibility would issue in both a more differentiated approach to our moral response to criminal conviction and a positive contribution to the form which the proper punitive social response should take. For the very process of establishing character responsibility would involve answering a wide range of questions which would generate some understanding of the meaning of the behaviour from the agent's point of view and an explanation of the behaviour, at least in some cases such as insanity. Accordingly, the meaning, form and function of punishment in cases of insanity would be different from that in cases of sane offenders – but this would result from an application of the usual criminal justice analysis rather than by dealing with insane offenders as in a special category from the start. But this solution still seems unpalatable, for our attitude to mentally abnormal offenders seems to be influenced by real doubts about the justice of judging them on the basis of the standards and practices of the normal criminal justice system. In view of that fact, we must turn to a third suggestion about how to accommodate the insanity issue within a conception of criminal justice which employs the character conception of responsibility. This would be that we cannot take it, in the case of insane persons, that their actions do in fact manifest settled dispositions, character traits, in any real sense, or at least in anything like the sense we take non-insane persons' actions to do so. The link between disposition and action seems to be severed by insanity, not because it alters the capacities of the insane person, but because it involves disordered thought and behaviour which is not patterned by the structure of thought (both in terms of reason and emotion) by which we normally communicate and interpret each other's actions. Insane offenders must thus be removed from the ambit of normal criminal regulation not because they lack normal capacities of understanding and control, but because they do not and cannot participate in the normal discourse which underpins the enterprise of criminal justice.[25] Abstract though this solution is, it is my conviction that the proper explanation for our attitude towards and treatment of insane offenders must be couched in some such terms.

The second obvious difficulty which arises for the character conception is that it, like the capacity conception, seems to rule out absolutely the existence of strict liability. In the previous chapter, I questioned the attitude of Hart's mixed theory to such a prohibition,[26] and at a later stage I shall hope to show that the different structure of my integrated account of punishment poses the problem in less intractable terms. But for the moment, I should point out that the character conception mitigates in one important sense the impact of an absolute bar on strict liability. This is because of the fact that it would lead to the raising of a broader, as well as a different, set of questions from those of the capacity conception. For in order to establish the inference from action to disposition, quite apart from the important evidence given by whether the actions seems to have been intentionally, recklessly or carelessly done, it would seem necessary in many cases to look more broadly at the defendant's attitudes as manifested in other relevant areas of behaviour. The details of where to draw the line, and in particular the extent to which at least recent criminal record should be taken into account, are obviously complicated and cannot be resolved here. But it does seem clear at least that this approach would require the law to broaden the focus of its time-frame[27] backwards to earlier stages (and even forwards, in cases of apparently genuine remorse), and thus the inquiry would be able to focus on inattention, indifference, carelessness in, for example, the design of a workplace or the setting up of a system of work within which someone has been injured, or the environment polluted, apparently without anyone's being responsible. Thus the focus of the character conception, which is broader than just subjective mental states, and which does not issue in an artificial, momentary conception of responsibility but raises a wider set of questions about the continuity of that action with other manifestations of the agent's disposition, might well lead to a situation in which strict liability would not be justified even on a theory which gave instrumental considerations a central place.

But perhaps the most fundamental objection to the character conception, for which I have claimed as an advantage its resonance with the purposive aspects of a legitimate criminal process, is that it indeed coheres too closely with an instrumentalist view and cannot really explain why it is *fair* to punish individuals who are character-responsible. A full response to this objection must await our final construction of the arguments for punishment: moreover, if the objection is put from the point of view of allegiance to the capacity conception as the proper, if isolated and impractical, conception of fair attribution of responsibility in criminal justice, and if my arguments so far have failed to dislodge or at least unsettle that basic judgment, then what I have to say now will probably also fail to convince. But I want to make some final, more positive remarks about the merits of the character conception in response to a less intransigent, but nevertheless persistent, form of this anxiety.

One particularly worrying idea which is raised by basing responsibility upon character is that it seems to imply that it is legitimate for the criminal law to make *general* assessments of the worth of offenders, thus taking us beyond a conception of *responsibility* or *attribution* towards a more global normative judgment of personality based on an isolated incident or set of incidents in a person's life. In this respect, it seems to be reminiscent of the rehabilitative ideal in punishment,[28] which gave rise to anxieties about a repressively paternalistic role for the state, which might seek through punishment to mould the characters of offenders in a way which reached beyond the framework prohibitions of the criminal law, to a broader and less acceptable form of 'social hygiene'. These apparent implications of the character conception must be dismissed if that conception is to retain its appeal. An important source of their strength lies, I think, in the analysis of this conception of responsibility in terms of 'character', and we can resist these implications by reconceptualising the notion in terms of 'dispositional responsibility'. Once we think of an attribution of criminal responsibility as focussing on settled dispositions, on the *practical attitudes* which actions manifest *towards the relevant norm or norms of the criminal law*, we begin to see that that focus is far narrower than any global and unacceptable judgment of personality or character in a general sense, although naturally the two phenomena are linked. Thus the idea is that it is only fair and right to punish a person when her breach of a criminal regulation manifests hostility or indifference towards, or rejection of, either that particular norm or the standards of the criminal law in general. Thus those whose 'criminal' actions are aberrant, in the sense of their being unconnected with the agent's settled disposition towards this aspect of the criminal law, as may be demonstrated by factors such as provocation, duress, reasonable mistake, self-defence and many other familiar excuses and justifications, may not fairly be punished according to the dispositional conception. It is important to emphasise that there is a crucial difference between the relevant idea of aberration and that of the offence being untypical in the sense of its being *unusual*; many offences probably are unusual for an agent when viewed in the context of that agent's life in general, and therefore the wider perspective just discussed would not necessarily generate the right judgments for the criminal law even if it were thought to be acceptable. The relevant concept of aberration or, conversely, centrality, relates rather to attitudes specific to the criminal law, and the practical attitudes which are reflected in a judgment of behaviour as 'intentional', 'reckless' or 'negligent' – in other words, a positive finding of 'mens rea' – will be as important to a positive attribution of dispositional responsibility as factors such as mistake and duress will be to its rebuttal. An offender, in other words, *can* be dispositionally responsible for an action (for example, one which she does intentionally) even though there is every sign that she is unlikely ever to do such an act again. But why, positively, is it fair to punish those who are dispositionally responsible for their offences? The full argument for this view must be built up gradually over the following chapters, but in the context of this one the important point has to do with the value of autonomy, the maintenance of and respect for which I shall argue to be one of the defining features of a legitimate criminal process. In this context, what autonomy requires is that the criminal process treat seriously the individuality and sense of identity of each citizen by responding punitively only to actions which are genuinely expressive of the agent's relevant disposition: with which the agent truly identifies, and can call her own. This seems to be a minimal requirement which we can infer from the often supported (and rarely spelt out) value of 'respect for persons'. Dispositional responsibility thus acts both as a threshold condition for justified punishment *and*, positively, as a clue to the proper punitive response: it coheres with both 'respect for persons' and the reductive and other purposive functions of the criminal process. To put the argument simply, what I am claiming is that a condition of dispositional responsibility for criminal liability represents both the least a fair system can do to satisfy the autonomy of its citizens, and at the same time the most that citizens can fairly ask it to do, given the importance of the functions of the criminal process. For although the value attached to autonomy also contributes to the justifying rationale for the system as a whole, autonomy is on our pluralistic conception only one of the basic political values internally related to the legitimate functions of the criminal process, and the fulfillment of other basic values adds to the positive and negative arguments from autonomy which ultimately combine to provide the strongest possible account of the justification of punishment. We must now move on to other issues relevant to the development of those arguments, leaving aside for the moment the dispositional conception of responsibility, which promises to constitute one important component of the final structure.

THE QUESTION OF LEGAL OBLIGATION

In this chapter we turn to the question of the nature of legal obligation. This is an important question for the theorist of punishment, although one little concentrated on by most writers on the subject. The importance of the question flows from the fact that any purported justifying argument for punishment presupposes, or proceeds from, a view about the nature of law in general, and of criminal law in particular. Within all legal theories, in turn, whether descriptive or prescriptive, there is implicit or explicit a particular view of the nature of legal obligation. And in some very influential legal theories, these views have been concerned with the place of sanctions in motivating obedience, and their analytic or contingent connection with the existence of legal obligation. Thus an understanding of the nature of legal obligation is clearly of importance to the task of producing justifying arguments for punishment, in the sense that it is necessary to the identification of just what it is which we are attempting to justify. For if, as is inevitably the case, the justifying arguments for punishment are bound up with justifying arguments for the existence of the law itself, the view that punitive sanctions are a conceptually necessary or morally desirable feature of the criminal law entails that any justification for the law itself must include a justification of punishment. My aim, then, is to draw some conclusions from the debate about the nature of legal obligation in terms of its implications for the justification of the imposition of punishment by legal authorities.

My main focus will be on accounts of the nature of legal obligation which claim to be descriptive or analytical. The difficulty of preserving a clear distinction between descriptive and normative theory – indeed the very question of whether a purely descriptive account is possible – has dogged studies of the issue of legal obligation perhaps above any other. How can there be a wholly descriptive account of the normativity of law? Do all such accounts merely represent crude sanction or probabilistic theories? In this chapter I shall try to keep this fundamental issue and indeed the importance of making clear whether the enterprise is primarily descriptive or prescriptive in mind, whilst focusing on the place of sanctions in legal systems. It must also be borne in mind that the issue of legal obligation reaches beyond the ambit of criminal law to legal regulation in general, and any conclusion about the place of sanctions in our understanding of legal obligation would also have those wider ramifications. Indeed the notion of sanction itself as usually conceived covers a variety of measures which certainly extends beyond the conception of punishment defined in Chapter 1. The question of the distinction between civil and criminal law will be addressed in the following chapter: for the moment, it is important to examine the general question of sanctions in the light of, whilst witholding judgment on, the widespread assumption that the appropriate sanction in the case of breach of the criminal law is a punitive as opposed to, for example, a compensatory one.

LEGAL OBLIGATION AND THE NORMATIVITY OF LAW

At first sight, the expression 'legal obligation' is highly ambiguous, and the strategy of most theorists, in an effort to keep separate descriptive and prescriptive questions, has, naturally enough, been one of dividing in the hope of conquering. The clearest division which has been made is that between the legal obligation having to do with our duty to obey the law, which I shall refer to as political obligation (and which will be dealt with in Chapter 6), and legal obligation in the sense of what is meant by a law's being *binding*, which I shall refer to as the question of legal obligation. The former is generally treated as a question of moral or political philosophy, thus being 'banished to another discipline', at least by strict positivist legal theorists who maintain that there is no logical connection between law and morality. The latter, on the other hand, can be taken as a question of analytical jurisprudence; in describing the content of a legal system, we use the language of duties and obligations rather freely, but apparently without meaning to make any final moral judgment about whether the laws we speak of as generating obligations ought to be obeyed. This second question is thus closely linked to that of legal validity; but not all valid laws directly generate obligations, at least for the private citizen. Some, for example, confer powers – probably a less problematic concept for analysis in descriptive 'social fact' terms. But even power-conferring laws are ultimately supported in the structure of legal norms by rules which impose obligations on legal officials to recognise and enforce those powers. Thus, in the end, the question of the nature of legal obligation must have a central place in any legal theory, and we return to the puzzle of how it is that we can talk in these frankly normative terms without taking a particular, committed position on the wider question of political obligation.

Nor is this a difficulty peculiar to positivist theory: perhaps the most sophisticated exponent of the divide and conquer strategy is in fact the natural lawyer, John Finnis,[1] who has distinguished four types of obligation relevant to legal theory: empirical liability to be subjected to a sanction in the event of non-compliance; legal obligation in the intra-systemic sense (or, in our terms, validity), where the premiss that conformity to law is socially necessary operates as a framework principle insulated from the rest of practical reasoning; legal obligation in the moral sense, or the moral obligation which some writers argue to be presumptively entailed by a valid duty-imposing legal rule; and fully fledged, independent moral obligation. We shall bear in mind this useful framework in considering the apparent contradiction with which we are confronted.

The relevance of sanctions to legal obligation

One traditional but now discredited set of answers to the puzzle of legal obligation is that the meaning of the claim that a particular legal rule generates an obligation is either that a sanction is likely or certain to follow on from its breach (the predictive account) or that another legal rule has prescribed that a sanction be imposed on breach (the sanction-rule account). The development of these views can be traced[2] through the works of Bentham and Mill and even into the 'normative' account given by H.L.A. Hart in *The Concept of Law*.[3] Hart, in fact, expressly dissociates himself from the sanction theories, emphasising the intelligibility and conceptual possibility of legal rules *not* backed up by sanctions, and distinguishing between the ideas of being *obliged* and being *obligated* by means of his famous analysis of the internal aspect of rules.[4] Nevertheless, when he addresses the issue of identifying which laws do actually generate obligations, Hart (who discusses the question only relatively briefly) appears to say that legally *obligatory* laws are those which are backed up by serious social pressure and which are most crucial to the maintenance of social life, sometimes even demanding behaviour running against strong inclinations[5] – which appears in itself to be a modified form of sanction theory. It seems that there is another strand in this modern positivist account, and that it is one inimical to the sharp description/prescription divide. We shall return to this question after examining the nature of the more purely sanction-oriented theories.

Another illuminating recent examination of the place of sanctions in the analysis of legal obligation is provided by Tom Campbell, who approaches the question as part of a rather different enterprise. In his book, *The Left and Rights*,[6] Campbell aims to establish that there would be a place for legal rights even in a utopian socialist society. In order to do this, he sets out to answer the Marxist objection that all laws are inherently coercive. He therefore has to produce an analysis of legal obligation (correlative to his interest-protecting conception of legal rights) which is not sanction-based. Campbell does very persuasively despatch some of the most famous sanction theories, essentially relying on the argument that the content of any particular duty-imposing legal rule is quite intelligible without any reference to a reinforcing sanction. For example, it seems perfectly sensible to say that the legislation making the wearing of seatbelts compulsory which was passed in New Zealand some years ago generated a legal obligation even before the deferred sanction provisions came into effect. Nor does it seem to be the case that our recognition of the legal obligation of the judge to apply and enforce both duty-imposing and power-conferring legal rules depends in the slightest degree upon the existence of sanctions threatened or applied on failure to do so. What we seem to be left with once we have dismissed sanctions as the explanation of the apparent propriety of the use of the concept of obligation in legal discourse is the idea that the law *itself* claims obedience, *claims* to create genuine obligations, independently both of any threat of sanction and of any separate or parallel moral argument.[7]

Indeed, the view that sanctions are not *conceptually* integral to laws is now widely held by legal theorists. What is more, recent writing has adopted a broad, differentiated approach to the concept of sanction itself. Honoré, for example, in his article, 'Groups, Laws and Obedience,'[8] emphasises that in some societies none of the 'remedial' norms would have to be punitive. Instead (or, of course, additionally) they could simply supplement the already existing rationality-, morality- or tradition-based reasons for obedience by offering rewards, attempting to induce conciliation and so on.[9] These remedial norms could all be conceived as dictating sanctions in the broad sense of legal responses designed to persuade or coerce legal subjects to obey primary norms, whilst clearly encompassing measures wider than the punitive sanction whose relationship with legal obligation is our principal interest. But a crucial point emerges from Honoré's assertion that it is fundamental to the idea of law that it is concerned with *obedience* in the sense that the very (apparently descriptive) statement 'X is a law' betrays a special posture with respect to whether or not it should be obeyed and how disobedience is to be justified. For this suggests that the place of sanctions in reinforcing legal duty-imposing rules can be seen as a empirical question, contingent upon factors such as the nature of the group subject to the laws and the content of the laws, instead of or as well as an analytic claim relating to the nature and function of law as a form of social regulation. Thus the debate about penal sanctions may be conceived straightforwardly as concerning the appropriateness or necessity of that particular form of sanction given the functions of the law and empirical facts about a particular society. Again, this is an issue to which we shall return.

Normative language and the adoption of points of view

Two sophisticated analytical attempts to explicate the concept of legal obligation may now be considered: each purports to stand firmly on the positivist side of the alleged line, and each satisfies more nearly than the others we have already considered the injunction that any such explanation should focus on the nature of legal rules themselves as guiding standards of conduct and the reasons or motivations which they (analytically or typically) generate.

First of all, let us consider Hart's account of the internal aspect of rules, which purports to explain the difference between merely being obliged (as one would be by the gunman's threat) and having an obligation under a rule. The internal attitude which some citizens and all officials adopt towards the rules of a legal system means that they treat them as a guide to or reason for their own behaviour and as a justification for the critical reactions they express or feel when others breach the rules.[10] This agent-centred analysis based on a particular kind of acceptance or adoption of rules by those subject to the legal system of which those rules form a part and where at least the officials of the system share this internal attitude shows, at least from the agent's point of view, why laws generate obligations. On the other hand, the account does not purport to tell us when or why the legal obligations ought, in the full-blooded moral sense, to be met, just as it does not require us to ask why it is that any particular agent has adopted an internal attitude.

Closely linked to this analysis is that offered by Raz, which relies on the viewpoints from which normative statements about what should be done according to the law are made[11] and which can be reasonably regarded as a supplementation of Hart's account.[12] In addition to the fully external and internal viewpoints, Raz adds a third; a detached viewpoint, which is said to be implicit in the work of Kelsen, who indeed introduced the notion of the special, restricted, legal and allegedly descriptive sense of 'ought' as a central idea in jurisprudence.[13] This detached viewpoint nevertheless generates normative statements, albeit not ones adopted by the speaker herself. For example, the carnivore who advises her (morally) vegetarian friend that she ought not to eat a particular dish because it contains meat acknowledges in her statement her friend's committed, internal viewpoint with respect to vegetarian norms, but the speaker does not adopt that viewpoint herself, nor does she in any way endorse the standard she tells her friend she ought to maintain. In this case, again, what is being offered is an account of legal obligation from a particular point of view: from this stance a legal order can be understood as generating obligations independently of the question of the moral worth of the rules in question. In line with positivist analysis, no questions are raised about the reasons why any particular agent should adopt the detached point of view, although the reasons would seem to be primarily practical (and its power in the prediction of sanctions seems not irrelevant) given that all the examples we are given consist of situations in which one person, perhaps a lawyer, is advising another about her 'objective' situation as regards the law. In contrast to Hart's view, however, the explanation of the use of normative language depends solely on reference to an individual commitment, and not also on a background of other committed attitudes within a society. It can thus be applied to a wider set of situations than can the social rule analysis.[14]

In the legal context, for Raz, it is the fact of the courts' adopting the belief, sincerely or as a pretence, that laws are valid reasons for action, which is necessary to the existence of a legal system and thus to that of legal obligations.[15] On this view, statements of legal obligation or what ought to be done according to law state what one has reason to do *from the legal point of view*: they tell us what we should do *if* legal norms are valid norms, but assume rather than state the truth of the condition. This concept of normative legal discourse as based on the assumption of the law's providing reasons for action is a clear departure from the perhaps more straightforward social rule theory.[16]

One set of criticisms of these types of account suggests that it may not be possible satisfactorily to explicate the notion of legal obligation without broadening the traditionally quite narrow focus of a positivist account. Both MacCormick[17] and Finnis[18] have argued that ultimately the legal theorist must, in order to give a full picture of the nature of law and of legal obligation, examine the *reasons* for the agent's adoption of that attitude. As such, they draw the boundaries of (descriptive) jurisprudence more widely than does traditional positivist jurisprudence. Several reasons for drawing the lines in this wider way can be suggested, although in my own view none of them ultimately destroys the fundamental positivist arguments when taken on their own terms. Let us examine the reasons suggested. First of all, it is argued that a legal order will only be stable if a hard core of the population (and especially the officials) do in fact adopt the internal attitude for *moral* reasons. In times of crisis (such as revolutionary situations, or the emergence of a system from a pre-legal state), systems unsupported by such a core of moral approval and endorsement will quite simply fail to survive or emerge. Now this may very well be true as a factual generalisation, but it does not affect the essentially conceptual positivist argument; nor does it establish a conceptual link between law and morality. It may be that a small number of officials will be able to maintain a legal order by use of their monopoly of force even where their moral enthusiasm for the system is not shared by the populace. It is equally true that we can imagine and indeed may be able to cite examples of systems maintained solely in and by the self-interest of a dominant upper class, unbuttressed by any moral beliefs whatsoever.

Secondly, it has been argued that (perhaps as a matter of consistency?) Hart should not have omitted (at least in the absence of some justifying argument) to use the central case technique,[19] used to such good effect in constructing the rest of his legal theory, when it comes to the internal attitude. The point seems to be that the burden is on Hart to explain why the technique of selecting a focal meaning of an internal attitude should *not* be used here, plus a positive assertion that it should be so used because of the practical significance of differences between various types of internal attitude. Certainly there is a whole range of viewpoints which could count as fully internal (as well as an enormous number of possible external attitudes). Such views might be based on moral approval or concern for the community; tradition; fear; self-interest and so on. And if a central case selection is to be made, Finnis and MacCormick certainly make out a good case for regarding volitional commitment or disinterested interest in others and moral concern as the paradigm upon which the other types are parasitic. For this does indeed appear to be the fullest form of acceptance, adoption, commitment, that we can imagine. But what is the significance of this? Does it once again reduce to the factual claim considered above? Or is it better understood as part of a prescriptive vision of the ideal legal system?

There are three main points at issue here. First, even if we allow the propriety of the use of the central case technique in the context of the internal attitude, this only establishes a relatively weak connection between law and morality. For, presumably, the link itself would *necessarily* exist only in central case legal systems. Secondly, the idea of an implicit reference to the moral element in the explanation of legal obligation in even non-paradigm cases seems to be tied up with the idea that legal validity or intra-systemic obligation presupposes as a framework principle presumptively moral obligation: when we use normative language intra-systemically, we are assuming through our discourse that legal obligations are prima facie moral obligations.[20] This is not a view endorsed by positivist theory, nor, I would argue, is it an accurate representation of the basis on which intra-systemic legal discourse proceeds, as reflection on the diversity of possible and actual internal attitudes illustrates. Finally, in the case of Raz's account, it is clear that the central-case technique could not be applied to his separate, third type of viewpoint. Of course, the critics of his account might wish to argue that we should apply the technique to the fully internal attitude to which detached statements refer, and on which they depend for their sense. If so, the arguments recited above will apply.

What does emerge, however, from the debate is the conclusion that the explanation of purely legal obligations does depend on what we might variously call commitment, adoption, acceptance or something like it. This commitment must be given by some of the agents subject to the legal system – most obviously the officials: but it is reflected in the normative language quite properly and commonly used by others who, though detached themselves, are acknowledging by the use of the language of obligations and so on the commitment of others. Apart from their relevance to the factual, systemic issue of stability, the reasons for the adoption, acceptance or commitment of others seem to relate rather to the concerns of political philosophy in constructing a normative theory of a just legal order than to an analysis of the concept of legal obligation. What really matters at this stage of our inquiry is the fact that certain individuals have taken a decision or adopted an attitude which puts them in a special relationship with the rules of a particular legal order: which means that those rules generate reasons (although not necessarily conclusive reasons) for action for them, independently of their moral status or the threat of sanction, by the very reason of their pedigree combined with the agent's adoptive attitude.

This discussion has, however, left one important ambiguity unresolved: can a person who does not adopt an internal or committed attitude be said to have legal obligations? Does someone who refuses to acknowledge or accept the rule of recognition of a system have obligations under it? Clearly, for the sophisticated positivist account, at least one (and more, for Hart) person must have (or have had, in the case of discourse concerning archaic systems, or be assumed to have, if the discourse is hypothetical) such an attitude in order for normative discourse to have a proper footing. It would be an extraordinary feature of this type of account if indeed it restricted the existence of legal obligations of those with internal attitudes, in view of the fact that the normative language which we are seeking to explain is used generally – for example, by a lawyer advising a non-law-abiding client. What we need to bear in mind, I think, is that what is in issue is the 'legal point of view': the point of view taken up by the person with an internal attitude is an attitude implicitly contained within the law itself. As we might put it, the law 'claims allegiance': it purports to generate reasons for action.[21] Naturally the types of reasons for action which it does generate will in fact differ for different citizens; but the viewpoint theory depends only on the *assumption* that laws are valid norms: no further inquiry need be undertaken with respect to the types of reason for action involved. Thus we do have an account of why normative language is used irrespective of the attitudes or commitments of the particular agents in question, which itself, however, depends on the existence of attitudes held by some agents corresponding to the stance taken up by the law itself.

The function of analytical jurisprudence

The defence of this kind of view is really tied up with the defence of a particular conception of the nature and limits of jurisprudence itself, and I anticipate that many readers, especially of a book whose main concern is a normative issue of political philosophy, will object to the conclusions I have drawn in the last paragraph by reason of the narrow view of the ambit of legal theory which I have assumed. So I want to break the flow of the argument to say a few words in defence of this methodology. Taken as a statement at large, it is clearly ludicrous to suggest that the question of why people adopt internal attitudes is of no interest. It is clearly a question of enormous importance for historians, sociologists, anthropologists, psychologists, legal theorists and indeed anyone who is concerned with reflecting on the nature and function of law as a form of social organisation. But to affirm this is not to admit that all interesting questions which can be raised with respect to the nature and function of law can be dealt with within the confines of one discipline or one mode of thought. The question of why people obey the law seems primarily to be one of sociology or psychology: that of why people ought to obey the law, one of moral and political philosophy: the question of what is meant by the claim that an individual has a legal obligation when that claim is not meant to imply a moral one also is, I would argue, a discrete question of analytical jurisprudence. I do not think that this necessarily means that the analytical jurist is not influenced in her task by certain cultural and other factors, and I am thus not claiming that the analysis of legal obligation would be a universal one, cutting across across cultural, geographical or historical borders. My argument is merely that within our own society and culture, there is an acknowledged and functional conceptual distinction between various different theoretical tasks which bear on the understanding of law, and that one legitimate and illuminating such task in this context is that of analytical jurisprudence. To reach a rounded understanding of the nature and functions of law, one has to draw on many disciplines. And although challenging and redefining the boundaries between them is a legitimate and important intellectual exercise, blurring them without explicit argument is likely to lead to confusion rather than breadth. The enterprise of those of us who do find it ludicrous that more legal theorists do not inquire into questions such as why people adopt an internal attitude to the law ought to be to encourage each other to extend our study and research into fields such as political philosophy, sociology and so on, rather than to pretend that jurisprudence encompasses them.

LEGAL OBLIGATION AND THE LAW'S CLAIM TO OBEDIENCE

Moving back to the main argument, we can relate our conclusions about the nature of legal obligation in an illuminating way with the arguments about the law's need to motivate obedience to itself[22] which seem to exceed the boundaries of a purely analytical approach. On the one hand, it can be argued that the origins of the shared commitments and understandings of the group subject to a legal system are unimportant; what matters is their present existence, and not their source, whether that is to be found in agreement, force, custom or some other factor. This equates with the positivist view of the lack of need further to analyse or differentiate the internal attitude: in each case, the present commitment to the norms of the system as guides to and reasons for conduct is the distinctive feature of a legal order. On the other hand, the idea that legal theory involves commitment and that the very statement 'X is a law' strikes a special position as to whether or not it should be obeyed seems to raise difficulties for the positivist approach. But the difficulty, I think, flows from a serious ambiguity in the notion of 'commitment'; it suggests a full, moral attitude – but it can also be used, as I have been using it, to mean something closer to adoption, which, as I have argued, does not necessarily have any moral flavour. However, linguistic ambiguities aside, on the commitment/adoption theory of legal obligation, we can reconcile this statement with the primarily descriptive nature of the enterprise. For both committed and detached statements of the law, using normative language, do strike a posture on the issue of obedience, in that they acknowledge the law's own claim to allegiance and the added reason provided by the agents' own adoptive decisions. Thus the idea of law's containing an implicit position on how disobedience should be justified can also be reconciled with this moderate interpretation so long as we bear in mind that *from the point of view of the agent with the internal attitude* the existence of the law provides *a* reason for action. The way in which this reason bears upon other reasons (such as moral ones) which the agent may have is a separate, very complex question which will have to be taken up again in chapter 6.

This restricted idea of making a commitment is parallel to the idea that membership of a group necessarily involves a sacrifice of freedom: in just the same way, adoption of an internal attitude towards the norms of a legal system, thus taking laws to generate legal obligations on oneself, involves a limiting of one's freedom to decide for oneself what one ought to do in a wide range of situations: there is a surrendering of autonomy to legal authority. The limited sense of commitment which I have tried to describe is also reflected in the idea of a group as constituted by a lack of professed rejection rather than express or, perhaps, whole-heartedly moral, acceptance. The origins of and reasons for the acceptance are unimportant from the point of view of exploring and developing the nature of a group as a tool for analysing and understanding the nature of law, although they will be crucial in constructing our ultimate normative vision of a just system of punishment.[23]

Before returning finally to the question of the relationship of sanctions to legal obligations, it will be as well to say a little more about the question of the relationship of legal obligation in the sense outlined above, and political obligation – the moral obligation to obey the law. Does our 'committed' view of legal obligation in turn commit us to the view that legal obligation entails at least prima facie political obligation, or can the two be kept separate, as positivists would wish? A moment's reflection shows that the question of political obligation can only be concluded by an inquiry into the *content* of identified legal obligations, and of the *reasons* for agents' adoption of internal attitudes to legal rules, which we dismissed as irrelevant to the question of legal obligation in the strict sense. Many types of reason have been put forward as grounding a prima facie obligation to obey the law: agreement; acceptance of benefits resulting in a corresponding obligation to accept the burdens of a legal system; consistency with objectively moral principles and so on. To anticipate that argument of Chapter 6, it is my own view that with a possible exception in the case of a very crude version of natural law theory in which only laws consistent with, and indeed derived from, objective moral principles count as laws at all (a thoroughly discredited view, even in the eyes of most natural lawyers[24]), none of these suffices to establish any general political obligation, at least within the underlying assumptions of liberal political philosophy.[25] But what is important here is that we can understand the idea of the agent's adoption of legal obligations without having to inquire into either the moral worth of the substance of the law or the moral assessment made by the agent herself of the content of the legal obligations. The 'legal point of view', for example, depends only on the *assumption* rather than acceptance of the idea that laws generate reasons for action; nor is it the case that such reasons would always be moral ones. It may be true as a generalisation of the facts in present-day economically developed countries that agents subject to their legal systems do regard their legal obligations as a species of at least presumptively moral obligations, but it would not affect our analysis if in fact they regarded the question of obedience of legal norms as a mere matter of prudence or convention. And despite the apparent credibility of the factual generalisation referred to above, the existence of many morally neutral or arbitrary laws reinforces the advantages of our non-committal analysis. Once questions of legal obligation have been determined, other questions remain for the agent to answer, concerning how she should weigh the legal reasons for action with, for example, moral ones. From a practical point of view, as Kelsen's theory assumes, there are strong reasons for the agent to work out for herself a system of priorities such that her obligations make up a 'non-contradictory normative field of meaning'.[26] But to assert a prima facie obligation to obey the law seems to be either to make a trivial claim or to underestimate the importance and frequency of conflicts, arising for all agents who go through this reflective process, between moral and legal obligations; and this is simply to miss out an important dimension of moral life within complex political society.

SANCTIONS AND EFFECTIVENESS

Let us now move back from the strict question of analytical jurisprudence to our original, wider question of the place of sanctions in legal systems. As we have already noted, one of the main functions of law identified by legal theorists is the task of motivating obedience to itself.[27] Clearly, if legal orders are to achieve their primary task of regulating the behaviour of and relationships between members of a group (again, the assertion could be taken as an analytic or a factual one, or both) constituted by shared understandings (which themselves become embodied in the law, for example in constitutional norms), it must have mechanisms by which it can reinforce already existing and perceived motives and reasons to obey, in the case both of citizens with internal and external attitudes. Some disobedience may be tolerated or even valuable, perhaps in the Durkheimian sense of providing instances for punishment which may in turn reinforce social solidarity through strengthening collective moral commitments to the content of the law,[28] but widespread disobedience would lead to dissolution of the group. Of course, if the shared commitments themselves have become seriously eroded over time it may well be that even a sophisticated set of interlocking remedial norms may not be sufficient to maintain the group. Moreover, as we have seen, it is quite clear that these remedial norms need not in any analytical sense be punitive, although as a matter of fact, it may well be that penal sanctions will be necessary at some stage in the interlocking sets of norms in many kinds of society.

One can, I think, draw an interesting analogy between this view of sanctions and their relationship with legal obligation and Kelsen's view of the relationship between effectiveness and validity.[29] For Kelsen, the effectiveness of a system was a necessary, but not a sufficient, condition of the validity of the norms of that system; if the system as a whole was not by and large effective, legal obligations (in our terms, not Kelsen's) would not be generated by it. Similarly, on the view we have been considering, the general effectiveness of common understandings and prescriptions is a necessary condition for the existence of the group and thus for laws to be created by it: hence the practical need for methods of enforcement. In Kelsen's legal theory, the other necessary conditions sufficing to ensure validity are not ultimately clearly enumerated, but within his framework, which distinguishes between the factual concept of effectiveness and the normative one of validity, we can accommodate our two notions; legal sanction and legal obligation. As a matter of *fact*, it seems likely that sanctions (including, perhaps, penal sanctions) will be necessary, at least in legal orders governing large and heterogeneous populations, in order to preserve and guarantee the general effectiveness of the system as a whole. But this does not entail that individually valid (and effective) legal obligations cannot exist without being backed up by the threat of sanctions. Sanctions are thus to be seen as a matter of lending credibility and effectiveness to the system as a whole, rather than as guarantees of obedience towards or sources of obligations arising from individual laws.

This approach has the great merit of putting punitive and indeed all legally institutionalised disadvantage-imposing sanctions in perspective: they are simply one technique among others (such as offers of rewards or conciliation) employed or acquiesced in by legal orders to motivate obedience. Legally operated sanctions exist alongside extra-legal motivations deriving from the reasons for adopting the shared understandings in the first place – which may or may not have been moral ones. What is more, there is an important area of interaction not only between institutionalised and non-institutionalised sanctions, but between different sorts of legal norms which may contribute to the motivation to obey the law. For example, Honoré equates sanction-stipulating (remedial) norms and constitutional norms as serving at least one purpose in common[30]; that of reinforcing motivation to obey. Thus any individual derivative norm is reinforced both by remedial (possibly punitive) norms and by the genetic norm from which it is derived – the authority enjoyed by the source of the law reinforces the reason to obey. This may, although contingently, be because just as the sanction gives most people a prudential reason to obey, the constitutional genetic norms give many citizens some form of moral motivation, highlighting as they do the ultimate, for instance, democratic pedigree of the norm in question. Thus an apparently morally neutral norm may be seen in a different light when the subject reflects that it has emanated from a democratically elected legislature, or a much-respected ruler; the fundamental reasons for adoption of the internal attitude may play an important role here in actually motivating obedience. This, I would argue, is where the arguments for the application of the central case technique to the internal attitude which we considered earlier make a particularly important contribution to our understanding. By the same token, one particular norm may be seen in a very different light by two citizens equally bound from the point of view of the law itself: one may be motivated to obey by the process of reflection just described, whereas the next may be motivated largely or exclusively by prudential reasons connected directly or indirectly with the existence of sanctions. Indeed, one can see how this structural feature of legal systems as a matter of fact increases their stability because it allows derivative norms to be challenged (morally) without necessarily (morally) challenging the genetic norms from which they get their validity. But none of this affects the analytical question of the existence of legal obligation. For it is the internal attitude itself, and not its origins, nor simply the sanctions which may be threatened for breaches of legal duty or promised for compliance, which constitutes and explains the concept of legal obligation.

Effectiveness and the justification of punishment

Let us now finally turn to the implications of what has been said about the nature of legal obligation for our central preoccupation, namely how the imposition of punitive sanctions by a legal authority may be justified. Clearly we are now moving away from the realms of analytical jurisprudence and indeed of sociological thought about law. But the relationship between this normative question and the analytical one of legal obligation is important. If, for example, we had concluded that there was a necessary analytic connection between the concept of legal obligation and that of punitive sanction, this would have led to the conclusion that any possible justification of the existence or adoption of a legal system or a set of laws would include or entail a justification of punishment: thus the primary question would be, can we justify having a legal order along with the punishments and/or threats of punishment which that entails, rather than treating the two normative questions separately. If on the other hand we conclude that the concept of law does not entail that of sanction, or does so only in a much looser sense, then the debate about the justification of punishment is not tied in so intimately with the outcome of that about the justifiability of law itself, but becomes part of a more open discussion about how particular (justified) legal systems may best motivate obedience to their prescriptions. Ultimately, however, the particular view which we have reached about the relationship between legal obligations and sanctions suggests that the upshot of the debate does not make such a clear difference to the starting point and parameters of that about punishment than might have been the case. For even on the basis of a contingent relationship, the justification for the existence and maintenance of an actual, effective legal *system* will involve us in justifying the sanctions which guarantee and maintain the effectiveness which we have described as a necessary condition for its validity. The justification of penal sanctions must thus be sought through arguments about whether we need to threaten and inflict punishment if we are to enjoy the moral benefits of a legal order, and the primary question then becomes whether those benefits outweigh the moral costs, including those of punishment, which having such a system involves. The contingent relationship need not always hold, and indeed we can not only find intelligible but also espouse as an ideal the sort of legal order of unsanctioned coordinating standards envisaged by Campbell.[31] But in the world as we know it, one who is convinced of the justifiability of legal systems necessarily faces the dilemma of sanctions; and anyone who supports the distinction between civil and criminal modes of legal regulation will have to confront the moral dilemma of punishment.

The salient features of the retributive/consequentialist debate on punishment have already been considered and do not need to be repeated here. What I want to do is merely to point out the close relationship between our conclusions on the relationship of sanctions to legal orders and legal obligation and one set of theories of punishment discussed in Chapter 2. For the idea of sanctions as backing systems as opposed to individual rules bears a close resemblance to the mixed, essentially rule-utilitarian theory of punishment espoused by John Rawls.[32] Rawls, as we have seen, argues that the ultimate justification for having *institutions* of punishment is the good effects which they can achieve, notably in deterring breaches of the law, preventing resort to self-help, maintaining respect for the legal order and so on. But in order to overcome the stock criticisms of such thoroughgoing utilitarian arguments for punishment, such as their justifying victimisations in certain cases, Rawls argues that at the individual level what justifies punishment is quite simply the fact of a rule of law having been broken. This along with the existence of the sanction-stipulating norm which is thus brought into operation explains and justifies individual acts of punishment.

I have suggested that these arguments do not really overcome the objections to utilitarian accounts, and in the light of the foregoing discussion of sanctions and legal obligation, both the attractions and the dangers of Rawls' view become clearer. Our conclusions so far have certainly led us towards some form of consequence-sensitive justification of punishment. The reason for the existence of sanctions has been said to be to provide a motive for obeying the law, and the reason for wanting to or being justified in motivating obedience to the law is most obviously the good effects (not in an exclusively utilitarian sense) in terms of efficiency, smooth coordination, social protection and general quality of life to which the existence of a stable legal system can contribute. Thus far we are in line with Rawls' analysis. But we are left with the problem of linking the arguments at the general and at the individual level. Would we not expect the general justifying arguments for the institution of punishment to dictate when we should apply punishment in individual cases? The problem for the rule-utilitarian here is that she must either keep hold of her utilitarianism at the cost of occasional, utility-directed breaches of the rules, or she must stick to the rules whilst acknowledging values other than the original utilitarian goals – perhaps most conveniently referred to as values of fairness or equality.

Our descriptive, non-sanction-based account of legal obligation shows that the mere fact that legal rules themselves may dictate sanctions (in whatever sense) in certain cases of breach in no way contributes to the moral justification of those sanctions in the large sense – yet Rawls' argument seems to be perilously close to asserting just this. How could the argument 'because X broke a rule' ever constitute a sufficient moral argument for punishment? It certainly furnishes the beginnings of an argument, most obviously in terms of the effects of the breach, such as harms to the victim, and social costs in terms of resentment and so on, but the argument is not fleshed out by Rawls, and, of course, if it were it would defeat the initial object of the exercise. For this was to find some limiting principle to overcome the difficulties of utilitarianism – and the argument which I have begun to sketch is essentially a utilitarian argument. This is not in any way to deny the reality of the problem which Rawls and other supporters of mixed theories are addressing; it is merely to suggest that much more needs to be said of the relationship between the arguments for penal sanctions at the systemic level and their application to individual cases, and that the answer lies in the direction of a tying together of the two strands of the argument at a deeper, normative level, in pursuit of an integrated consequence-sensitive theory which incorporates a distributive principle, absence of which in utilitarianism gives rise to the problem of victimisation among many others.

CONCLUSION

I have defended a general characterisation of law as a system for the reinforcement of group pressure by means of the adoption of rules of various interlocking kinds. Implicit in this characterisation is a view of legal obligation, as a matter of analytical jurisprudence, and also a view of the contingent relationship between such obligations and sanctions in the systemic context, as a matter of descriptive sociology. That contingent relationship makes the justification of punishment dependent upon at least part of a general political philosophy which would provide a justification for the maintenance of a legal system. This mode of analysis pinpoints what is of importance in the distinction between institutions of punishment and individual acts of punishment and the relationship between that distinction and that between systems and individual laws. The existence of individual duty-imposing laws does not entail that of sanctions of whatever kind and thus does not logically link the question of the justifiability of punishment with that of the justifiability of law: the existence of a legal system, however, involves the function of motivating obedience, in which sanctions of various kinds are likely to be necessary, thus the punishment debate relates closely at an empirical level to the desirability of having legal systems. This approach also emphasises that no theory of punishment can ignore the problem of justifying punishment in an unjust society: if the system itself is unjust, the connection we have identified renders the idea of an independent justification of punishment a nonsense. This conclusion would be too obvious to merit explicit statement were it not for the fact that most writers have attempted to produce justifications of punishment which deal with that issue in isolation from its context in moral and political philosophy. Given this fact, it is obvious the direction in which our discussion must now turn – to the fully normative questions of the nature and limits of the criminal law and the political obligation which citizens are often argued to have to obey it.

CHAPTER 5

THE NATURE AND LIMITS OF THE CRIMINAL LAW

The next two chapters are concerned with two specific problems of political philosophy and their connection with theorising about punishment. Having defined punishment as a state response to breaches of the criminal law, it is obviously necessary to say something about the nature, scope and functions of the criminal law, and, having done so, to explore the relationship in which citizens stand to that law: the problem of political obligation. Without some understanding of the factors relevant to these broader questions of justice within political society, a justifying argument for punishment must be incomplete.

In this chapter I shall put forward what I shall call a functionalist view of the criminal law. I use the term in a broad sense, the idea being that what identifies the criminal law of a society is a particular set of ends, functions and purposes to which it is centrally directed, those ends being pursued in a distinctive way, that is, by the laying down of standards of behaviour generally backed up by the threat of the application of punitive state power in the event of disobedience, and indeed by its application in that event. Clearly, different societies at different times pursue different policies and goals through the criminal law, and this might be thought to render the enterprise of functionalist analysis as I have defined it either illegitimately ethnocentric if of a relative degree of specificity, or, if general, useless, in the sense of its being too abstract to be illuminating, or at the very least unlikely to form a basis for the (separate) development of principles with any critical cutting edge with respect to particular systems of criminal law. I shall try to overcome this difficulty by keeping in mind two separate distinctions. The first is between two levels of generality in the specification of the functions of the criminal law. The first is relatively abstract, and explores the place which the criminal law occupies in the constitutional theory and legal structure of different societies and the connection between the establishment of a criminal justice system and the preservation and protection of what are acknowledged to be the most important values in any given (relatively developed) society. The second level is more particular, having to do with specific functions which the criminal law may serve and the various ways in which it can do so. Naturally, what I shall have to say about the second level will be largely an extrapolation from the UK system or others very like it. But even at the first, general level, my comments will be restricted to societies in which the criminal law has come to be distinguished from the civil law, and in which it plays a part not dissimilar to that which it plays in the present 'western' world. I shall have some specific coments to make about the criminal law in radically poor or inegalitarian societies, but in general my remarks have no bearing on, for example, so-called primitive societies: if these are analytic truths and valid prescriptions in any sense, they are only so for a specific type of legal system.

The other important distinction which must be borne in mind is that between the descriptive and the critical aspects of my remarks. Part of the chapter will be devoted to a functionalist analysis, an attempt to extrapolate the primary functions of criminal law and to understand its social meaning, in the sense of its instrumental and symbolic significance for members of a society and the role it plays in social life: inevitably my starting point will be informed by the role which penal law plays in the UK. But since the ultimate enterprise is to construct a normative theory of criminal law, the goal will be to elicit the set of principles which seem to inform the social conception, and then to turn those principles back on actual systems to see how far they match up to a rationalised or idealised version of the social conception. This, along with arguments about the nature and relative importance of the basic values the maintenance of which is so closely connected with our reasons for having a system of criminal law in the first place, should be sufficient to provide a useful critical framework within which to evaluate the justifiability of particular types of criminal law and of punitive social responses to their breach. The critical framework will be at a fairly high level of generality, and any detailed discussion of the nature of the fundamental political principles which I take to inform that framework must be postponed until a later chapter.[1] What I have to say will, I hope, be sufficient for the limited purposes of the present argument.

THE NATURE AND FUNCTIONS OF THE CRIMINAL LAW

The first level of generality

Perhaps the most important feature of the criminal law to which attention needs to be drawn is that it is merely one amongst several methods of social control in society. Morality, religion and custom, amongst others, provide alternative and often complementary normative systems for the control of behaviour and indeed attitudes, with their own distinctive types of sanction. The civil law, the education system, the family and many other institutions also play an important part. What is it, if anything, which makes the criminal law distinctive amongst these other norms and practices? Or, to ask a slightly different question, what are the facts, beliefs and principles which should underpin a political body's choice to proscribe certain sorts of behaviour by means of the criminal justice system?

I shall frame my answer to these questions in terms of what I shall call the principle of urgency. This principle dictates that the criminal law be invoked whenever a particular sort of behaviour poses a real threat to the values considered to be most fundamental in that society, creating an urgent need for a state response adequate to curtail that threat and even to educate other citizens who might have been influenced or tempted to adopt similar behaviour in the future. The principle of urgency relates directly to the distinctive *means* used by the criminal law, which involves not only the threat of penal sanctions but also the element of 'moral analogy': a breach of the criminal law is regarded as the type of legal infraction most threatening to the framework values of the community, and this is reflected in its public characterisation as a serious social wrong. Moreover, the notion of criminal law as concerning fundamental interests is reflected in another distinctive aspect of its method, in that the community, in the shape of the state, takes not only responsibility (this is also ultimately the case with civil law) but also the initiative (and effectively a virtual monopoly) in its enforcement. This both reflects and reinforces the view that the interests which it seeks to protect and the values it aims to uphold are those regarded by the community as part of its basic framework and indeed identity. Thus a particular conception of the ends to which the criminal law is typically directed and the distinctive features of its means are interrelated – they reinforce one another.

The basic values the protection of which is the central end of the criminal law will have to do with the very reasons for the existence of the society as such – with the advantages and goods which human beings might reasonably have come to hope and indeed expect to attain through their social interactions in political society. They will have to do with fundamental needs and interests which liberal theory argues predate political society and which it is generally acknowledged that society must respect.[2] Others would argue that these needs and interests are in fact socially constructed; that they arise through the living of social and political life. For now, we can set this question aside,[3] for it is not so much the origins of these needs and interests, or their relativity or universality, which is important. What matters is the fact that at a very high level of generality some such set of values is publicly acknowledged, commands a significant degree of consensus and relates directly to the framing of the criminal law. We might expect to find some indication of what these values are taken to be in the constitution of a given society, perhaps in a bill of rights. There is an analogy here, I would argue, with the 'minimum content of natural law' argued by H.L.A. Hart to constitute a 'natural necessity' in any legal system:[4] given the basic facts about human nature and bodily design (which is, of course, not to claim that those facts have not changed somewhat over history under social influence, nor to deny that they may change again) it will be necessary for a legal system to embody certain basic protections of factors such as physical integrity, freedom from dishonest dealings in certain circumstances and property (although, of course, this need not take the form of private property). To sketch a very bare list, which I shall develop further in my discussion of the second level of generality, basic values might be expected to be concerned with physical integrity, property, health, sexual autonomy and the protection of such social and collective interests as the preservation of the society itself, protecting the environment, the maintenance of some degree of public order and ultimately the upholding of its framework of shared understandings and common values. The criminal law is often understood as being concerned with the prevention and mitigation of *harms*: I have chosen to push the analysis back one stage to focus on the values and interests whose violation came to be identified as relevant harms. I do so in order to emphasise the fact that the idea of harm is not 'objective' or self-defining: to understand the nature of criminal law, we need to know how it comes to be that certain things are *recognised* as harms by the criminal law. To achieve this, we have to look beyond the criminal law itself to the wider system of values in a society.

How does this basic conception of the criminal law relate to broader political principles and conceptions of justice? One way of explicating the connection would be by means of Rawlsian original position:[5] what would people under a veil of ignorance agree to as the subject matter for the state's exercise of some of its most coercive powers, with the attendant costs and risks to personal liberty entailed? Alternatively, we could imagine a hypothetical initial contract made at some point in history between the founders of a political society, an agreed constitution which would set the terms of mutual cooperation and political regulation for the years to come.[6] I prefer, however, not to employ these devices, useful though they may be in terms of conducting thought experiments or making more explicit intuitions which we share. I shall instead conceive the dominant fundamental interests as being actually embodied in the mutual understandings and indeed political institutions and practices which exist in any given society.[7] Again, I should stress that I am not implying that the specification of such fundamental interests is universal, nor even that consensus could realistically (if ideally) be envisaged at anything other than a high level of generality.

Identifying such values at any decent level of specificity will be difficult, given the controversial nature not only of the values themselves but of their relative importance and the means by which they should be protected. All these factors may be the subject of grave disagreement and indeed political faction-fighting: those embodied in the law and political practice will change according to such factors as which group is politically dominant at any one time. To employ this conception is not to assume a wholly consensus model of society or a society of relatively static values. It is, on the other hand, to view the practice of politics and of lawmaking as an enterprise directed at establishing and enforcing a basic set of standards which, notwithstanding disagreements, apply to all members of society for as long as those standards are supported by the political institutions. It seems preferable to attempt this task, acknowledging the lack of consensus and the constant process of incremental or indeed radical change even in a *relatively* stable and homogeneous society, rather than to pin the conception to some actual or hypothetical past agreement. For such a vision threatens to rob present citizens of any real opportunity to shape the basis of political co-operation, whilst, in the context of the real world, where freedom of movement between societies is limited, also denying them the possibility of joining some different arrangement – even were there to be a wide range of choice among different types of political organisation.

Before moving on to the lower level of generality, we must consider some further normative principles which I shall argue should underlie the conception of the criminal law which I have characterised. Starting out from a basic (untested and indeed untestable) assumption that some form of political organisation is necessary to the protection of the most important interests which human beings may have and indeed to the very development of human potential, one basic principle will be that the criminal law is justified in protecting the security and existence of the community itself. How broadly such security is conceived will of course be very controversial; some writers have taken the extreme view that changes in the values adhered to in society constitutes a change in the society itself, thus justifying the use of criminal sanctions to preserve the status quo.[8] It is certainly true that in our society the criminal law is in general used in a conservative rather than a dynamic way; to preserve existing distributions of power and resources rather than to change these patterns. Fierce debates arise over the lifting of criminal prohibitions, such as that on homosexual behaviour,[9] and when use of the criminal law has been advocated for the purposes of 'social engineering', as was the case with the original proposals for Race Relations legislation in this country (and as indeed is still the case in the limited form of the offence of incitement to racial hatred) this tends to be met with deep suspicion. The general feeling is that social change should be effected by means less coercive, and indeed subtler and more effective than those of the criminal law. I shall return to the question of use of the criminal law for the purposes of righting unjust distributions at a later stage, but here it is sufficient to say that the conception of social security which I am employing is a narrow one which focuses on the protection from threat of subversion at the constitutional level, as exemplified by the criminal laws against treason, and, more controversially (at least as far as their scope is concerned) the protection of official secrets.

Starting out from this basic assumption, then, for what purposes ought the state to use the criminal law? I shall argue for the place of two fundamental values as the basis for the state's protection of the list of interests I sketched above: that of autonomy, on the one hand, and of welfare, on the other.[10]

Implicit in this conception is, of course, a *general* view about the proper principles on which the practice of politics should be conducted, and I would certainly acknowledge the relevance of these values to the resolution of other questions of political and prescriptive legal philosophy. However, my direct concern is to explore the implications of the two principles of the nature and ambit of criminal regulation, gradually moving down from this high level of abstraction to a more concrete set of principles specifically apposite to the criminal law. Thus the primary question could be framed in terms of what scope the criminal law might have in a society committed to creating and fostering an environment in which citizens can decide to lead their lives in a variety of ways, without undue interference from other citizens or the state, in which their socially acknowledged fundamental interests are protected and respected, and in which an adequate level of welfare is within the reach of every member of the community.

People within society, then, value the preservation of areas of, at least perceived, freedom of decision and action: one of the main dangers of the criminal law is the way in which its coercive methods can erode personal autonomy. But on the positive side, criminal law can also foster autonomy by restraining citizens' or the state's encroachments on various kinds of personal freedom and integrity. As for welfare, by this I mean the fulfillment of certain basic interests such as maintaining one's personal safety, health and capacity to pursue one's chosen life plan. The concepts of welfare and interest which I am employing are not, to borrow Brian Barry's term,[11] entirely want-regarding, for some sane adults may in fact not want certain of their interests to be protected. The conception of welfare which I shall be using is importantly ideal-rewarding or objective.[12] This is not to say that preferences are irrelevant, however: one important way of identifying the interests to be acknowledged by the concept would be in terms of the set of basic preferences which the reasonable or perhaps average person could be expected to want. In case this sounds like a recipe for a dull and conformist, or unduly paternalistic society, let me emphasise that we are talking of very basic goods: health, physical security and so on: my arguments for limiting the ambit of criminal regulation within these boundaries will be given in a later section. Thus the criminal law can be conceived as a set of norms backed up by the threat and imposition of sanctions, the function of which is to protect the autonomy and welfare of individuals and groups in society with respect to a set of basic goods, both individual and collective. The framework values of welfare and autonomy will be more fully developed at a later stage: this brief specification should be sufficient for present purposes. From this positive conception of criminal law I shall argue for a more specific set of limiting principles.

The second level of generality

Before moving on to the question of limits, let us move down to the second level of generality, in order to say a little more about the diversity of functions which it is open to the criminal law to fulfill within the ambit of the general conception. As soon as we move away from the high level of generality, we can identify a multitude of diverse and often competing possible functions, many within the general conception, but perhaps even more which lie outside its range. For the tools created in the criminal law are powerful and dangerous and can be used not only to promote autonomy and welfare, but also to create or perpetuate oppression and inequality (as does the present UK criminal law, it has been forcefully argued, of men over women[13]), to maintain the status quo, to (at least attempt to) engage in social engineering of various kinds, both legitimate and illegitimate: the general conception can be imaginatively used or corrupted and distorted. In order to illustrate the diversity of functions and of ways in which those functions can be pursued, I shall revert to my list of basic interests, and give some selected examples of the ways in which they may be protected by criminal law and the side-effects and incidental goals, which criminal regulation may have.

Let us begin with a clear case: that of offences which threaten directly the social value of physical integrity. Quite apart from standard laws prohibiting homicide and assult,[14] there is also the possibility, realised in the UK system, of laws regulating the conduct of road traffic and of the carrying on of work in factories, shops and so on.[15] Here the criminal law is involved (for example, in fixing a speed limit) in a complex judgment about the acceptable level of risk of physical and mental harm, taking into account costs of enforcement, utility of traffic circulation at certain speeds or of production at a certain rate or of a certain kind, the autonomy of citizens who choose to take certain risks, and so on. Here we see that the criminal law's function is not simply to protect personal safety, but also to define what *level* of personal safety should be protected: it defines as well as defends the social good in question. Hence the great importance of negligence liability, which sets a standard of reasonable behaviour or safety which must be maintained – an idea which, as we have seen, sits unhappily with traditional conceptions of responsibility in the criminal law.[16]

The law relating to property may take many forms, but taking the simple example of theft, we can see that the criminal law not only protects property rights as such but, in doing so, maintains a particular distribution of holdings and preserves the status quo.[17] This, of course, raises difficult questions about the status of the law if these holdings themselves are unjust. This subject will be taken up in the next chapter. An interesting example of the differing weight accorded to the principle of autonomy in the specification of the interests protected by offences against property and those against the person in English criminal law is that fact that consent of the victim (and even a genuine belief in the victim's consent) is always a good defence to a charge of theft or criminal damage, whereas it is not a defence to assaults other than trivial ones.[18] Thus one is held able to consent to the taking of one's property, even if one thus leaves oneself completely destitute (and therefore, in a sense, harmed), but not to a physical injury of even a moderate kind, with certain specific exceptions. In the case of personal integrity, the 'objective' or reasonable-person conception of welfare holds sway, and this relates to the importance which is attached to that particular interest in our society. These distinctions, examples of which could be multiplied, are evidence of the complexity of values embodied in actual systems of criminal regulation, about the ordering of which a normative theory must be able to provide some guidance.

What bite could our very general principles flowing from the welfare/autonomy conception have in identifying unfairness and answering such questions? Let us take an example from the English law on sexual offences. The law goes to some lengths to protect the sexual autonomy and integrity of men and women, as well as to protect the young from precipitate sexual experience.[19] Yet distinctions are made both between men and women and between heterosexuals and homosexuals. Since the legal definition of rape covers only vaginal intercourse, only women can be raped;[20] however, indecent assault upon men was until recently punishable far more severely than that upon women.[21] The age of consent differs as between homosexual and heterosexual behaviour between consenting adults in private.[22] Women cannot be raped by their husbands, at least during cohabitation.[23] These examples *may* reflect considered judgments about the need for social protection based on facts about certain kinds of sexual behaviour as opposed to others, but they certainly also reflect attitudes which differentiate between the relative value of men's and women's, heterosexuals' and homosexuals' sexual autonomy, and a controversial attitude towards the nature of the marital relationship, which are illuminating and, on the face of it, exhibit an unequal concern for the welfare and autonomy of some groups over others, which seems to be unjustifiable even within the very general normative conception sketched so far. Quite apart from this, sexual offences raise the ugly spectre of how far the criminal law should protect a citizen from so-called 'moral' harms – again, a question best tackled in the context of the further development of our normative arguments about the ambit and limits of the criminal law.

Many other examples could be given, exhibiting a diversity of possible legitimate functions for the criminal law – the protection of health by prohibiting the sale of adulterated foods or of drugs, the protection of public order, maintenance of the fair and efficient administration of justice through laws on perjury or contempt of court, and protection of the environment are just a few. Some of the goods which can be protected by the criminal law conduce most obviously to individual human interests, others focus rather on social and collective interests. I shall not multiply these examples, for I hope I have already said enough to illustrate the diversity of possible specific functions of the criminal law, the possibility of its abuse, and the existence of different 'spheres of justice'[24] possibly requiring different distributive solutions even within the framework conception of criminal justice which I have offered. But I should emphasise that in all these cases it is *serious* threats to or encroachments on these interests which are the proper focus of the criminal law: as we have seen, many other kinds of regulation, legal and otherwise, also conduce to the protection of many of our most fundamental interests, and it is only where the behaviour in question represents a direct threat to and rejection of a basic social value that a criminal law response conceived in this way is appropriate. This very general principle, which I think is deeply embedded in the social meaning of the criminal law in our society, has, however, a considerable critical force when applied to our actual system of criminal law which is, as we shall see, in many respects far more extensive than the principle would dictate. Having sketched this positive picture, it is time to move to the argument for the major limiting principles which delineate the proper scope of the criminal law.

THE PROPER AMBIT OF THE CRIMINAL LAW

We turn, then, to the enterprise of developing some more detailed normative principles governing the ambit of the criminal law thus conceived. Such principles will inevitably be relatively abstract and yet, I shall argue, they provide a criticial cutting edge against which our own criminal law may nevertheless be found seriously wanting.

The principle of fundamental interests

This principle rules out the application of the criminal sanction to the violation of or threats to interests other than those considered as fundamental, those recognised at the constitutional level, in a society. It follows fairly directly from the conception of criminal law outlined above. It will be to some extent culturally relative, given that different societies value different sorts of interests, although, as I have already suggested, given certain contingent facts about human behaviour and physique, there will usually be a common core to the criminal law in different societies at a similar stage of economic development. Why should the criminal law be limited in this way? There are two main reasons. In the first place, it is at least plausible to believe that an inflation of the ambit of the criminal law may devalue the currency of its threat and therefore its efficacy in really important areas. Doubtless this is hard to test, and judgments about the boundaries of fundamental interests are difficult to make: but in most societies there is, as I have argued, some publicly acknowledged hierarchy of dominant interests and, on the conception of the criminal law which I have put forward, its major role will be to protect those seen as most important. As we have seen, the lack of criminal sanctions with respect to certain behaviour by no means removes all social disincentives to its practice: a good example would be the decriminalisation of certain kinds of homosexual behaviour, for which many other less formal sanctions unfortunately undoubtedly persist. Where the criminal law encompasses behaviour which does not threaten fundamental interests, or which does so in such a way as not to express any clear or direct rejection of or indifference to the values which underlie them (as must be the case with many of the less serious offences, often of strict liability, which exist in systems such as our own), it exceeds what is ordinarily understood as its proper ambit, and threatens its own symbolic and, ultimately, instrumental functions.

The second reason for this principle is more important. This is that the criminal law draws upon the vast array of state powers, exercising coercion relatively directly. Whether or not we can truly be said to be free to do what the criminal law forbids, the threat of punishment certainly affects our autonomy in the relevant area of behaviour. My freedom to do X is not, at least according to common sense, as great if X is punished by a substantial fine or a term of imprisonment, as if it was not so punishable. The values which we attach to privacy and the sense of control which we aspire to feel over our own lives (whether it is genuine or not) would be seriously diminished by a more intrusive and widespread criminal law. Related to this reason is the increasing likelihood, as the ambit of the criminal law widens, that the legislator is using the law for illegitimate purposes: for example, to protect the interests of some at the expense of those of others, or for the legislator's own ends.

This seems an appropriate point at which to pause to consider two issues already touched upon; those of the use of the criminal law to proscribe 'moral' harms, and its use for purposes of social engineering. The debate about the former, and particularly discussions of Mill's famous 'harm principle' limiting the interventions of the criminal law to the prevention of 'harm to others',[25] has raged amongst lawyers and philosophers for generations,[26] and any contribution made here to an already rich literature will inevitably be a modest one. But some remarks at least are called for on the issue of how far the sorts of laws over which the debate has agonised – for example, laws prohibiting obscene expression of various kinds, blasphemy, certain types of consensual sexual behaviour and the use of drugs for non-medical means – would fit in to the fundamental interests conception of the criminal law.

A distinction must be made between paternalistic considerations on the one hand and arguments about moral harms per se on the other.[27] As far as paternalism is concerned, I have already indicated that the conception of interest being employed would permit at least a limited practice of paternalism by means of its identification of certain basic interests in objective or ideal-regarding terms. Thus no one should be allowed to consent to a serious physical assault, unless for medical purposes: ironically, the issue of consent to death, as in cases of euthanasia, is more complex. This is not the place to explore fully arguments about paternalism and the consent defence, but, taking the example of laws prohibiting the non-medical use of certain dangerous drugs such as heroin, I would argue that paternalistic prohibition can be justified on the basis that what the criminal law aims to do is to protect fundamental interests not only in a momentary but principally in a *dynamic* way:[28] it protects not just individual actions in pursuit of fundamental interests, but the continuing possibility and opportunity of all citizens to pursue their interests, seek their welfare, exercise their autonomy. This gives a limited place for paternalistic legislation prohibiting the harm of inflicting or possibly even seriously risking grave, long-term and certain damage to one's own capacities for pursuing one's own future good. This seems a relatively secure footing for paternalism, explicating the way in which and the extent to which causing or risking harm to oneself can constitute a genuine personal and social harm which should be acknowledged by the criminal law, whilst leaving room for the general operation of the principle of autonomy.

Turning to the problem of moral harms, how far should the offence felt by someone who hears her religion ridiculed, or the disgust felt by someone who witnesses some obscene exhibition, or reads pornographic material, or even that felt merely as a result of the knowledge that pornography or so-called 'deviant' sexual behaviour actually goes on, count as a harm to which the criminal law should seek to respond? After all, recent history has seen an increase in our understanding of the reality of 'psychic harms', the real distress they cause, and an extension of their legal recognition, as in the awarding of tort damages for pain and suffering. The attractions in this context of some form of compromise solution such as that adopted by the Williams Committee,[29] on the basis that the real interest in not being subjected to offensive or embarassing displays without actually seeking them out would justify some measure of restriction, at least in public places, but that in a society based on equal consideration of fundamental interests, criminal prohibition aimed at preventing offence or disgust by mere knowledge of certain practices would never be justified, are evident. It seems that acknowledgment of a basic interest in avoiding offence of this kind, however deeply felt, would be inconsistent with the principle of equal protection of fundamental interests of those who choose to express their sexuality, to take that example, in the given ways – and, I would argue, those interests should take priority. However, two reservations must be made. The first is that as our state of knowledge increases, it is possible that we shall come to understand that, for example, pornography causes harms more serious, subtler and more direct than we presently acknowledge. For example, feminist writers in the USA and elsewhere have argued persuasively that the existence of pornography seriously harms not only the women who participate in making it but also all women, whose most fundamental interests are violated by a degraded conception and indeed objectification of their gender and sexuality, male violence against them and general sexually discriminatory practices to which pornography substantially contributes.[30] Pornography is, on this view, both a symptom of and an important means of perpetuating men's oppression of women. Doubtless it will be a long time before this argument is generally accepted, even among women, and many complex additional issues arise about the desirability of criminal regulation, but it provides a good example of how our changing understanding of the nature and causes of harms may shift the proper boundaries of the criminal law.

My second reservation has to do with cultural relativism. It is not too hard to imagine a society which placed far greater emphasis on moral harms than does our own – an example might be a society which has an established religion at the very core of its social, cultural and political life. In such a society the gravity of offence and the social discord caused by blasphemy might be very much more serious than it is in our society. Given the dynamic nature of societies and the great value of conscientious expression, it is hard to imagine a case in which the legal right to pursue one's interest in expressing dissent or in worshipping any religion could justifiably be removed; but in some kinds of societies a wider range of restrictions could probably be justified because of the different priorities accorded to different values therein. We must always bear in mind that the application of the fundamental interest conception of harms will produce different results according to the different standards and self-perceptions of different societies. In considering both of these problems, it seems that we are pushing at the limits of the traditional liberal political framework. How far we shall indeed have to abandon or modify that framework in resolving the problem of punishment will have to be considered more fully at a later stage.[31]

Moving to the issue of social engineering, any ideal-regarding innovations introduced by political institutions will of course be limited by the principle of fundamental interests, on whose specification, as we have seen, preferences have an important although not decisive bearing. According to this principle, any deliberate shaping of behaviour and attitudes by means of the criminal law must be restricted to that which directly and seriously threatens *fundamental* interests. But given that no system is ever perfectly just in practice, and that our knowledge and understanding of, and attitudes towards, different kinds of harms changes over time, it may be justifiable for the legislator to legislate somewhat in advance of popular attitudes, on the basis either of convincing factual arguments not yet generally known or acknowledged, or on that of injustice such as existing unequal protection of certain interests or, more probably, the interests of a certain group, which could be mitigated by a change in the criminal law. The principle of fundamental interests counsels caution but not despair in the use of criminal law in a dynamic way.

The principle of legitimate purposes through equal consideration
This principle also follows directly from the fundamental interests conception of the criminal law, and is separated from the principle of fundamental interests more as a matter of emphasis than of substance. It dictates that the only justification for the legislator's use of the coercive apparatus of the criminal law is in a genuine and necessary attempt to protect interests which are or are potentially fundamental to all citizens. If criminal legislation aimed at the protection of non-fundamental interests is illegitimate, that aimed at furthering the interests of those with political power, or of any one group at the expense of those of another, or aimed at maintaining or imposing tyranny or oppression, is also and more fundamentally illegitimate.[32] This principle is in part a principle of the equal consideration of the fundamental interests of all individuals and groups, and partly a substantive principle of legitimacy aimed at preventing the use of the criminal law for improper purposes – for example, using the criminal law to enforce draconian tax levies aimed at pursuing in the name of nationalism or some other ideology a war which runs counter to the interests of most individuals and groups in society. As such, violation of this principle of equality might be regarded as one specific instance of substantive impropriety, but the equality principle can, as I shall try to show, be pushed a little further.

The principle of equal impact

If the criminal law properly aims to protect and uphold fundamental interests, it is also incontrovertibly true that its methods, when invoked, adversely affect (albeit justifiably) those very interests. It is thus important that an egalitarian principle bear not only on the distribution of interest-protection in the substantive law, but also on the potential impact of the law's application. The principle of equal impact dictates that in so far as possible criminal laws should be framed in such a way that all adult citizens not suffering from some form of mental incapacity (such special circumstances, along with factors such as duress and provocation, would of course have to feature in the range of excusing conditions in order for this standard to be met) should have a roughly equal, or at least not grossly disproportionate, opportunity of complying, at least in so far as their social and economic situation bears on that level of opportunity. In other words, the impact of the threat embodied in the law (as opposed to the impact of law-enforcement[33]) should be relatively equal. It would also dictate that all citizens should have an equal chance of exploiting the criminal process, as defendants, witnesses or complainants, in order to vindicate their fundamental interests.

By way of illustration, let me give a few examples of current laws and facts about the English criminal process which I take to violate this principle. The laws controlling sexual behaviour do not have a roughly equal impact as between homosexuals between the ages of 16 and 21 and heterosexuals of the same age because of the disparity between the relevant ages of consent. As such the fundamental interest in sexual expression is unequally protected and unjustifiably curtailed. More controversially, the impact of the law of theft is clearly grossly unequal in its impact upon the very poor, at least given the absence of a defence of necessity or irresistible impulse excusing those who steal food out of starvation and, more radically, the lack of any mitigation for those who suffer greater temptation to violate property laws given their poor financial position. At the level of practice, research suggests that women who have been raped or subjected to domestic violence are less likely to have their claims considered seriously or investigated thoroughly by the police, or are disbelieved and subjected to humiliating cross-examination far more stringent than that employed with other sorts of victims, thus violating their real opportunity equally to exploit the criminal process.[34] Similarly, poverty and the lack of a fixed address affects the likelihood of making bail, which not only increases relative chances of mistaken incarceration followed by an acquittal but also quite probably prejudices the possibility of adequately preparing a defence. In the same vein, prosecutors' perceptions of what constitutes 'real' crime can mean that certain sorts of offenders (such as persistent thieves and burglars) run a far greater risk of detection, arrest and prosecution than do other groups (such as the so-called 'white-collar' criminal who 'misappropriates' her employer's property, the speeding or even drunken motorist, the negligent factory owner).[35]

The difficulty with the principle of equality of impact is, of course, to establish its proper limits. How can a state properly respond to the fact that, to use examples from the UK, the young and those in lower socio-economic groups (and indeed men) are statistically over-represented in the criminal population,[36] given that the enterprise of criminal law is to protect the fundamental interests of all? Can and should the criminal law be prevented from perpetuating and entrenching patterns of disadvantage and injustice which exist in society? And how can these problems be reconciled with its important aims, pursued on the basis of a dispositional conception of responsibility which acknowledges the need to deal with citizens as they are, irrespective of certain unavoidable inequalities of capacity for compliance?[37]

Obviously, it would be impossible to have a perfectly just system of criminal law in an unjust society. In the first place, if the political will to remedy the injustices by other means does not exist, it will not exist to do so by the criminal law either; moreover, the criminal law will inevitably reflect disadvantages in instances of unequal impact such as those I have described. Furthermore, as we have already seen, there are limits to the extent to which the criminal law can and should be used to remove unfair disadvantage, partly because other means such as civil law and education will often be more effective, partly because to use the criminal law in a pioneering and reforming way may involve an illicit degree of intrusiveness and thus violation of the principle of fundamental interests and in particular the value of autonomy, and partly because the criminal law lacks certain tools (such as directly redistributive potential) which are needed to wipe out some forms of injustice. Thus violation of this principle will often operate not, or not only, as a sign that the criminal law or its administration is in need of reform, but more importantly as a sign that wider social change and political action is called for. Perhaps the most difficult issue here is the extent to which violation of the principle of equal impact affects the existence of political obligation, and I shall be discussing this in the following chapter. But for the moment I merely want to underline the intuitive importance of the principle and the way in which it exemplifies the continuity of problems of justice in different areas of political action. The different spheres of justice may be to some extent distinct and indeed complex, but injustice in one sphere (such as in the distribution of economic resources) will almost inevitably lead to injustice in others (such as punishment or education). It is simply not open to a just government to plead inevitability, for it has power in many spheres. In the UK, the facts about socio-economic and other forms of bias in the distribution of offending suggest that the principle may have been violated in important respects. Some positive response (for example through a widened range of mitigating excuses, as far as the criminal law is concerned) in both legal and other contexts such as the welfare system is clearly needed.

How should the limits of such a response be drawn, bearing in mind the importance of maintaining the central functions of the criminal law? Here I think we need to draw on two distinctions: that between internal and external factors influencing the opportunity to obey the law; and that between external factors over which the state has or should have some influence, and those over which it has none. Internal factors would be such things as a hasty temper or a poor memory – factors which are bound up with an individual's character and over which she herself probably only has limited control. Here in practice the state could have little influence, and even if it could, attempts at influence would be ruled out by the value which I have argued should be attached to individual autonomy. I have already suggested in chapter 3 that the necessary condition of offending should be that the action in question is a central expression of the offender's settled disposition towards the criminal law, and it is undoubtedly the case that on a strict capacity view of equal opportunity to comply, this is unfair, since the character (whether mutable or not) of some individuals makes it harder for them to comply with the law. That is just one place where an inevitable element of moral luck enters into the criminal law:[38] the state can and should do nothing to change our varying characters: it must simply concentrate on the criminal law's legitimate function of protecting basic interests and maintaining reasonable standards for peaceful co-existence in society. The capacity-theorist's dream of a perfectly just society in this respect is quite simply unattainable.

External factors, on the other hand, are those which are extraneous to the person herself – factors such as lack of money, the existence of racial prejudice, the fact that a pedestrian happened to be on the crossing as one drove carelessly over it, and so on. Here it is clear once again that there are limits, both to the possibility and to the propriety of state intervention to equalise external factors, and moral luck enters the picture once more. It may be true that had no one been on the crossing at that time, had there not happened to be a car coming in the other direction as I swerved, the criminal harm would have been prevented and I would have been innocent of any offence, or guilty only of a lesser one, even though the degree of my negligence was the same. This is a matter of luck about which political institutions can do nothing (the position could be slightly mitigated by abandoning negligence liability, but only at the cost of serious detraction from achievement of the law's legitimate functions). The same goes for the fact that I happen to have suffered some outrageous treatment in the absence of which I would never have assaulted my victim – within certain limits (exemplified by the compromises reached by various legal systems on the question of provocation) the law has to require a certain standard of resistance to bad luck if it is to achieve anything at all. But some external factors the state can and should influence. The vast disparity of wealth and the enormously unequal distribution of a variety of social goods (such as real educational opportunity) can hardly be doubted to have an impact upon different people's real opportunities to obey the law, especially where the disadvantages and inequalities in question have been such as to affect the person's fundamental interests. It should be noted that in this instance there is a possible link even with internal factors: an upbringing in conditions of gross deprivation might well be likely to affect someone's *capacity* throughout her life to obey the law – to affect, in a sense, her character. Again, the importance of preserving the efficacy of the criminal law probably rules out any state response through the criminal law to this fact, but once again it illustrates the continuity between different areas of state responsibility, and the importance of a political response at some other level. The existence of racial prejudice and gender discrimination creates disparities not only in terms of real opportunity for and costs of compliance but also of the treatment of citizens within the criminal process, as complainants, defendants or witnesses. The state may not be able to wipe out discrimination and disadvantage overnight, but it can and should work gradually to remove them, making due allowance through principles of mitigation for the victims of interim inequalities of impact in the criminal law.

The principle of consistent pluralism
Our discussion so far has implicitly acknowledged that, both within its particular functions and even at the most general level, a criminal justice system legitimately pursues a plurality of values. This brings it face to face with the apparently intractable problem, adverted to in our discussion of the mixed theories of punishment, of weighing and balancing the claims of conflicting values which are incommensurable. Even at the level of general principle, where we have identified two main values, those of welfare and autonomy, it would be foolish to imagine that one always acts as an absolute constraint upon the pursuit of the other; and at the particular level of pursuit of a variety of specific goals and the protection of a multitude of particular interests, any rigid system of absolute values constraining the pursuit of others is clearly out of the question. If we wish to maintain a pluralist position, we have to confront the problem as best we can. What I would argue the principle of consistent pluralism can offer (I am extrapolating here from the ideas of Brian Barry[39]) is the modest prescription that the legislator make consistent, conscientious, informed and sensible balancing judgments between the various values acknowledged as fundamental over reasonably lengthy periods of time both within the criminal law itself and across the broader spectrum of political decision-making in general. It is the difficult responsibility of every political society to work out some coherent ordering of its values, within the framework of its deepest guiding principles. This ordering may change over periods of time and should be responsive to changing social and economic conditions (the diminishing relative value of autonomy in the context of gross poverty is an example which comes to mind here) but the requirements of consistency should survive these changes. This principle is clearly connected with that of equal consideration of interests; it would offend both principles to value the welfare of certain groups relative to autonomy higher than that of others (in the absence of relevant difference between them such as infancy). A good example here would be the paternalistic argument for the differential controls on homosexual and heterosexual behaviour between the ages of 16 and 21: it might be argued here that the law paternalistically protects the alleged welfare of actual and potential homosexuals between

those ages more highly than it does their autonomy, making the opposite ranking for heterosexuals. In the absence of strong countervailing reasons for the differentiation, this would be an example of violation of the principle of consistent pluralism. Another would be the different ages of legal sexual intercourse for men and women;[40] again, the connection with the principle of equal consideration is obvious, as is the implicit stereotypical and sexist assumption about the relative capacities and scope for autonomy of teenage males and females.

The principle of efficiency

Given the costs of enforcing the criminal law and the impact on autonomy of criminal legislation, it can, I would argue, be inferred from the general functionalist conception that no criminal law should be passed which either does not prima facie have a good chance of achieving or is not necessary in order to achieve its (legitimate) purposes. There are various different sorts of inefficiency; difficulties of enforcement or detection (which can lead to intrusions on privacy and the existence and abuse of prosecutorial discretion which may further discriminate against certain groups), ineffectiveness of detection and punishment to deter or underpin an adverse social judgment of the conduct in question (a good example would be the prohibition of the sale of alcohol in the USA in the 1920's) and relative inefficiency in the sense that the costs, both economic and social, of criminal enforcement outweigh the benefits to be gained by regulation itself, or because some other less costly and more efficient means of enforcement exists. It is hard to improve upon Bentham's thorough classification of such 'cases unmeet for punishment',[41] and his argument holds good even outside a utilitarian ethics. We may disagree with Bentham about the range of functions which the system should have, but we can nevertheless agree that such cases of inefficient and unnecessary punishment are an illegitimate use of the criminal process. In current English criminal law, such an argument could be made about the widespread existence of 'regulatory' offences, generally based on strict liability and concerning infractions of the social interest in, for example, public health or safety. The infractions concerned are generally relatively petty in terms both of the threat or damage they present to that interest and the attitude towards it which the offending behaviour expresses. The offences could thus be said to violate this principle in the sense that they could be dealt with as effectively outside the criminal sphere thus avoiding the devaluation of the currency of criminal prohibition which, as I have argued, is typically and properly conceived as relating to much more serious forms of interest-threatening behaviour. Legislation which violates the principle of efficiency should be repealed or modified so as to comply with it.

The principle of residual autonomy

This limiting principle, which flows from the importance attached to autonomy, and which relates rather to the nature of the punitive response than to the substance of the law, dictates that no punishment should be so draconian as effectively to coerce compliance, thus detracting from the sense of decision and responsibility amongst those subject to the law. Unreflectively, this may seem odd; are there not some sorts of behaviour which are of such unequivocal evilness (for example, cold-blooded killing for financial gain) that an absolutely coercive sanction, or even preventive detention, should be instituted? Clearly, the appropriate severity of sanction and hence of erosion of autonomy will vary with the type of behaviour, but for two reasons I would argue that we should adhere to the principle of residual autonomy. In the first place, attitudes to certain forms of behaviour change; 'mistakes' are made; this militates against draconian or absolute punishments such as capital punishment. Secondly, and more strongly, whether or not determinism is true, we value our sense of freedom, decision and control in the planning and living of our lives enormously.[42] One aspect of this is our opportunity to express our disapproval of the criminal law by disobedience; another is to be able to plan our lives so as to minimise its intrusion into them. Radically coercive and severe sanctions reduce this sense of autonomy to practically nothing – almost as much as would retrospective criminal legislation, which would, of course, also be ruled out by this principle. A society in which there is no real opportunity to do what is acknowledged as wrong is one in which the social and moral significance of compliance with the criminal law is seriously diminished.

CONCLUSION

What all these remarks add up to is a more detailed conception of the nature as well as the limits of the criminal law on the basis of which we shall try to reconstruct a set of arguments for punishment. On this conception, the function of the criminal law is regarded as being to aim for and protect equally the fundamental interests of all citizens and groups in their own welfare and autonomy. The criminal law is properly invoked in response to serious and direct threats to and violations of those fundamental interests through behaviour which expresses a rejection of, hostility or total indifference to the basic framework values which the society acknowledges. Its distinctive punitive and public means both reflect and reinforce its functions of interest-protection and the upholding of framework values. We have seen that this conception has a considerable critical edge in the assessment of current English criminal law, which in important respects is unfair and over-extensive when judged according to the principles I have enumerated. Exceeding this proper ambit constitutes one important form of injustice which can be perpetrated by the criminal law. It is also the case, however, that failure to fulfil its function, omission to fill up the space within these boundaries, can be an important source of suffering and injustice in political society. A fuller specification of the general political principles which underlie the functionalist conception will be an important part of the argument of the final chapter of this book. Before reaching that stage, we must turn to the specific question of whether criminal law conceived in this way generates a duty of obedience on the part of citizens.

CHAPTER 6

POLITICAL OBLIGATION

The subject matter of this chapter relates closely to that of the previous two. In chapter 4, I argued that there was no necessary connection between legal obligation and any moral obligation to meet our legal obligations, and that as a matter of empirical fact, sanctions for breach of legal obligations were overwhelmingly likely to be necessary to achieve the functions aimed at by most legal systems, even if not for each individual legal norm. Given this practical importance of penal sanctions and the threat of them as a cornerstone for most criminal justice systems, at least in the sorts of societies which are our focus, and given the thesis of the separation of legal and moral obligation, it is clearly important, if we are to produce a *justification* of punishment, to give an account of political obligation: how do the arguments which justify punishment relate to the reasons why citizens ought to obey the criminal law? If political obligation cannot be explained and defended, where does this leave the enterprise of justifying punishment? If we have no obligation to obey the law, can we justifiably be punished for breaking it?

In answering this fundamental question, there also arises a set of no less important supplementary issues. What sort of obligation is political obligation? To whom is it owed, and in respect of what sorts of behaviour may it exist? This latter question was, of course, largely the subject matter of Chapter 5. Furthermore, we have to consider whether, where political obligation is said to exist, it exists with respect to all or only to individually justified criminal laws; we must ask what types of injustice may exist in the criminal law and criminal process and whether all of these have the same, and what, effect on political obligation.[1] I shall of course refer to the attitudes which each of the model theories of punishment would take towards these complex questions, but my main aim is to develop an understanding of the implications of the position taken in the last chapter on the nature of the criminal law for political obligation, and, ultimately, the justification of punishment. I shall thus once again exploit the idea that the main function of the criminal law is that of maintaining by distinctive means a basic standard of security, autonomy, interest-protection and respect for these fundamental values in society. Any obligation to obey the law, then, would contribute to the maintainance of a standard of behaviour and awareness sufficient to achieve this end with respect to the most important aspects of social and personal life.

THE NATURE OF POLITICAL OBLIGATION

The concept of political obligation has to do with the existence of a set of conclusive reasons for obedience to the criminal law of a political society. Why, then, do we speak in terms of obligation rather than straightforwardly in terms of the reasons for obedience themselves, so as to make the values involved explicit? I am not myself convinced that this is indeed the right course, and I shall argue that any satisfactory account of political obligation will have to take account of and be sensitive to a complexity of reasons, so that to talk baldly in terms of the general presence or absence of obligation in a society is to oversimplify the issue. In addition, the eliciting of the various reasons why members of a society ought to obey the law is necessary in order to engender a healthy attitude of social responsibility towards the content of the criminal law: women and men in political society should not be content unreflectively to obey the criminal law. The value of autonomy and indeed the possibility of tyranny requires that we reserve the possibility of evaluating the law and the responsibility for deciding whether or not it ought to be obeyed.[2] Conversely, the valued functions of the criminal law dictate that the ideal social attitude should also give due weight to the demands of that law.[3]

However, the idea of political obligation does have two attractive features. The first is its apparent conclusiveness, which renders it a useful if dangerous political tool. But it must be remembered that it is conclusive in the sense that a judgment of political obligation represents the *conclusion* of a complex argument about the justice of the demands of the criminal law.[4] It may not be feasible to go through this argument in all its stages every time we are confronted with an instance of criminal regulation, hence we find it useful to educate ourselves into a general attitude favourable to obedience. But to indoctrinate this attitude without also articulating and scrutinising its basis would result in a society in which obedience would be both less valuable and quite probably also less stable: it would not flow from real personal decision or commitment. The second advantage of casting the arguments about why the criminal law ought to be obeyed in terms of political obligation is that this does bring out the important factor that that obligation is owed *to* some other person, set of persons, or institution. Of course, our responsibilities and debts to other members of society will form an important part of the argument about why the law ought to be obeyed, as well as about why we have different reasons for obeying the law of our own state from those for obeying that of other states. Framed in these terms, questions about whose interests are affected by our obedience or disobedience to the criminal law are brought out especially vividly; but, again, we must not lose sight of the fact that obligation expresses the closing stages of an argument about our relations with the state and with each other, and about the legitimate powers of the state. The conclusion of this argument is not foregone.

AN OBLIGATION TO OBEY THE LAWS OF A SYSTEM?

What I have said so far should be sufficient to indicate that I do not think it useful or legitimate to speak in terms of a general *obligation* to obey all the laws even of a system which is substantially just. Yet many discussions proceed on just this assumption.[5] What might the basis for it be? One obvious possibility would be a social contract view, on which citizens are regarded as being bound to each other and their government by the terms of an initial (actual or hypothetical) agreement so long as the state does not breach those terms, that initial agreement including the term that criminal laws properly enacted must obey.[6] Another possibility would be the 'mutuality of political restrictions' argument according to which we are obligated to each other to comply with laws on the basis that each forbears for the benefit of others and in return receives the benefits of others' compliance, forfeiting the right to this benefit where she fails to comply herself.[7] We can see here some analogies with the retributive view of punishment: those who offend breach the contract, or take an unfair advantage, or create a moral disequilibrium, which can only be redressed by punishment.[8] But it is sometimes justifiable to break a contract; even if the conception of hypothetical social contract is not too artificial to have any real force,[9] surely the mere fact of actual or supposed agreement cannot conclude the question of the propriety or lack of it of future disobedience for all time – at least not in an area as crucial as that of the criminal law. Similarly, the idea of a mutuality of political restrictions seems to cover a multitude of sins; what if some of the restrictions are far more burdensome for one group than for another? Mutual forbearance and cooperation certainly provides *a* reason for obedience, but hardly a conclusive one. The mere fact of membership of a society, even if it had been by agreement, or would have been agreed to, seems insufficient to found political obligation in this strong sense.

For the utilitarian, of course, the very idea of general political obligation would be out of the question: as with the more straightforward case of promise-keeping, the act-utilitarian would have to assess the negative and positive consequences of particular acts of obedience and disobedience in order to take the course with the highest balance of utility.[10] Even the rule-utilitarian would reserve her powers of judgment as to the utility of the rule itself before unreflectively obeying it. As we saw in Chapter 2, John Rawls has argued that a form of rule-utilitarianism can be applied to *systems* of laws: to institutions and practices.[11] The same difficulties mentioned in that context apply here. Once again, we seem to be pushed in the direction of a pluralistic approach which acknowledges *both* the importance of the effects of disobedience *and* questions of the fair distribution of the burdens and benefits of a criminal justice system in society.

Given the objections to the notion of general political obligation considered above and the moral importance of reserving to the individual the possibility of judging a law to be too wicked to be obeyed,[12] how have defenders of general political obligation sought to reconcile it with the value generally attached in liberal theory to individual responsibility for evaluating laws? One common response is to modify the claim and to argue that in a generally just society there is a *presumptive* or *prima facie* obligation to obey the law.[13] This is an odd notion, for, as I have argued, the very concept of obligation expresses something definite, conclusive; what could a prima facie obligation be other than the assertion that there are always some reasons, many of which will have to do with our mutual social responsibilities in political society, for obeying the laws of a generally just system? And if so, why not express it in those terms? Those who espouse the prima facie obligation doctrine (like rule-utilitarians) want to have the best of both worlds, and with good reason. They wish to exploit the determinate, conclusive aura of the concept for the purposes of apparent clarity and certainty, because it cannot be denied that in a generally just and healthy society it will be useful and legitimate to engender a popular attitude that the criminal law, concerned as it is with our most important interests, is to be obeyed. On the other hand, they wish to maintain that citizens keep a residual and important responsibility for judging the criminal law and evaluating their own moral position with respect to it, and that sometimes, even in a generally just system, an obligation to obey particular laws cannot be established. In the context of a generally just society with a well-intentioned government it is perhaps permissible to speak in terms of a presumption that the criminal law ought to be obeyed; but the really important task is to elicit the reasons why that is so.

It seems necessary, then, to examine some of the most important of these reasons. Not taking an unfair advantage *vis-à-vis* other law-abiding citizens has already been mentioned and is clearly an important factor. The existence of a high level of cooperation in a political society with a well developed state apparatus can undoubtedly achieve many goods which would not have been possible without it, but it also risks special dangers. Thus the existence of such a society involves the adoption of mutual responsibilities which are at least partly reinforced by the criminal law. On our functionalist conception of that law, it aims at achieving a certain set of personal and social goods, the achievement of which can be sacrificed or diminished by individual or collective acts of disobedience. Indeed, several of the goods aimed at, such as public peace and national security, only exist or have any real value if the level of compliance with a legitimate set of criminal regulations is very high; and even in other areas where mutual dependence is less extreme, individual offences cost dear in terms of both economic and social resources. In addition, systematic patterns of disobedience can subtly or overtly undermine the system itself, or the efficacy of individual laws within it, and can detract from its long term capacity to achieve its ends. Of course, it has been argued that acts of disobedience actually fulfil a positive function in society, upholding moral values and increasing the sense of social solidarity.[14] It is certainly true that there is always a sense in which an offender and her offence are *used* by society to the best possible (for example, educative or deterrent) effect, but this does not mean that the offence is necessarily valuable on balance. After all, by definition, at least within our conception of the criminal law, an offence causes or risks very serious personal, social or collective harms. It is the criminal law's functions of reducing or mitigating the social and personal impact of such harms, the state's substantive concern with protecting the welfare and autonomy of its citizens, those citizens' commitment to a political society aimed at securing those goods equally for all, that are the basis for the strong and numerous reasons why in a generally just society, one where the criminal law does serve equally to protect the fundamental interests of all its citizens, it is usually right for them to obey that law. But whilst there are several important arguments for obedience deriving from the nature of generally just systems, these do not seem sufficiently compelling to ground the idea of conclusive political obligation given, as I shall argue, the primacy of the question of the justice of the particular law in question.

OBEDIENCE TO JUST LAWS

If we are to reject the idea of a political obligation to obey the laws of a generally just system, what should we say of that of an obligation to obey individually just laws within a system? To answer this, we have to formulate a conception of what counts as a just law. This is clearly a complex question, but the general framework of the conception has already been developed in the previous chapter, and all I shall do here is to reiterate the conclusions drawn there. A just law would be one which both fulfilled some of the positive functions of the criminal law and observed its limiting principles. It would thus be aimed at protecting even-handedly some fundamental collective, social or personal interests, and would have a reasonable chance of achieving that aim without undue prejudice to the interests of any particular group, leaving room for the exercise of residual autonomy and being enacted as the result of a conscientious effort on the part of the lawmakers fairly and consistently to judge the relative weights of competing basic interests. If a law is in this sense just, its breach constitutes by definition a real and immediate threat or harm to important social and personal interests, and on the face of it there will be a good reason for some form of state response. This is only true, of course, given also that the criminal law generally institutes an adequate array of defences and excuses so that those who suffer from certain sorts of internal and, more typically, external difficulties in complying, those whose offences do not manifest a genuine rejection of the fair demands of the law, should not be proceeded against, or should be able to defend themselves. The strength of the argument also depends on the existence of fair and efficient practices within the criminal process as a whole.

What form should society's response towards breaches of a just criminal law take? The obvious priorities would seem to be to curtail and discourage future such acts and to mitigate some of the harmful side-effects of the present act, such as resentment, resort to self-help and so on; thus the consequentialist arguments for punishment or something like it are very strong. The consequentialist case for obedience to a just law is a clear one, given not only the harms directly caused by offences but also the costs involved in their detection and prosecution, never to mention the anger, anxiety and secondary hurt and resentment which they cause. But, of course, all this can be described without having to draw on the idea of an *obligation* to obey: the consequentialist reasons for obedience or disobedience will vary to some degree in every case, and at least a thorough-going utilitarian would reject any general notion of obligation to obey just laws because she might always be able to imagine a possible case where disobedience had better consequences than obedience. In order to ground the notion of obligation to obey more securely it would be necessary to have a different theoretical base. We need to draw on that underlying the mixed theories, which emphasises the parallel value of fairness; or, as I have argued, that outlined in chapter 5,[15] which emphasises the pursuit of the dual goals of welfare and autonomy in the context of a consistent pluralism, in order to reach the conclusion that citizens should always obey laws which are just according to the principles espoused. This might justify, though it would clearly not necessitate, talk in terms of the conclusive concept of obligation. On this view, fair criminal laws would be seen as so central to the protection of fundamental interests in society that it would practically always be wrong to break them given the breach's direct and indirect impact upon the welfare and autonomy of other citizens and indeed on the offender herself as a member of the society.

The clearest alternative to a purely consequentialist conception of political obligation is, of course, that which flows from the retributivist view of punishment set in the context of some form of social contract theory. On these views, as we have seen, it is the breach of a hypothetical or historical agreement, or the upsetting of the existing distribution of advantages *vis-à-vis* compliance with the law, which makes breach of the criminal law wrong. I have already discussed what I take to be the serious problems which such an approach encounters; it also has important limitations as a complete account of the basis for any obligation to obey individually just laws, despite the intuitive plausibility it holds in this area. My argument is that on a pluralist view such as that referred to above, we can develop an account of the 'obligation' to obey just laws which combines the intuitive strength of the idea that it is based on the effects of compliance with just laws, with the equally important intuition that it has also to do with mutual cooperation and forbearance. The vision of a society which endorses the functionalist view of the criminal law is one in which the whole enterprise of criminal regulation is aimed at securing social and personal benefits which it would otherwise be hard to protect. The reasons for obedience, in this framework, will not be only those of self-interest; they will be cooperative and altruistic as well. My forbearance from breaking just laws not only recognises the benefits which I will gain from their observance, but also implicitly acknowledges the similar benefits which all others have to gain, as well as acknowledging the harms to which offending may lead both directly and indirectly, which I and others have at least approximately equal interests in avoiding if proper limiting principles are met. In other words, there are strong reasons for obedience to just laws in terms not only of the social costs of disobedience (which will typically outweigh the gains to the offender), but also in terms of the moral demands which a just law makes on the citizen in straightforward terms of the rightness of forbearance from action which directly or indirectly threatens and expresses rejection of interests or values acknowledged as fundamental in a certain social context. An individually just law which is genuinely and effectively aimed at the promotion of welfare and autonomy in the given sense makes a moral claim on the citizen's obedience. This moral claim is reinforced by the existence of a background system which is just, but that added strength is not sufficient to ground political obligation irrespective of the justice of the particular law.

It is still not clear how usefully even within this conception we can speak of an *obligation* to obey the law, rather than of a set of strong reasons for compliance. I would argue that the conclusiveness of the discourse of obligation can attract some support within a pluralist as opposed to a straightforwardly consequentialist framework, but doubts remain as to whether it adds anything to the debate to frame it in terms of obligation. More will have to be said about this at a later stage when the background political conception has been more fully developed. Leaving this question open for the moment, let me reiterate that the argument for obedience to the law has to refer to its substantive justice and the benefits of compliance for society as a whole and the citizens and groups of citizens within it. It is as much a matter of good will, support and tolerance, the preservation of the community and the welfare and autonomy of those within it, as it is to do with self-interest. As such, these reasons have more truly to do with our responsibilities to each other in political society than with any relation between the individual and the state; but as the representative of all citizens and the administrator of the criminal justice system which should be for the benefit of all of them, it is perhaps permissible to talk in the shorthand of a duty owed to a (personified) state as well as to each other, if we do indeed choose to talk in these terms.

Just laws in unjust systems

So far, I have been assuming that these just laws which there are such strong reasons to obey exist within a system which is *generally* just. What different should it make if a just law exists within a substantially or even moderately unjust system? To answer this fully would involve us in a discussion of the various types of injustice, and this detailed discussion will be the subject matter of the next section. But a few specific comments are called for here. For an act or even rule-utilitarian, these different background considerations would make no real difference, in that the assessment of the justification of any particular action, decision or rule will be made afresh each time the question of obedience arises, and will as a matter of course take into account such effects of obedience as the disutility of supporting an unjust system by supporting one of its occasional just laws. The fact of general injustice may affect the outcome, but not the process of reasoning. For the social contract theorist, on the other hand, the question would presumably be whether the degree of injustice in the system as a whole was such as to render the agreement null so as to invalidate all purported exercises of power by the government. If so, there would be no political obligation to obey even the incidentally just laws of the unjust government; if not, there might still be an obligation to obey the just laws along with an obligation conscientiously to object to the unjust laws of the system.

On the pluralist view which I have defended, the matter will probably also be one of degree. Relevant factors will be whether the system as a whole on balance furthers the fundamental interests of its subjects; whether disobedience to its just laws could materially affect its support of unjust laws; what the type of injustice is; how it bears upon the potential offender; what the alternative forms of government would be likely to be should widespread and general civil disobedience be effective to undermine the stability of the existing regime; the consequences for members of society in terms of their welfare and autonomy, and the resentment, insecurity and costs of a particular act or strategy of disobedience. Given that this is a consequence-oriented position, general principles rather than hard and fast rules must be developed; we can enumerate relevant factors, but given the multiplicity of possible instances of background injustice, it would be impossible to produce a neat set of prescriptions for the well-intentioned citizen. Given that many systems may not be substantially, let alone perfectly, just according to the conception of justice sketched above, this analysis calls further into question the usefulness of analysis in terms of political obligation, with its absolute and conclusive ring. Once again, if we wish to respect the value of at least a sense of residual autonomy, we will wish to encourage citizens to make judgments about background injustices and their effect on the strength of the case for obedience to the criminal law. The conclusion will depend on the type of law under consideration, the possible strategies for combating injustice, and the type of injustice. It may well be that disobedience to just laws is *not* often an effective strategy for protest against and changing unjust ones, and that the harm to the victim's interest, social security and solidarity from offending will outweigh any benefits. But we can imagine legitimate cases – for example, (and on the assumption that the situation is such that the laws themselves are not fundamentally tainted with the background injustice) withholding tax payments from or violating the public order laws of a government committed to apartheid; playing Robin Hood and stealing from the rich to give to the poor in a society of radical poverty. In such cases we might even be tempted to say that the laws broken were tainted by the injustice of the system as a whole. I shall return to the question of civil disobedience and conscientious objection in the next section. Meanwhile it is sufficient to note that whilst it is neither sensible nor useful to speak in terms of generalised obligation to obey the laws of a system, neither is it sufficient to focus upon individual laws in isolation from the system as a whole. Our social responsibilities differ according to the general justice or injustice of the system to which we are subject, and the justice of individual laws can rarely be conclusively evaluated without reference to the system as a whole.

OBEDIENCE TO UNJUST LAWS

Many different forms of injustice can be perpetrated by means of the criminal law. Since I have put forward the view that any argument for an obligation to obey the law must rest largely on the effects of obedience and of disobedience, and since the conception of justice which I have sketched has an important consequence-sensitive element, it follows that the reasons for obedience to an unjust law are likely to be considerably weaker, if indeed they exist at all, than those for obedience to a just law. By definition, an unjust law is one which does not serve the proper ends of the criminal law. However, once again, it would be misleading to give a straightforward prescription that unjust laws should not be obeyed; this will depend on the type of injustice, its bearing on offender and victim, the effects of disobedience, and background considerations about the general efficacy and fairness of the system as a whole. It is to such a classification that I now turn.

Types of injustice

Once again, the retributivist and the utilitarian will give differing answers to the question of what constitutes an injustice in the criminal law, flowing from their own differing and particular conceptions of justice. Enough has been said in the previous two sections to indicate the line which they would respectively take. Our approach to the various issues we have considered has suggested that the conceptions of distributive justice underlying the major theories of punishment are unsatisfactory in important ways, and from now on I shall concentrate on the implications of the political principles based on welfare and autonomy which I have sketched and defended. On that view, there would be four main types of what I shall call public injustice: injustice according to the conception of justice embodied in the constitutional principles of the society, possibly calling for what John Rawls has distinguished as civil disobedience as opposed to conscientious refusal.[16] In the first place, a law might violate one of the limiting principles; it might go beyond the proper ambit of the criminal law, in the sense of focussing on non-fundamental or sectional interests, being an instrument of tyranny or oppression, favouring the interests of one group at the expense of those of another, not reflecting a judgment flowing from a consistent welfare/autonomy pluralism. Secondly, a law might, although aimed at protecting some basic interest, operate in practice in such a way as to disadvantage grossly unequally different groups in society, due to their social situation as being poor, subject to prejudice, or members of a certain class, religion or gender. Thirdly, a law, although apparently satisfying the first two conditions, might have no chance of achieving any of the benefits at which it aims, or might only be able to do so at an unacceptably high cost in economic and human terms. Finally, a law might be drawn, enforced and sanctioned in such a coercive way as to leave no real room for a sense of choice or decision as to whether to obey or not.

What should the response of a conscientious citizen be to each of these types of injustice? Leaving aside the question of effects for a moment, in the case of the first type of injustice it would surely be right to refuse to obey, given that the legislative power entrusted to the government has not been used for its legitimate purposes and thus becomes not a constitutional exercise of authority but a brutal and tyrannical use of power, which citizens may indeed have a responsibility to resist in the name of preserving a system based on the guiding principles I have described. In the second case, the issue is somewhat more complex in that the source of injustice is a set of background unfairnesses or inequalities not *directly* related to the criminal law, such as poverty or racial discrimination, or an injustice perpetrated by some executive actor in the criminal process, such as a police officer, prosecutor, probation officer or judge. Obvious examples would be the way in which type of dress and hair style can affect probabilities of arrest, and the extent to which being poor can affects one's chances of being convicted of theft, or one's being homeless one's chances of being granted bail and indeed of being arrested.[17] Luck may have its necessary ambit, but it should be limited to areas where it is inevitable and not those where external factors could be changed. These injustices are not, in a sense, on the *surface* of the criminal law, yet ultimately the responsibility, either for the background injustices or the actions and prejudices of the executive officers and justices, must rest with the state, which has a special power to attempt to change the situation. In such cases, the effects of civil disobedience will often make it an unfeasible political strategy, but there may well be cases in which disobedience could be justified. In the third case, disobedience could also often be justified, by subsumption from the arguments given in the first type of case: if no proper benefits can accrue from that exercise, the exercise of coercive legislative power will be illegitimate. Finally, in the fourth type of case, although disobedience will generally be ruled out for pragmatic reasons, a justification for disobedience will exist, again as a direct result of violation of the limiting principles.

Before moving on to the question of effects and the bearing of injustice on offenders and victims, we must consider one final, slightly different, type of injustice, which I shall call the conflict of critical morality. This category, which corresponds with that which Rawls analyses in terms of conscientious refusal,[18] exists where, although a law satisfies the public conception of justice embodied in a society's political institutions, an individual's or group's personal or peculiar critical morality does not endorse that public conception or, as is often the case, whilst endorsing the public conception at a general level, disagrees about the morality of a particular concretising application of that public conception, such as the judgments reached about prioritising and balancing interests, or the conception of particular interests adopted. Examples would be the refusal to serve in a (publicly) just war on pacifist principles, refusal to pay taxes partly spent upon nuclear weapons of defence on moral grounds, refusal to wear a seatbelt on libertarian principles, or to wear a crash helmet which would interfere with the wearing of a turban on religious principles.

In my discussion of political 'obligation', I have stressed the importance and desirability of maintaining within political society an area for the exercise of personal critical judgment, indeed as one of the cornerstones of continuing democracy. It is also true that societies such as our own are relatively heterogeneous; we must beware of assuming a high level of consensus and of under-estimating the extent of conflicting interests and conceptions of the good conscientiously held by members of the community. Are these factors not given insufficient weight if we insist that conscientious objectors of these sorts ought nevertheless to obey the law? I would argue that they are not, because, despite the importance of individuals' autonomy and, to some extent, distance from their state, the fact remains that the central function of the criminal law is based on mutual cooperation, forbearance and even altruism for the general social and personal good *in a narrow range of exceptionally important areas*. Given the social aspect and importance of criminal law, allowing conscientious refusers to disobey with impunity would be to risk a sacrifice to some of the important benefits the law can attain, and indeed to contravene the very nature of the criminal law as a collective enterprise. We can maintain, however, our allegiance to the two types of values by means of an analysis which employs the device of points of view; whilst we can accept that, from a particular citizen's point of view, a law is unjust, and she retains her personal autonomy to break it if she feels she must (hence the fourth category of injustice), she must nevertheless be regarded from *society's* point of view as having broken the law, and thus a state punitive response may be justified.[19]

Naturally, there are also problems of proof with cases of conscientious refusal; this compromise solution has the added advantage of avoiding these. We should say, with Rawls, that a just system will be such as to leave the citizen a real possibility of putting her own conscientiously held beliefs before her publicly acknowledged social responsibilities: but the state must nevertheless vindicate its own public judgment of the justice of its criminal law by treating her as an offender (though perhaps also by mitigating her punishment) if the social benefits of the system as a whole are not to be diminished. Furthermore, such conflicts of critical morality underline yet again the importance of the principle of fundamental interests, which confines the operation of the criminal law within a relatively limited ambit.

The bearing of injustice on victim and offender

Having discussed the various types of injustice, let us now turn to the more specific question of how that injustice bears upon offender and victim. Again, what I shall have to say is, I think, implicit in the general principles expounded in chapter 5. In this context there could be three specific kinds of unjust law; those which treated both victim and offender unfairly; those which treated only the victim unfairly; and those which were unjust only in respect of offenders. Our analysis will depend not only on these distinctions but also on that between direct and indirect disobedience, which I shall develop in a later section. For now, it will be sufficient merely to give some examples in order to draw some general conclusions.

First of all, what should be said of laws which treat both potential and actual victims and offenders unfairly? Examples are somewhat difficult to produce, but a general type of injustice which might bear on citizens in this way would be a law which had no chance of achieving its aim, thus unjustifiably affecting the offender's freedom of action, whilst also failing to give to victims the protection of their fundamental interests which is the function of the criminal law. Another possibility would be a law which violated the principle of equal consideration of interests with respect to both offenders and victims. Perhaps more likely is a situation in which one particular type of injustice bears on the law's application to the offender and another on its application to the victim; for instance, a law which was disproportionately difficult for one group of potential offenders to comply with, and also unfair to victims in discriminating between the level of protection accorded to one group of victims as opposed to another in relevantly similar circumstances. Let us take an example of this mixed kind as our illustration. Imagine a law against assault which penalised assaults on women less severely than those on men, assuming also that the incidence of assaults on members of each sex was roughly equal in severity and frequency, but under which both sets of penalties were so draconian that they violated the principle of residual autonomy. I have already argued that violation of that principle, although it would render disobedience an unlikely strategy, could justify it. Does the added injustice to victims add to the case for disobedience? Clearly not to this law itself, for breach of that law would both cause direct harm to the victim and compound the injustice embodied in the law. Whenever a victim is affected adversely by a direct act of civil disobedience, that adverse effect tells strongly against *direct* disobedience by the offender, and the law's injustice to the victim cannot affect the argument. And if we are speaking of disobedience by the (potential) victim, who then by definition becomes an offender, once again it is difficult to see how *direct* disobedience, which implies the creation of another victim, could be justified.

What of a law, then, which was unjust only to victims and not to potential offenders: could this ever justify disobedience to that law? This depends, of course, on the types of injustice to and effect of disobedience on the victim; but I think that on the given conception of the criminal law, it would not be possible to produce a case where injustice to victims *per se* could justify disobedience to the unjust law. This is because the types of possible injustice relevant to victims, that is, failure to protect their fundamental interests, either incidentally or by design, perhaps due to a failure to comply with the requirement of consistent pluralism, perhaps out of tyranny or prejudice, and unfair discrimination in the protection of fundamental interests of victims and offenders, would mean that *direct* disobedience would serve only to compound and further the injustice perpetrated by the law itself. There is one other general sense in which victims often are, I would argue, treated unfairly by criminal justice systems. This is in the fact that the proper state response to offending may be geared to general preventive or socially protective goals and do little to right the wrong done to the individual victim. With the gradual introduction of principles of compensation and restitution within criminal justice systems,[20] it seems that this unfairness is beginning to be removed; but in any case it is clear that this injustice has no bearing on any justification for direct disobedience.

Finally, then, what of laws which are unfair not to victims but only to actual and potential offenders? It should by now be clear that the types of injustice enumerated in the previous section are mostly ones which do bear directly on the offender; for they consist in a use of the coercive power of the criminal justice system for illegitimate purposes and in unjust ways, and the true victims of these injustices are potential offenders (all members of society) whose autonomy is curtailed by the threat of punishment, and those actual offenders who are detected and punished on the basis of unjust laws. It is right, therefore, to focus on offenders in a chapter on political obligation; but, as not only potential offenders but also potential victims ourselves, it is as well to remember that there are two sides to the coin of injustice in any criminal justice system.

The effects of disobedience

It is both a consequence of the general position I have defended and a proviso on what has so far been said in this chapter, that an individual act of disobedience must be largely evaluated in terms of its effects. I mean 'effects' to be taken in a broad sense, not only to cover the direct consequences of disobedience for offenders and victims, but also its wider ramifications and implications for the system and society as a whole. Thus disobedience which causes grave and particularly irreparable harm to a victim (disobedience to 'victimless' crimes will often be easier to justify because of this) or which seriously threatens the stability of a generally fair system which would be likely to be replaced by a less just one, or which, as a response to a less grave form of injustice, will cause graver unfairnesses or will exhaust substantial amounts of resources devoted to enforcement, which could have been directed at more pressing social goals, will not be justified. These examples may sound far fetched in the context of individual acts of disobedience. But in the context of widespread civil disobedience as a political strategy, the effects in terms of costs, impetus for change, harm to victims and threat to public peace and security can be substantial. It is the responsibility of anyone who considers, whether as an individual or as part of a group strategy, breaking a law in the name of public injustice, to evaluate the effects and implications of her action and of the strategy as a whole and her likely contribution to it, and to balance these with the effects of inaction and of alternative strategies of protest, taking into account the relevant probabilities of both desired and undesired outcomes resulting, and to evaluate them in terms of the public conception of justice outlined above. This may seem a Herculean task, but once again we should remind ourselves of the valuable social functions towards which a just criminal law is directed, and emphasise the social responsibility which citizens have towards each other when determining their position *vis-à-vis* any particular penal law.

Background considerations of justice and efficiency

These factors can be dealt with briefly since they have already been discussed in relation to types of injustice and the effects of disobedience. But it is important to consolidate the argument that background fairness, unfairness and unfair inefficiencies in the political system as a whole cannot be kept entirely out of any legitimate process of reasoning about the issue of civil disobedience. The fact that a particular law operates unjustly with respect to one particular group, be it the poor, women or an ethnic minority, because of some background injustice strictly separate from the criminal law (unfair inequality in the distribution of resources, sexual, racial or religious discrimination) *should* bear on our thought both about how far a member of the disadvantaged group is justified in disobeying the law in question and on how the state ought to respond to such disobedience. This is so because, whilst the injustice is not directly perpetrated by the criminal law, it is perpetuated by the 'even-handed', formally fair application of that law, and because it is ultimately the state which must act to resolve the unfairness, albeit in some other sphere of its governmental responsibility. By contrast, but by the same token, the fact that a criminal justice system which is as a whole just and efficient generally contributes to the realisation of the public conception of justice must also bear on our evaluation of acts of disobedience, and specifically on those which threaten the stability of the system as a whole rather than militate towards changes in particular laws within it. In a just society, there will be strategies other than disobedience for changing the law; the effects of disobedience are costly in many respects, and background considerations of justice dictate that someone who wishes to remedy specific injustices within a generally just system be required, if not to exhaust, at least intelligently and genuinely to exploit other strategies for reform before offending against a socially beneficial system by disobedience.

Direct and indirect disobedience

So far, for the sake of simplicity, I have generally been assuming that the act of disobedience is directed at the specific law which offends against the public conception of justice – the case of direct disobedience. It is clear, however, that a draconian punishment, or the fact that the law is unfair to the victim, or the type of injustice, which may bear on the way in which the law is enforced, will often mean that direct disobedience is not a suitable response to injustice. Whilst it may be useful to protest against seatbelt requirements by refusing to wear one, it would hardly be sensible to respond to an unjust difference between punishments for assaults on men and women by assaulting members of either sex, nor to protest about capital punishment by committing a capital offence. Nor would it often be useful to protest about the unequal application, both by the enforcement agencies and inevitably, due to background inequalities, of the law of theft by stealing (unless, perhaps, one does so in order to redistribute). This raises the possibility of what I shall call indirect disobedience; disobedience to a just law, or to a law which is not unjust to oneself, as a response to the existence of injustice in the framing or application of other laws. To put it in another way, what bearing does the existence of some injustice within the criminal justice system have on the reasons for obedience to other laws within it? Does any instance of injustice affect all reasons for obedience? And to what extent do we have to distinguish between injustice perpetrated directly by the criminal law and background injustice from some other social sphere, which is merely reflected in or perpetuated by the operation of the criminal law?

The practical difficulty and disutility of direct disobedience in many instances means that, at least at the level of political strategy, acts of indirect disobedience are typically more common – acts such as criminal damage (for example, in the form of indelible graffiti), public disorder, disruption of meetings, failure to pay income tax, and so on – than are acts of direct disobedience as strategies directed towards protest and reform. The question here is really one of the extent to which it is proper for citizens to use breach of the criminal law as a means of political protest against injustice of any kind, and, as such, I think certain additional principles must guide its use. In addition to what has already been said about effects, injustices and back-ground considerations, a more stringent principle of effectiveness and one of appropriateness should be brought to bear in the case of indirect disobedience. Both of these principles flow from the great importance of the criminal law and from the added risks to its stability and respect for it involved in indirect disobedience which is directed at individually just laws, thus causing real harms. Before accepting the use of indirect disobedience as a political tool, any citizen should be confident that it has a reasonable chance of success (in the relative sense of not causing more harm and distress than it has a probability of preventing, measured in terms of the degree of harm caused discounted by the probabilities of their occurrence) and should have exploited all other avenues of protest to which they had access and which had any reasonable hope of having any impact – political lobbying, use of the media, and so on. Here the principle of effectiveness runs into the requirement of appropriateness; to preserve the social benefits of the criminal law, we must maintain the view in society that breach of its just precepts in the name of graver public injustice should only be undertaken as a last resort. In any generally just system, there will be other possible strategies of protest; these should be exploited before the inevitable harms involved in breaching just laws are accepted.

It seems to follow from this argument that, whilst the threshold level of justification is high, once it is reached, the state has no justification for inflicting a punitive response. Indeed, by desisting from punishment, the state would acknowledge its responsibility for the injustice and make a public commitment to attempt to remedy it (once again, we must distinguish between conscientious refusal and civil disobedience in this context). Should it make any difference that the injustice lies outside the ambit of the criminal law, for example in racial or sexual discrimination, or unjust distributions of resources? I would argue that this should not make a difference to the kinds of argument required to justify disobedience or punishment. Reasoning about criminal justice must be insulated from the rest of practical political reasoning to the extent that this is necessary to preserve the central legitimating functions of the criminal law (assuming the system to be generally just), but not beyond that point. It is fundamental to the view of punishment which I wish to defend that it be set, as a moral question, in its political context. Without an appreciation of the interplay between arguments, values, injustices in different spheres of political action, a crucial dimension on the problem of punishment is (and often has been) lost.

Injustice by omission

A few words at least must be said of the problem of injustice perpetuated or, more controversially, perpetrated by the criminal law through its omission to protect certain fundamental interests rather than by the positive content of its actual laws. Doubtless such injustice will generally offend against the principle of equal consideration of interests, for we can imagine a law which which by its framing or in its application protects particular interests of one group more effectively, or acknowledges the interests of one group more highly, than those of another (for example, the employers of blue collar workers from employment-related offences such as theft or fraud more effectively than those of white-collar workers, or men in relation to indecent assault more effectively than women). But we can also imagine a system in which a value recognised as fundamental within the public conception of justice was quite simply unprotected. Since there is by definition no actual law, direct disobedience is clearly out of the question; and since it is highly likely that the omission in question will be one concerning a value which is just emerging in social consciousness to wider recognition, or one which certain groups are trying to advance, indirect disobedience would rarely be within the principle of appropriateness given other, safer, less costly and more legitimate avenues for reform. It is, however, important to remember that criminal justice systems cause or support injustice not only by action but also by omission, and that the positive principles of the functionalist conception are as important as the negative limiting principles.

Judging the justice of disobedience

Finally, in cases of disobedience informed by the public conception of justice, an important question arises about who should have the final say as to whether or not the law in question did indeed violate that conception of justice so as to render punishment an unjust and inappropriate response. Can it be left to the citizen to avow her good intentions and put before the courts her reading of the injustice involved? Or must it be left to the court or some other organ of the state, which might thus be thought to be acting as judge in its own cause? Again, given the importance of the criminal law as a collective enterprise, it is clear that some body which represents the society as a whole and its conception of justice, or rather that dominant in its present political institutions and practices, rather than some particular person or group, must have this responsibility. But the importance of the state not being judge in its own cause underlies the crucial significance of the principle of the independence and impartiality of the judiciary – an ideal hard if not impossible to attain in any society of divided and diverse interests. The difficulty is to think of any better solution than the traditional (varying) western conception of judges and courts with power (implicit in the UK) to interpret the constitutional values at the pinnacle of the legal system. We would have to imagine political facts very different from our own, and a judiciary very unlike our own, to conceive of a case of a judge in this country explicitly condoning an act of civil disobedience (even of a direct kind) on the basis of the law's failure to comply with the public constitutional conception of justice (perhaps the few cases in which national law has been found wanting in the light of principles of EEC law come closest to the sort of reasoning which would be involved).[21] Moreover, since that conception will itself be controversial, at least in matters of interpretation, due to the existence of competing conceptions of the concept at both its general and particular levels, this will inevitably give the judiciary enormous power. This is not the place for a treatise on controlling that power;[22] suffice it to say that the question of whom a system entrusts the final decision to, on what basis, and subject to what controls, will be among the most important questions which have to be taken in the framing of a constitution.

CONCLUSION

I have gradually built up a complex picture of the process of reasoning which should underlie the debate about political obligation. A certain degree of complexity is, as I have argued, inevitable if we are to avoid the pitfalls of a simplistic subscription to the notion of political obligation. In particular, I have argued that it is crucially important to acknowledge that the type of injustice involved affects the types of reasons relevant to the justification of disobedience, although not the process of reasoning itself. But we may summarise the argument, by way of general conclusion, as maintaining that on the basis of a pluralist conception of justice, (as yet partially described and incompletely argued for), civil disobedience has to be justified by reference both to its rationale – its defence of public justice – and its effects – its contribution to that commitment – taking into account all side-effects and long term implications. The important task which remains is that of further developing the political principles underlying these arguments in order to work out their implications for theories of punishment.

CHAPTER 7

PUNISHMENT AND THE LIBERAL WORLD

We are now ready to return to our central question of the justification of punishment. During the last four chapters, we have built a sharper appreciation of the issues which have to be tackled in producing a set of justifying arguments; in the next and final chapter we shall draw all the threads together in order to say, in the light of what has gone before, what is the best that can be said for punishment. But in this chapter, I want to return to the traditional theories and some of the moral and political ideas underlying them, in an attempt to draw out certain common themes which, despite their differences, they share. In this way I hope to crystallise both what has been illuminating and what has been unsatisfactory in the history of justifying argument, and to lay the ground for the arguments of the concluding chapter by exploring in some detail the general political assumptions on which traditional theory has proceeded.

LIBERALISM AND THEORIES OF PUNISHMENT

What is striking about the traditional theories of punishment expounded and examined in Chapter 2 is that they can all be located, at least in their modern forms, at some point within the liberal tradition in political theory. This contention will, of course, be controversial, given the notorious difficulty of defining the concept of liberalism, which has indeed been the the subject of much debate in philosophical journals.[1] I would certainly not deny that there are many different conceptions of liberalism, nor could I hope to do justice to the richness of the liberal tradition in developing a model of liberalism for the purposes of re-examining some of the most familiar arguments for punishment. My aim, rather, is to draw out some central liberal themes and to explore how they are related to the strengths and weaknesses of theories of punishment. To that end, I shall sketch a model which I take to incorporate the defining features of and the key issues addressed by liberal political theory.

Liberal individualism

Despite the wide variety of conceptions of liberalism endorsed even by modern theorists,[2] it would be hard to deny that some form of individualism has been centrally associated with the liberal tradition. By individualism, I mean some assumption of the moral significance of the individual, which moreover proceeds from characteristics which can be abstracted from any particular social environment, and a taking of individuals as the primary focus of concern in the moral assessment of any particular set of political arrangements. A central example of liberal concern for the individual is the principle of taking persons seriously as moral agents worthy of respect and concern, which appears in various guises in many versions of liberalism. It can be traced from Kant's injunction that persons should be treated as ends in themselves rather than as means[3] through to Dworkin's principle of equal respect and concern.[4] It can be seen at work in Hart's principle of fairness[5] and in the utilitarian prescription that each person should count for one in the utilitarian calculation and no one for more than one.[6] This last example is especially clear in the work of modern consequentialists such as Peter Singer, who espouses a principle of equal consideration of interests.[7]

The individual is thus the primary focus for moral concern as far as liberalism is concerned, and this is most clearly evinced by the view of early liberalism that man (the liberal individual is still predominantly male . . .) comes into society bringing with him a relatively fixed set of 'pre-social' rights and interests, which must be respected by subsequent political arrangements.[8] The most obvious modern statement of this theme is to be found in Robert Nozick's *Anarchy, State and Utopia*, in which it is argued that in any society the set of rights and duties is just that which existed before its formation: no new obligations arise, on this extreme view, in political society. It is hardly surprising that the 'communitarian' critics of liberalism[9] have levelled the charge that it presupposes an inadequate and artificial conception of human nature which generates an impoverished view of the ambit and potential of life in political society. According to such critics, humans are to a large extent social and socially constructed beings: it is both necessary for them to live in some form of society, and the conditions, norms and expectations of that society will play a large part in determining their attitudes, behaviour and indeed physical and mental capacities.[10] Thus the idea of an original 'state of nature' inhabited by human individuals without cooperation or social structure becomes, even at the level of thought experiment, ludicrous: since survival in such a state would be well nigh impossible, it seems an eminently unsuitable starting point for reflection on the proper form of political society. We should rather recognise that humans have to be understood as social beings whose very 'personhood' is influenced by the kind of society in which they live. Needs, rights, interests, preferences, and conceptions of rationality are not timeless, objective, pre-social phenomena; they develop *through* social coexistence and are constantly subject to revision and modification.

It is, of course, clear that this caricature version of the primacy liberalism attaches to the individual has been substantially modified by theorists such as Dworkin[11] and Rawls.[12] Moreover, they have responded vigorously to the suggestion that all liberal theory in some way fits the caricature.[13] These writers and others like them certainly acknowledge the importance of human social existence and even some measure of social determination of human nature: they also defend a much fuller conception of the state than did early liberals and their intellectual descendants such as Nozick. Have they succeeded in shelving, or modifying sufficiently, the underlying conception of fixed, pre-social, individual human nature which has been criticised? Surely the very idea of an (albeit hypothetical) original position[14] in which individuals are abstracted from all but the most basic knowledge about the nature of their society, or of the auction in which individuals bargain for parcels of goods,[15] has a stronger resonance with the unfashionable social contract theory (the ultimate in individualistic methods of legitimating social arrangements) than these theorists would care to admit? Enough has been said at least to support the proposition that some form of individualism lies at the heart of liberal theory: although I have so far concentrated on some negative aspects of that liberal concern, it also has important positive aspects. I shall return below to the implications of this feature of liberal thought for the justification of punishment.

The other features of liberalism which I shall discuss relate closely both to individualism and to each other. I have separated them as an expositional device in the interests of clarity: some degree of overlap is, nevertheless, inevitable.

Freedom and the rational, responsible person

Another distinctive feature of liberal thought is its vision of humans as essentially rational beings, capable of reasoning about the best means to chosen ends, and able at least to some extent to govern their emotions both in engaging in the process of reasoning and in acting on its outcome. Thus in the liberal view of morality, reason is privileged over emotion: the role of intuition tends to be played down, rationalised (as in Rawlsian reflective equilibrium) or excused. There is also a tendency to regard rationality as a value-free, universal concept, and consequently liberal approaches to different cultures have often been criticised as naive or ethnocentric.[16] This view of rationality at the core of human nature is well reflected both in the utilitarian view of persons as rational calculators and, somewhat differently, in the Kantian vision of the rational agent which finds its way, in modified form, into Rawls' original position and Dworkin's auction.

Closely related to the liberal vision of rational persons is the notion of humans as free and responsible agents, capable of understanding and controlling their own actions. Here again there is a considerable divergence between the utilitarian and other liberal traditions, the former being substantially less committed to the notion of free will than the latter (indeed, this division between utilitarian and non-utilitarian versions of liberalism arises at many points, as the debate on punishment brings out so clearly). But for the purposes of model-building, I shall identify as a centrally important feature of liberalism the vision of the individual as an autonomous agent capable of choice and control, aware of her environment and, at least in some respects, capable of shaping it to her own ends. Both rationality and the capacity for responsible action are thus for liberalism at once factual features of human nature and sources of normative limits on the ways in which human beings may be treated, particularly by political and other public institutions. These features above all others seem to entail the distinctively liberal focus upon the moral value of freedom.[17]

Paternalism and neutrality

The vision of the liberal person sketched above has traditionally fostered in liberal theory a distrust of paternalism and a positive view that human beings should be allowed to exercise their 'natural' capacities without being unduly interfered with (the so-called 'negative' conception of freedom[18]). This issues in a serious concern with the limitation of state power and a particular resistance to the idea of citizens having any conception of the good foisted upon them by their government. Thus a relatively minimal or at least restrained state should essentially create a framework within which individual diversity may flourish. Important (and varied) examples of this kind of thinking are to be found in Mill's discussion of paternalism and his statement of the harm principle;[19] in Dworkin's identification of liberalism in terms of a distinctive neutrality as between conceptions of the good;[20] in Ackerman's principle of neutrality;[21] and in Bentham's assertion that pushpin is as good as poetry.[22] We can, of course, find counter-examples: theorists who in other respects defend liberal values whilst adopting a perfectionist stance on the question of conceptions of the good.[23] What is more, it can very persuasively be argued[24] that the very idea of neutrality is fraught with ambiguity and even incoherence. For surely any political theory worth the name is inevitably perfectionist at least to some degree, in that the very purpose of such a theory is to provide a coherent set of values and prescriptions for the conduct of political life, and in so far as it dictates that certain decisions be left either to individual decision or put to a democratic vote, that is as much a conception of what constitutes a good life (that is, one in which individuals have a wide measure of free choice) as a theory which specifies the structure and values in more detail. Moreover, since many forms of life can only be pursued against a certain backcloth of public goods and facilities, the achievement of any strong form of neutrality by anything other than a minimal state would seem to be well nigh impossible. This is not to say, of course, that there is not a relevant difference between theories which purport to espouse neutrality and those which endorse perfectionism, nor to deny that liberal theories have tended to be of the former kind. It is simply to question whether the relevant difference is genuinely expressed in terms of neutrality as between different conceptions of the good, rather than in terms of the more slippery area of disagreement over how best to respect the autonomy of citizens in political society. For the purposes of our model-building, however, liberal concern with neutrality, and particularly liberal anti-paternalism, must count as important features of liberal thought, especially in the modern tradition.

Rights, justice and equality

Harder to pin down, because of its breadth, is the concern of liberal theory with the values of justice, equality and individual rights. Especially in the public sphere,[25] a concern with just distributions as between the primary subjects of liberal theory, individual human beings, has received an enormous amount of attention,[26] and even utilitarians, whose unitary principle has difficulty in accommodating satisfactorily a plurality of values, have felt constrained to give an account of the place of justice among moral and political values.[27] The relationship between the value of justice and liberal individualism is not difficult to see; in a world of scarce resources peopled by essentially separate beings with conflicting claims and preferences, principles of fair distribution will clearly have a high priority. This perhaps accounts (at least in part) for the absence of the concept from the main modern rival to liberalism, Marxist theory, which in some of its forms regards justice as an essentially bourgeois preoccupation.[28]

Another concept generally occupying a central place in liberal theory (and rejected by many Marxist theories) is that of individual rights, claims which operate with a special weight to defeat arguments from general background political considerations such as general social welfare.[29] Again, the link with individualism is obvious, as is considerable diversity within the liberal tradition. Leaving aside act-utilitarianism's general rejection of the concept,[30] two main views have been put forward regarding the origin of such rights. In traditional liberalism, they tend to be seen as 'natural',[31] deriving from human pre-social interests, nature and needs. More recently, Dworkin[32] has argued that political rights are (at least in part) defined by reference to defects in the operation of the democratic process, where the vote is corrupted by the existence of 'external' preferences influenced by, for example, racial prejudice. The influence of the liberal conception of individual rights is, of course, easy to see in the constitutional structure of many countries, perhaps most notably in the constitutionally privileged rights entrenched in the USA.

The concept of equality cannot claim such an exclusive relationship with the liberal tradition as can those of rights and justice, yet it features strongly in modern liberal theory, where a major preoccupation has been to develop and defend a distinctively liberal conception of the concept of equality.[33] Again, a wide variety of such conceptions has been proposed: a right to equal concern and respect for all citizens;[34] equal consideration of interests;[35] equality of welfare;[36] equal counting in the utilitarian calculus;[37] equality of resources;[38] equality as the exclusion of irrelevant reasons;[39] and, last but not least, equality of opportunity.[40] I shall not attempt to reduce or distil from this diversity; suffice it to point out that a concern for some form of human equality flows naturally from the liberal view of distinctive human nature, although doubts can be (and have been[41]) raised about the independent importance of the concept, sometimes in the light of the existence among human beings of different capacities and degrees of rationality and responsibility.

These, then, along with the key concept of freedom discussed above (and indeed embedded linguistically in the very name, liberalism) form the conceptual framework of values within which liberal theory is typically constructed, and the linguistic counters with which liberal discourse is carried on. It is worth mentioning, however, another distinctively liberal concern often associated with liberal equality; the ideal of the rule of law. Liberals have often (and quite often unfairly) been accused of focussing on the issue of formal fairness and equality, the treating of like cases alike, at the expense of concentration on substantive issues.[42] This criticism has been most justly levelled in the legal context, where 'equality before the law' has sometimes been highly valued to the exclusion of any proper questioning of the substantive definition of what count as like and unlike cases, which may, of course, be extremely iniquitous.[43] But the value attached to formal equality by liberals in the legal context relates to a cluster of more or less formal values often collectively defined as 'the rule of law'.[44] These values include consistency as between laws, possibility of compliance, congruence between declared rule and official response, non-retroactivity, clarity, relative stability, publicity and generality, all of which relate more or less directly to one of the other identified features of liberalism, conducing to a situation in which the rational, responsible individual is free to plan her life so as to avoid as far as possible the coercive intervention of the criminal law. As such, the rule of law is central to the liberal-legal ideal, and is of particular interest in the context of our primary question of punishment.

Welfare

Another concern professed by much of the liberal tradition is the welfare of individuals, be it in terms of their happiness, the satisfaction of their preferences, or the extent to which they have achieved their own objectives or are well off in terms of some 'objective' measure of goods or resources.[45] This aspect of political morality seems so obvious as hardly to bear any specific mention – yet its importance to modern political theory is probably to be attributed to the pervasive and continuing influence of utilitarianism and the various forms of consequentialist and consequence-sensitive theory it has spawned over the last two centuries. Whilst it is clear that most liberal theories do not share utilitarianism's exclusive focus on welfare, however defined, it is nonetheless true that most liberal theories attach great importance to welfare, either directly, as in Rawls' difference principle[46] and Dworkin's conception of background political justification relating to general welfare,[47] or indirectly, through the affirmation of goods such as individual rights, which are valued at least in part because they generally contribute towards human welfare or flourishing, even if the weight given to those goods is independent of their actual contribution in any particular case. Bentham's trenchant arguments for the centrality of the capacity for suffering[48] have left their mark on liberal political theory, even if they have not been straightforwardly incorporated.

The distinction between public and private spheres

Another distinctive feature of liberalism, closely related to the value attached to autonomy, is that it generates a relatively stringent conception of the limits of state action (already mentioned in the context of paternalism). Obligations imposed by the state are seen as prima facie fetters on individual freedom and thus subject to a heavy burden of justification. The working out of the threshold of proper state action has often been framed in terms of a distinction between public and private spheres, perhaps most famously expressed in the Wolfenden Committee's assertion of the existence of a realm of private morality which is 'not the law's business'.[49] Such allegedly conceptual distinctions tend, of course, to be slippery, and many writers have noted that any attempt to pin down a relatively specific conception of the public/private distinction turns out to be very difficult to realise. Moreover, the distinction is often appealed to *as if* it generated a clear limit to proper state action whilst it is in fact being used to cover a value judgment whose premises, legitimate or illegitimate, are suppressed.[50] A good example of shifts in the distinction along with developments in political ideology is the fact that according to nineteenth century laissez-faire doctrine, the public sphere encompassed only a limited state, the market being regarded as part of the private sphere, a set of relationships and exchanges between private individuals, with which the state should not interfere. In more recent times, most would accept that the sphere of legitimate state action includes (at least some) intervention in the operation of the market; now it is the family and family life which tends to represent the ideal liberal conception of the private sphere. This is not the place for a full discussion of the public/private distinction and its significance: suffice it to say that although it can all too easily be used as a mystifying shorthand for 'that which should and should not be regulated', there remains a core of significance in the idea of privacy as part of liberal ideology, which relates once again to liberalism's principle of taking the pre-social individual as the starting point for the construction of political principles. As far as punishment is concerned, state punishment fits easily into the public sphere, and private chastisement (within limits) into the private. But it is worth noting that the influence of the ideology underlying the distinction is often clear, at least in British society, in the operation and application of the law, the clearest example being that of police reluctance to intervene or prosecute in cases of domestic violence.[51]

Lack of emphasis on public goods

A last feature of liberalism which I want to mark out is a negative implication of many of the other features already noted. As a result of its emphasis on the autonomous flourishing of individuals and its hostility to perfectionism, liberalism has been slow to develop any conception of public goods or virtues, or indeed any thorough conception of common social values. Goods such as the attainment and maintenance of the background conditions for peaceful, stable, secure and rich social existence tend not to be given a central place in liberal theory, and to be valued instrumentally through their contribution to the fulfillment of individual rights or utilities. As with many of the preceding arguments, this is less true of modern liberals such as Rawls and Dworkin (and especially of writers such as Walzer[52]) than it was of earlier writers. Nevertheless, when compared with writings in other political traditions (for example, those of Finnis[53]), the difference in this respect is still striking (and this is not surprising given the clear threat that a committment to such values may present to neutrality). Thus it may be that, if some of the strongest arguments for punishment have to do with the upholding of common goods or public virtues, liberalism will have difficulty in accommodating the best that can be said for that practice.

Liberalism and consequentialist versus non-consequentialist reasoning

One final issue must be mentioned. This has to do with the location of liberalism within the fundamental moral distinction between consequentialist and anti-consequentialist positions. It is quite clear that those whom I have, implicitly or explicitly, identified as standing within the liberal tradition nevertheless stand on different sides of this particular distinguishing line. The extreme positions here could be represented by Kant and Nozick on one side and by Bentham on the other, with writers such as Rawls and Dworkin standing somewhere in between. The issue is further complicated by the fact that the definitions of consequentialism and the various forms of anti-consequentialism are themselves controversial,[54] some writers defining consequentialism broadly so as to include, to take a topical example, the 'goal' of restoring the moral equilibrium in a retributive sense, others defining it restrictively so as to include only more direct or tangible results of human actions. It is quite possible to define consequentialism so broadly that it swallows up all other theories: for our purposes, it will be useful to employ a narrower definition so as to preserve a significant distinction. Most crudely, one could say that consequentialist theories value certain goals as states of affairs, evaluating the moral status of an action exclusively in terms of its actual or intended effects, generally in contributing to the realisation of that valued state of affairs, such as aggregate happiness. Thus consequentialism focuses only indirectly on the means used to achieve the valued goals, and finds no place for the acknowledgment of any intrinsic goods or actions valued irrespective of their effects. Deontological and other anti-consequentialist theories, on the other hand, focus less on some endstate and more on the moral propriety of actions and decisions in respecting rights and duties: such theories evaluate situations not only in terms of end results, but also on how such results were or should be achieved.

From this rough and ready characterisation, it can be seen that most modern liberal theories (like their counterparts in the punishment debate) attempt to incorporate both a non-consequentialist (typically a rights-respecting) element and a consequence-oriented element. A good example would be Dworkin's theory in which consequentialist reasoning is assumed to play a large part in background political justification, whilst rights operate as trumps over that background process of reasoning.[55] Similarly, in the context of punishment, Hart's mixed theory of punishment pursues a goal, subject to fairness-based side constraints.[56] We must, of course, draw a distinction between thoroughgoing consequentialist theories and those which are merely consequence-sensitive, taking consequences into account as one important but not exclusive criterion in evaluating moral and political actions. In this sense, modern liberalism (like modern theories of punishment) has a clear pluralist element, and much attention has been devoted to the issues both of how the different elements within a pluralistic theory accommodating incommensurable values can be related to each other in a coherent whole and of the nature of incommensurability itself.[57] This will be one of our main preoccupations in developing an adequate set of arguments for punishment: possible solutions might be the prioritisation of a set of principles or values;[58] making one set of values (such as respect for rights) act as absolute or near-absolute side-constraints on the pursuit of others;[59] recourse to intuitionism in balancing the values;[60] or the idea of a principle of consistency, already discussed in chapter 5.[61] It seems fair to conclude, however, with the observation that in terms of the structural quality of its moral framework, the liberal tradition has in the past been relatively divided, but that modern political theory is attempting to draw out what is of value in the two main aspects of the tradition, and to forge a reconciliation in terms of a pluralistic political philosophy.

In conclusion, I have tried to identify what I take to be some of the central themes of liberal political thought. It is clear that no one theorist will fit the paradigm, because not all liberal theories fully exemplify each of the features, and because even those who do may meet them in different ways. But we now have a model within which to locate our theories of punishment and evaluate their strengths and weaknesses in the broader context of those of a background political ideology.

THE THEORIES RELOCATED

Retributivism

It would obviously be a mistake to claim that retributivism as a principle of punishment can be located exclusively within the liberal tradition. For one thing, retributive thought about punishment predates liberal thought on the subject, and a retributive position is still defended by some who would not identify themselves as liberals.[62] Furthermore, retributivism has been argued by at least one writer to be the appropriate conception of punishment within Marxist political theory.[63] But since I take the most powerful statements of modern retributivism, especially in recent years, to be importantly located within a scheme of liberal values, my enterprise here will be to try to bring out more specifically than I have done so far the attractions of retributivism for liberals, and the connections between retributive principles and the liberal values outlined above.

Retributive principles as traditionally presented are clearly located within the anti-consequentialist tradition in moral thought; in their pure form, they deny the relevance of the effects of punishment to the moral evaluation of its threat or infliction. There is a significant resonance between retributivism and liberal individualism, most obviously when retributive arguments are fleshed out, as I have argued they must be, in terms of some background conception of political obligation.[64] On a social contract view, it is the (hypothetical) fact of individual agreement or the argument that agreement would have been given under certain conditions which obligates the individual agent to other members of society and, in a sense, to the state. On a mutuality of political restrictions view, the fact that the individual benefits from the forbearance of others generates an argument of fairness for her forbearance too. This in turn links up with the liberal view of persons as rational, responsible and autonomous agents; retributivism makes strong assumptions of voluntariness and responsibility, whereby it is argued that the agent's free, informed choice to commit an offence means that she *deserves* to be punished. In one extreme form it has even been claimed that the offender has willed her own punishment, has chosen or consented to be punished, or has a right to be punished:[65] the deepest rationality of the offender as agent would allow her to see that she should be punished in the given circumstances. Punishment under these conditions does thus not violate the autonomy of the offender as a person, it rather respects her as such.

It is this aspect of necessary voluntariness or choice which reconciles the retributivist with the liberal injunction against paternalism: if the offender has freely chosen to offend, and if the criminal law is legitimated in one of the ways discussed, it cannot be argued that she is having certain values foisted upon her when the just punishment is exacted. But there is, perhaps not surprisingly, a tension between at least some forms of retributivism and the modern liberal ideal of neutrality. Whether cast in terms of a 'reaffirmation of the right' or linked, as some significantly retributive approaches have been,[66] with the idea of atonement, retributivism can evince a strong element of affirmation of particular conceptions of the good. The extent to which it does so will of course depend on the substance and ambit of the criminal law, although one might argue that any such retributivist is automatically committed to the affirmation of whatever conception of the good is enshrined in the criminal law. And since having *any* criminal law inevitably rules out or at least renders very difficult the pursuit of certain conceptions of the good (for example, those which harm other people in particular ways), we can once again raise doubts about just how substantial this particular liberal ideal really turns out to be. Moreover, if punishments will always foster those conceptions of the good implicitly endorsed by the criminal law, this produces a possible tension for any liberal theory of punishment and not solely for retributivism.

The framing of retributive arguments for punishment in terms of the concepts of justice and rights also constitutes a clear link with liberal discourse. Retributive principles typically regard the individual subject of punishment as a rights-holder whose claims to autonomy and non-intervention must be defeated by arguments from desert generated by responsible action, which gives rise to 'a right to be punished' or a forfeiture of some or all of the offender's civil rights. Particularly in modern forms of retributivism, the argument is often framed primarily in terms of justice – indeed, the position is referred to as the 'just deserts' or 'justice' approach.[67] These positions proceed from a central, axiomatic principle of just deserts and criticise other theories for failing to respect the paramount value of justice (which, in the context, seems to be conceived in exclusively retributive terms). Equality, too, has a role to play: the value of treating like cases alike is often stressed and indeed flows logically from a consistent application of retributive principles – although discussion of the contribution of retributive punishments to any more substantive ideal of equality has been scarce indeed.[68] As far as a commitment to the advancement of welfare is concerned, however, retributivism departs significantly from other forms of liberalism in punishment. In so far as retributivism is concerned with human welfare, it could only be so in terms of a highly perfectionist view (for example, one on which it is defined as contrary to human welfare to live in a society in which relationships of justice disturbed by an offence are left unrighted) which effectively robs the concept of welfare of any independent status within the set of justifying arguments, or, indirectly, because of a contingent connection between retributive punishment and certain aspects of welfare such as the satisfaction of grievance desires.[69] Indeed, this divorcing of the retributive principle from any effects in terms of human welfare relates to the criticism that it is mysterious or pointless, and explains, I would argue, why few people find it possible to defend a purely retributive position in the context of the modern partial acceptance and integration of utilitarian or welfarist thought. Thus, as we saw in chapter 2, we have witnessed the development of several 'weak' retributivist, consequence-sensitive theories of punishment.[70]

Thus a retributive principle of punishment can be accommodated within, and seen to proceed from, a number of the liberal values identified above. It remains to consider more fully how this relationship connects with the strengths and weaknesses of the retributive tradition.

Utilitarian theories

Where do utilitarian theories fit into the model of liberalism I sketched earlier in the chapter? We have already noted that, whilst utilitarianism indeed endorses some form of individualism in the sense that it counts the utility of each individual in society, it does so in a very different way from other forms of liberalism in that it, in one form, aggregates and, in another, averages the sum of utility *across* individuals. It has thus been accused, variously, of violating a principle of the separateness of persons,[71] and of failing to respect persons as individual moral agents, since it endorses the use of one person as a means to the ends of others given that one person's disutility may be outweighed by the utility of others. The problems thrown up by this feature of utilitarianism for the issue of punishment have already been considered.[72] Utilitarianism is also consistent, of course, with the idea that preferences are socially constructed, as it is with the possibility that some individuals achieve utility through the satisfaction of the desires of others, although it is axiomatic at least for Benthamite utilitarianism that individuals (pre-socially or in society) are motivated solely by the pursuit of utility.[73] Thus although utilitarian theories of punishment are individualistic in the sense that they focus upon the motivation of individuals via the threat or infliction of punishment as an incentive to various ends, it can be directed to diffused social goods such as general deterrence or education – although these in turn will, of course, be valued solely by reason of their contribution to general utility, calculated by way of the sum of individual utility achievements. In other words, traditional utilitarian theories value social goods only instrumentally, principally because they take individual human preferences as the basis for the ultimate determination of value, stopping short of incorporating any perfectionist element. We shall have to return in the final chapter to the place which a consequence-sensitive theory which did incorporate such an element might give to public goods as part of its argument for punishment.

Another distinctive feature of the utilitarian strand of liberalism which we have already touched upon lies in the importance which it attaches to individual responsibility: utilitarian theories of punishment would be modified rather than undermined by the truth of determinism, and insofar as utilitarians have endorsed a principle of responsibility, this is only due to its contribution to overall utility.[74] However, both rationality and freedom have played an important part in the utilitarian tradition. The very conception of the utilitarian person, motivated by her desire for happiness or preference-satisfaction, envisages a rationally calculating individual who is capable of choosing the proper means to a desired end – a feature of such theories which has come in for particularly fierce criticism in the context of criminal justice as an unrealistic view of the behaviour and motivation of potential offenders.[75] What is more, even though utilitarianism itself generates no distinctive or intrinsic value for human freedom, utilitarians such as Mill have been centrally concerned with explicating the value of liberty within the context of a utilitarian political morality.[76] There has certainly been both room for and evidence of tension between the deterministic and freedom-seeking conceptions espoused by utilitarians of different varieties and in different contexts.

As far as hostility to paternalism and neutrality as between conceptions of the good are concerned, utilitarian theories certainly fit the liberal model, as is clear from the writings of both Bentham and Mill.[77] Indeed, utilitarianism could be said to be entirely agnostic as between different conceptions of the good: it merely affirms the desirability of a life efficiently devoted to the maximal pursuit of utility. But this is not to say that utilitarian writers have not on occasion endorsed what are effectively perfectionist arguments ('ideal' utilitarianism, and even classical arguments such as Mill's defence of free speech would be examples[78]), nor that a utilitarian system of punishments will not reflect and further any conception of the good endorsed by the criminal law. Consequentialist theories can quite clearly be perfectionist, and one can easily produce goals for punishment (some, such as rehabilitation, have actually formed the basis of many criminal justice policies) which aim specifically to endorse, further or indoctrinate some specific conception of the good and which are strongly paternalistic in nature. We shall have to evaluate these different strands within consequence-oriented principles of punishment in our final chapter.

Moving to the place of the concepts of rights, justice and equality, we find once again that utilitarian theories depart significantly from other strains of liberalism. As we noted above, act-utilitarians such as Bentham have no room for the idea of rights in their moral and political reasoning, and the difficulties encountered by rule-utilitarianism's attempts to incorporate such concepts have already been explored.[79] Utilitarians such as Mill have certainly attempted to give some special place within their scheme to the concept of justice but, once again, its place cannot be secure if the utilitarian principle is to retain its ultimate primacy.[80] In a sense, it is wrong to accuse utilitarian theories, both generally and in the context of punishment, of failing to embody concepts of justice and equality. Utilitarianism does have such concepts: a just distribution is that which contributes best to overall/average utility: individuals are equal in that all of their preferences count, and diminishing marginal utility will favour in many contexts more rather than less equal distributions. But these ideas are contained *within* the unitary principle of utility itself, and are therefore incapable of generating limitations on the pursuit of utility. Hence utilitarian theories generate an exclusively instrumental approach to the problem of punishment, including a less rigorous espousal of the rule of law than than adopted by other liberal accounts of punishment.

It is, of course, in its acknowledgment of and focus upon the value of human welfare that utilitarianism is most clearly located within the liberal tradition – or perhaps it would be more accurate to say that a concern for human welfare is utilitarianism's most important and lasting contribution to modern liberal thought. Hence it has become increasingly difficult to maintain a *purely* retributive position in punishment, as it has to hold a *purely* non-consequentialist view in ethics. The exclusivity with which utilitarianism focuses on effects and on human utility has been rejected, but the relevance of such factors is acknowledged: hence the move towards a pluralistic approach in both penal and general political theory.

Moving to the two last features of liberal thought, though utilitarians such as Mill have contributed to the development of the public/private ideology, it is in no way dictated by the principle of utility itself. Moreover, as we have seen, that principle is neither friendly nor hostile in itself to the development of public goods or common values; how far it supports their pursuit will depend on the utility functions of the individuals in any given society. It would, however, be possible to give a central place to such values in any ideal or perfectionist form of consequentialist theory. In the context of punishment, as we have seen, utilitarian theories have indeed often been used in support of practices of punishment aimed at promoting public goods such as the preservation of common moral values or the maintenance of a certain level of social protection. But a limitation remains that the logic of the principle of utility dictates that such goods be valued only by reason and to the extent of their contribution to the aggregate via individual utilities.

Thus, utilitarian theories of punishment occupy a secure place in the liberal tradition, although one which, as we would expect, differs in material respects from that of the retributive theories.

Mixed theories

The place of mixed theories of punishment should be relatively easy to locate, given that many of the relevant points have been anticipated in our discussion of the retributive and utilitarian theories. Naturally, the weak retributive theories fit most closely with the feature of liberalism which we identified as having greatest resonance with the retributivist or backwards-looking tradition: the rational, responsible and autonomous individual who deserves punishment in the name of justice is at the centre of the principle, a necessary feature of justified punishment. Yet arguments from the pointlessness of punishing when no good effects or no advantages in terms of human welfare are in view are defeated by the supplementation of the retributivist principle with a consequentialist sub-principle which acts as a constraint on the fulfillment of the central retributivist one; only punish when some good effects may be gained by doing so. As such, weak retributivist theories can be seen as a response to the perceived weaknesses in the exclusively non-consequentialist brand of liberalism and can be located within the modern move to a more pluralistic conception which seeks to accommodate right-, duty- and goal-based concerns within one coherent political vision.

The same is, of course, true of the mixed theories which put a utilitarian general justifying aim at their centre, but constrain its pursuit by the operation of distributive principles generated by the value of fairness. Here, the starting point is a different form of liberalism, which focuses exclusively on human welfare, and the modifying response is to the counter-intuition that it must at least sometimes matter *how* one achieves desired effects, that indeed features of states of affairs other than their effects are valuable, that distributions across individuals (and groups) are important, and that respect for persons as free and responsible agents must in some sense be accommodated within an adequate political and moral conception. It is interesting that, in a sense, the disquiet expressed by Hart in his article *Between Utility and Rights*[81] at the tendency in political theory to focus on one of these features at the expense of the other, and at the lack of a theory adequately combining the two, is effectively foreshadowed in his earlier work on punishment, which does indeed focus on both utilitarian and non-utilitarian concerns and seeks to accommodate both. Once again, the connection between the move to mixed theories of punishment and that towards a less monolithic conception of political value in the liberal tradition generally is clear. If one upshot of our discussion of liberalism is, crudely, that its tradition contains at least one fundamental division – that between consequentialist and non-consequentialist approaches – it is clear that most modern theories of punishment reject the division as presenting a false dilemma and keep one foot firmly on each side of the dividing line.

THE STRENGTHS AND WEAKNESSES OF LIBERALISM IN PUNISHMENT

The enormous strength and attraction of liberal political thought, both generally and in the context of punishment, is perhaps best illustrated by the sheer fact of its almost exclusive hold on the attention of political philosophers during the twentieth century, with only Marxism really acting as a challenge from the left, at least until the recent welcome development of 'communitarian' approaches to political theory.[82] One could say, of course, as a Marxist might, that liberalism is simply a political ideology whose time has come, one which is appropriate to prevailing historical conditions and political consciousness. There is clearly an important element of truth in this observation, but it does not do complete justice to the strengths of liberalism. What is more, I would argue that it is of prime importance for political philosophers and legal theorists on the left to 'take liberalism seriously', and to produce not only a critique of liberal theory but also a coherent set of alternatives to it. The relative failure to do this has, I think, been at least partly responsible for the continuing hold the liberal vision has had in moral and political thought and discourse.

Let me try to illustrate this point by way of a more detailed discussion of what I take to be the strengths of liberalism in the context of punishment. First and foremost is the fact that liberalism actually confronts and takes seriously the need for a justification: it acknowledges the moral problem of punishment, and engages in producing arguments and programmes for reform and the design of ideal institutions of punishment. It may be true that such theorising is often somewhat utopian and tends not to pay sufficient attention to political and social reality; but *some* vision is clearly necessary if change is ever to be undertaken. It would be unfortunate if the Marxist view of reformism and its largely deterministic view of the process of social change was allowed to act as a damper on the sort of left theorising which could ultimately result in some amelioration of conditions in the real, pre-revolutionary world. Some degree of realism about the potency of political theory is clearly healthy, but total scepticism and refusal to engage in debate simply gives the ground to liberal orthodoxy.

Closely related to this strength of liberalism is its development of a sophisticated conceptual framework (notably of rights, equality, liberty and justice) through which it explicates a coherent set of political values, used to specific effect in contexts such as punishment. Again, a degree of scepticism about the possibility of total coherence may be in order, but critics of liberalism have been all too quick to applaud the fact that liberalism has effectively made these political concepts its own – hence Marxist labelling of concepts such as justice or rights as inherently 'bourgeois'. Of course, there have always been exceptions to this tendency,[83] which has moreover been associated more closely with some political concepts than with others. But by adopting the posture I have described, political theory to the left of liberalism has, until recently, surrendered this powerful conceptual framework to liberalism. Yet in order to construct a viable alternative to liberalism, either an alternative set of concepts must be constructed (examples of such construction are to be found in both communitarian and feminist writings in political theory[84]) or at least some of the 'liberal' concepts must be borrowed and modified within the alternative theory. Whichever course is chosen, it has to be admitted that, in terms of the adequacy of its conceptual tools, liberalism still lies well ahead of any of its non-Marxist left-wing alternatives.

Another strength (although in a different sense of weakness) of liberalism is that it takes seriously the possibility of the abuse of power vested in the state. Punishment being an especially potent and vivid form of such state power, it has been an important part of liberal theorising about punishment clearly to expound the limitations on the legitimate power to punish and, at a greater level of specificity, a number of procedural safeguards at various points in the criminal justice system – as indeed this concern generates a special momentum to theorise about punishment in the first place. Again, it would be wrong for critics to continue to allow liberalism to claim this concern as exclusively its own: indeed, some current moves in the direction of a critical focus on power in general and its structuring and constraint may well be the direction in which a more satisfactory alternative to liberalism might be developed.[85]

Another strength of liberal theory is, I think, its acknowledgment of the importance to human beings of their sense of their own relative power and freedom, and of their own individuality and diversity. It cannot be denied that we all have a sense of ourselves as to some extent separate persons: and once again, liberalism's acknowledgment of that sense constitutes both a strength and a weakness in the tradition. I have already argued that this value could, at least in modified form, survive the truth of determinism, although of course much of liberalism makes quite strong assumptions about the possibility of freedom and genuine capacity-responsibility. I would argue that liberalism has been too easily allowed to make the value of autonomy and indeed the acknowledgment of the possibility and importance of human diversity (especially in Anglo-American thought) its own, and that the value we attach to our sense of freedom and the power at least to some extent to shape our own lives and our environment, through individual, political, social or community action is one which the challengers to liberalism must account for in reconstructing political theory. Such an account might, of course, take the form of the claim that the sense of that value is itself something which our socialisation and the nature of our society has developed in us, and that it, too, therefore, is open to change. Leaving aside the possibility of such reconstruction for the moment, we should note that in the context of punishment, this strand of liberal thought has been particularly associated with distributive principles and the notion of responsibility as a necessary condition for punishment, and with values such as certainty and publicity of the content and mode of application of criminal prohibitions, as well as with a concept of the proper limits of criminal regulation.

Last but not least, it cannot be denied that liberalism has a particularly strong basis in the intuitions of many citizens in current 'western' society. Many of its values are embedded in actual political institutions; our public political discourse operates within a liberal framework and largely employs liberal concepts of justice, equality and so on. In a sense, we are socialised into a liberal world-view. This makes the task of thinking ourselves beyond it exceptionally difficult; even though we may acknowledge at one moment certain of its defects, our appreciation of how to put them right at another may well be affected by other liberal values. Inevitably, we find it hard to reassess the basis of values which are at the foundation of current political thought and which we tend to take for granted – there is a temptation to ignore the radical challenge which the theory of the social construction of human nature and indeed of value poses for political philosophy. Doubtless my own arguments meet that challenge only very imperfectly; it seems to me, however, that ideal and normative argument about political issues is an important enterprise, even if its conclusions are more myopic that its authors generally believe!

But liberalism, too, has its weaknesses, which are often related to its strengths and several of which have particular relevance to our primary question of the justification of punishment. First and foremost is, I would argue, liberalism's failure to develop, and relative lack of interest in, public goods and collective values. For, on the face of it, some of the salient goods which can be promoted and fostered by practices of punishment, such as social cohesion or at least the mitigation of particular sources of social discord, can only be explicated properly in the context of a political vision which gives a central place to the value of community and which acknowledges the extent to which humans are indeed social beings who identify, discover and create themselves in a certain social context and through their interactions with other human beings, social institutions and practices. Despite significant advances in this respect in recent liberal theory,[86] there remains a residue of distrust of the social, of the primacy of the individual, which precludes liberal theory from properly acknowledging the social component of human determination and welfare. Of course, in the utilitarian tradition, it would be perfectly possible to accommodate collective values to the extent that they contributed to utility in the given sense; and to the extent to which modern liberal theory has given a place to such values, it has generally been through its welfare-oriented elements. But, at least in the context of punishment, the underlying view of individual human nature implicit in liberalism has meant that the goals have tended either to be straightforwardly reductive (general deterrence or incapacitation) or else primarily individual-oriented (rehabilitation or individual deterrence). Thus even if not one of its logical implications, this feature of liberalism has tended to constrain the imagination of what the feasible and desirable goals of punishment might be. This feature also clearly relates to neutrality, in the form of an (I think mistaken) anxiety that an acknowledgment of social values means a rigid imposition of one ideal form of life, rather than merely an already inevitable facilitation of one (adequate) range of options rather than another. As I shall argue in the next chapter, these difficulties can only be overcome in the context of a consequence-sensitive theory of the criminal process which abandons the ideal of neutrality and adopts an explicit albeit restricted perfectionism.

By the same token, a residually pre-social view of human beings who are seen as entering society as it were protected by or imbued with a set of rights, needs or interests which it is the function of the state to protect poses, in the context of punishment, a particularly intractable problem of justification. For since punishment inevitably violates, prima facie, some of the offender's central pre-social rights or interests, a very heavy burden of justification will rest on the state to explain why such rights and interests are dissolved, or may justifiably be violated, or are not violated under the given conditions. It can hardly be doubted that a political theory which acknowledged more firmly the inevitably social nature of human life would take a less stringent attitude towards the visiting of disadvantages upon persons in the expectation of fostering important social goals – although this is certainly not to say that our sense of our own individuality should not be respected at all. But it seems certain that the Kantian phobia about using persons as means to ends (the logical consequences of which are already rejected by modern liberalism[87]) would have to be dropped as an important feature of political value.

Am I being unfair to modern liberalism? It is, of course, true that in many spheres, liberal theory has moved beyond the early minimal conception of the 'night-watchman' state, towards a fuller conception of a state which can and should contribute to social welfare more positively, for example, by providing certain sorts of facilities, goods and services. But, once again, because of the relative lack of emphasis on social goods and values, and the primacy of the individual, this development does not seem to have filtered through to liberal thought about punishment so that, as we have seen, even those theories which incorporate a consequence-oriented element have been relatively unimaginative about what the *social* goals of punishment should be. This point also ties up with the argument made above about the tendency to deal with punishment as an isolated issue, which has no doubt also contributed to a lagging behind of penal theory in terms of a focus on public goods.

Another incidental feature of this kind of liberal assumption is that it tends to generate an exclusive focus (reproduced, of course, in this book) on *state* punishment rather than on the exercise of punitive power flowing from any other relationship of authority. As we have seen, a distinction between public and private spheres, and between public and private power, is central to liberal ideology, and it would indeed be foolish to deny that exercises of state power exhibit certain distinctive features which generate both special questions of justification and special supporting arguments. But it has been argued[88] that in the context of the modern welfare state, where many technically 'private' bodies (such as multinational corporations) wield what is, in terms of extent and quality, to all intents and purposes equivalent to state or public power, it is inappropriate to exclude from the ambit of political analysis all exercises of private power. This could well be of relevance to the issue of punishment, in that very powerful private bodies (for example, trades unions and the stock exchange) have and exercise punitive powers (most obviously in the form of expulsion from membership) which seem to call for similar kinds of justifying argument as do exercises of state punitive powers. Returning to an earlier discussion, if our alternative political theory does indeed use power as one of its central organising concepts, it may well be that the (in this book, definitional) focus on state punishment will have to be abandoned or modified along with the public/private distinction in its various forms. For a refusal to apply our political values in at least some 'private' contexts will effectively result in a consolidation (albeit by omission) of the pre-existing power relationships in those insulated spheres.[89] And although it can be argued that private punishments can ultimately be reviewed through the state's public legal apparatus, it is not clear how this affects the substantive justification which is called for by such practices.

Finally, we noted in our discussion of the central features of liberalism that it assumed a conception of the person as an essentially rational being – or at least one whose salient characteristics included a capacity for rational thought and action. It is, I think, quite clear that this emphasis on rationality has produced a somewhat naive view of human nature, which in turn has had several very important and adverse effects on liberal thought about punishment. Leaving aside the dubious propriety of taking the concept of rationality as (although valued) objective, eternal and universal, its features being identifiable in a value-neutral way, one clear implication of the liberal assumption of rationality is that it generates a number of prescriptions in specific contexts, perhaps most importantly the value of *consistency*. This is clearly at play in the principle of procedural justice that like cases should be treated alike, and in elements of the ideal of the rule of law, such as that of congruence between official action and declared rule and relative constancy through time. The ideal of individuals planning their lives so as to avoid the interventions of the criminal law, which helps to generate Hart's argument from fairness,[90] like Duff's vision of the criminal trial as a process of rational discourse[91] in which an offender participates as a moral agent, and equally the utilitarian view of the rationally calculating potential offender, weighing up the costs and benefits of offending, proceeds from the liberal conception of rationality. The most obvious difficulty which this feature presents in the context of criminal justice, as elsewhere, is what might be called the argument from real life: despite the fact that few would deny any moral relevance to the ideas of planning and decision, to the sense of our own relative power and freedom, it simply is not the case that people behave in the totally rational way this assumption suggests. Human motivation, as one would expect, is far more complex than the liberal vision would indicate. This point is of wider importance than just to the issue of how citizens react to the threat of punishment; it bears on the general question of the significance we attach to the institution of punishment, which seems to be far greater than would be justified merely by a calculation of its direct and indirect contribution to the prevention of offences or the mitigation of their seriousness. Thus whilst any full account of the sociological and psychological basis of human motivation and the formation of attitudes and beliefs must remain outside the scope of this book, it seems clear at least that an appreciation of the emotive and symbolic aspects of human attitudes to practices such as punishment and the threat of punishment must form an important part of the informational basis from which our reading of the traditional theories and our own normative thought about that practice should proceed.

This is not to say, of course, that security of expectations should be accorded no political value at all: it is merely to deny it the central place accorded it by liberal theory. What is more, this insight also sheds light on other, less often explicitly acknowledged, implications of liberal commitment to rationality and consistency. It seems to flow from theories with a retributive element that all offences must be punished, as a matter of both procedural and substantial fairness. In the context of procedural fairness, our discussion suggests (as indeed utilitarian theory is able to and has acknowledged) that this would not amount to an absolute or central value: other strong reasons may come into play to push us in the direction of the selective and indeed strategic enforcement envisaged in chapter 8.[92] Given the argument from real life, the assumption of rationality and the argument from planning, whilst important, do not seem to constitute sufficiently secure foundations for strong principles such as Hart's limiting distributive principle and the retributive principle of perfect enforcement. Moreover, this value attached by liberalism to rationality and consistency also generates severe embarassment about (and indeed wholesale sweeping under the carpet of) moral luck, an inevitability which no political theory is likely to applaud, but with which every political theory must learn to live.[93] Finally, liberal rationality tends to play down the potential symbolic effects and aspects of punishment. Although the idea, for example, of denunciation, has received some illuminating attention from liberals in recent years,[94] there has equally been a tendency, especially in the utilitarian camp, to dismiss such effects as somewhat mysterious and nebulous, unworthy of our serious attention and analysis. This view relates directly to the liberal view of human nature and rationality, which I have suggested is unduly simplistic. Like the affirmation of common values, I take its symbolic aspects and its place in our emotional lives to be important to the justification of punishment, and thus liberalism's lack of interest in them to be at least part of the explanation of the lack of an ultimately convincing liberal account of punishment.

CONCLUSION

We have now, in the light of our set of central features of liberal political philosophy, located the traditional theories of punishment in their proper political and theoretical context, and we have evaluated their strengths and weaknesses in the light of those of liberalism itself. Having explored the problem of punishment from several different points of view – through straightforward expósition and critique of the traditional theories; by examination of related political questions; and in the context of a particularly influential political tradition, it remains to try to reconstruct the best that can be said for punishment from the various materials we have considered. It is to this task that we finally turn.

CHAPTER 8

PUNISHMENT AND COMMUNITY

We turn, then, to the enterprise of reconstructing a set of justifying arguments for punishment. In the light of what has gone before, this enterprise must be located firmly within a general moral and political framework, and the claims which it generates will be dependent on a particular background social context. However, as the title of this chapter suggests, I shall allow myself to engage to some extent in utopian thinking – to imagine what punishment *could* be in a world somewhat different from our own in certain specified respects. As explained in the preceding chapter, my aim is to preserve the strengths of liberal theory in the context of criminal justice, whilst transcending its weaknesses by moving away from some of its central tenets in important ways. Of course, the tendency towards ideal thought in theorising about punishment is hardly new: almost any conceivable theory, as we have seen, makes background assumptions about the fairness of the laws or the system which punishment sanctions. Moreover, we have also seen that the problem of justifying punishment in a (fundamentally or partially) unjust society is bound to be complex for any theory except one which insulates the problem of punishment from the rest of moral and political reasoning in an unacceptable way. But it may well be thought that in moving away from certain liberal assumptions – assumptions which are at the moment in some way embedded in social consciousness in 'western' societies – I am moving towards a theory which is more radically utopian than are the traditional theories as defended in modern political thought.

Conversely, others will feel that actual social conditions and political consciousness inevitably constrain any theorist's appreciation of what is valuable or desirable, that conception itself being a product of complex social factors whose ultimate normative status is of dubious validity. I do not mean to deny that these are real and important problems, and I can offer only a partial solution to them. Certainly, the community conception of criminal justice which I shall defend builds on and in important respects reproduces some of the values which I argued to be implicit in our current social conception of criminal justice examined in developing the functionalist conception of criminal law in Chapter 5. But if we fail, in the name of realism or anti-utopianism, to try to imagine ourselves into different kinds of possible societies, our critical perspective on our own forms of social organisation is likely to be even more limited than it has to be. This is not to say that there is no difference between ideal theorising and political strategy, although in my view there should be a link between the two. After my discussion of the ideal vision, I shall return to the gap between the ideal and the actual so as to assess the insights we may be able to gain from the new conception of punishment in appraising, understanding and struggling to reconstruct our own practice of criminal justice.

Two other preliminary issues must be mentioned. These have to do with the concept of the nature of crime which is implicit in any theory of punishment. Indeed, it might be thought para-doxical, in one sense, to speak of punishment in terms of 'ideal' theory. Might it not be argued that in an ideally just and utopian society there would be no crime, or at least no need for formal punishments as a response to breaches of social norms? Is punishment not inevitably part of what has been called 'non-ideal theory'?[1] The way in which we classify our theorising is hardly a matter of great urgency, but the light in which we see our subject matter does seem likely to be an important influence on our thinking about it. Should we see crime as an eventually expungeable phenomenon, caused only by alienation, class conflict or background social injustice; or as an inevitable feature of human individuality or even original sin; or, somewhat more agnostically, as an inevitability or at least likelihood which is unfortunate given the suffering which both crime and punishment entail, yet which creates genuine opportunities to strengthen social bonds through affirmation of framework values? In my own thinking about punishment, the assumption has been the agnostic one, although many of my arguments presuppose or are consistent with the view which implicates factors such as class conflict and social disadvantage in the incidence of crime.

Secondly, it is important to be sensitive to the fact that it is all too easy to theorise about punishment on the basis of some fixed yet unarticulated conception of crime, and to suppress the insight that crime is a social construct – that what counts as crime in a society is a product of social decision, and that the nature and pattern of offending in that society must depend upon the nature of the society and its conception and definition of crime. In these concluding arguments, I have tried to keep in mind the dangers inherent in seeing crime in terms only of individual, and not also social, responsibility. It is necessary, then, to look beyond the surface of the criminal law, the practice of which is structured in terms of individual responsibility, both because that structure obscures the broader social functions of criminal law and, more particularly, because it obscures our view of the relationship between crime and punishment, the social functions of which I shall argue to be at the core of its justification.

THE PRIMACY OF THE SOCIAL

The main adjustment which I shall make to the liberal assumptions on which many modern theories of punishment are constructed is in adopting a view of humans as essentially, necessarily and primarily social beings. In other words, in speaking of the ideal planning or construction of a society, we cannot take our conceptions of what is right or just from any idea of what would be chosen by individual moral agents deciding to get together and form a society afresh. And this is because, to put it bluntly, the conception of an a- or pre-social human being makes no sense. What individual human beings perceive as the proper boundaries of autonomy around themselves, what they regard as just distributions, how they regard their relations with each other and a thousand other questions central to political philosophy, are ones which we simply cannot imagine being answered outside some specific social and institutional context. The idea of constructing the just society out of the imagined values and preferences of a set of pre-social beings could only have been conceived on the basis of a distorted and unrealistic set of assumptions, adopted in the everlasting pursuit of some 'objective', universal grounding for (liberal) political philosophy. The liberal assumptions are, as Bernstein has argued, tied up with the 'Cartesian anxiety';[2] if no objective grounding can be found, there is a fear that chaos will ensue as all normative argument will descend into the mire of total relativism or subjectivism in which anybody's values and opinions are as good as the next person's or the next group's, thus undermining the role and basis of political philosophy as it traditionally conceives itself. It is implicit in my enterprise that political philosophy *can* be reconceived in a way which retains its validity whilst resisting the Cartesian anxiety.

Let us now drop these liberal assumptions, and give instead a central place in our thinking about punishment to the impossibility of humans existing outside some form of society, and to the fact that our conception of ourselves as persons is inextricably linked with our relationships with others – with friends, family, fellow citizens, colleagues, neighbours – and with social institutions. What I want to emphasise is not only that relationships, interpersonal contacts, understanding, mutual support and fulfillment of obligations are among the things which human beings tend to regard most highly (hence our conception of psychopathy as mental abnormality in terms of lack of a sense of responsibility or sensitivity to others),[3] but also, and more fundamentally, that we actually *define ourselves* to an important extent in terms of those relations (in order to test your reaction to this claim, imagine the self-description you would give if asked, and count up how many of its elements refer to your position relative to that of other persons or communities). Add to this the clear fact of human interdependence, both physical and emotional, and the influence of social circumstances on values and culture, and it soon becomes obvious just how different these assumptions are from those of classical liberalism.

What difference does this make to the enterprise of justifying punishment? In the first place, and negatively, it in no way removes the need for a justification. For my aim is to try to preserve the strengths of the liberal vision, and liberalism's concern for welfare (in terms of the suffering or other disadvantages encountered by both victims of crime and punished offenders), its concern with our sense of our own autonomy – the value we attach to some degree of human diversity and distinctiveness, which we wish to preserve, dictate the need for strong arguments in support of the practice of punishment. What the new assumptions do, rather, is to relocate the question of justification in such a way as to allow more to be said about the social benefits which can flow from punishment and to dictate that more weight be attached to those social benefits than has usually been the case, at least outside utilitarian theory. Our assumption of the primacy of the social prompts a shift of emphasis in which the maintenance, stability and continuing development of society is a necessary condition for the flourishing of the people within it, and in which one would therefore expect the contribution which punishment can make to such a goal to be valued very highly. Thus the recurring and fundamental preoccupation within the Kantian strand of liberal theorising about punishment – that individuals should never be sacrificed to diffused social goals – seems to present us with something of a false dilemma. For if individuals have a fundamental interest in the maintenance and development of a peaceful, just society to which they belong and through which their personal development and many of their interests are realised and indeed constructed, the alleged moral boundaries which dictate that individuals never be used merely as a means to social ends begin to dissolve. The problem of distributing punishments fairly, of course, remains, and will be addressed below: we shall not entirely abandon the idea of individuality as generating moral limitations, but the strength and exclusivity of the liberal conception will have to be modified in a fundamental way.

THE IDEAL OF COMMUNITY

The starting point for our reconstruction of normative arguments about punishment, then, must be a particular vision of political society, and in this context I shall sketch a conception which is in certain important respects different from the traditional liberal ideal. The definition of a community, and of the distinction between a community and a society or indeed any other group of associated persons, can be developed in many different ways, most obviously in terms of size, extent of shared goals, or degree of common values and conceptions of the good.[4] A religious order, for example, is often cited as the central case of a community: relatively small, homogeneous and organised around a shared conception of value. A political grouping such as a state, on the other hand, might well be seen as a central instance of a society: an association of persons for certain limited purposes, identified by a lower threshold of common goals and values, creating a framework within which diverse forms of life, including the formation of communities and other groups devoted to particular ends, can develop and flourish. In developing my own account of community, I shall not be much concerned with this often-used distinction between society and community, although all of the features which I have mentioned so far will be important in sketching the conception. The idea is rather to develop, in the light of the assumption of the primacy of the social, a conception of what a political society such as our own might ideally become, particularly in terms of the relations between, and what unites and identifies, its members.

In the first place, any community must be identified by the existence of a certain threshold of shared goals and values. It is, of course, clear that the nature and extent of these shared goals and values will vary enormously from community to community, depending on cultural, economic and material factors. In some communities, the (from our perspective) relatively minimal goal of survival might almost exhaust the public culture; in others, a wide array of shared ends and indeed conceptions of the good acknowledged as legitimate will be publicly endorsed. Nor is this variety a matter of open choice – it will be constrained, and sometimes even determined, by prevailing material conditions. But within these constraints, it is clear that the setting of the threshold – the extent of commitment to common values or shared goals, and the ambit left open for human diversity, will be to some extent a question open for political decision. Thus a question arises as to the proper means to be adopted in a community for the making of social choices, and we must advert, albeit briefly, to this fundamental matter. It is important, however, to avoid setting up yet more false dilemmas: it will sometimes be the case that a fuller adoption of common goals and values will straightforwardly detract from the amount of freedom individuals or groups have to pursue different goals and forms of life – but this is not necessarily the case. For often, a common commitment to the pursuit of shared goals will actually enhance the possibility of the development of different forms of life.[5] For example, a public commitment to providing a certain level of goods and services in the context of health, education and welfare, or facilities or subsidies for the arts and sports, will increase the opportunity for diversity and development at the personal level. Once again, we should be suspicious of the collective/individual, public/private dichotomies which our thinking has inherited from classical liberal thought.

How, then, would common decision-making be accomplished in an ideal community? If we acknowledge that human beings and human nature are essentially socially developed, we must also acknowledge that the process is circular or continuous. Just as human beings go through a process of socialisation, so too they react to and have some capacity to act upon their social environment, which thus develops incrementally over time. The nature of this process is beyond the scope of this inquiry,[6] but even this brief allusion gives rise to certain rather obvious conclusions about appropriate methods of social decision. It points in the direction of some democratic conception in which citizens have the fullest possible opportunity to shape their own community and take on part of the collective responsibility for its maintenance and development. On the face of it, what seems to be indicated is some form of participatory rather than merely representative democracy,[7] through which people not only participate in decision-making, but are also shaped and made aware, their identity with the community reinforced, by the experience of participation itself. Here, I would argue, lies an important key to understanding the ideal of community – one less often discussed at least in the modern tradition than are common values, but of at least equal significance. This feature lies in a commitment to, the adoption of responsibility for, the community of which one is a member. This commitment, realised ideally through participation in the process of government and administration, can be seen as the ultimate expression of the vision of humans as primarily social beings: if community is essential to human existence, commitment to community is a more 'natural' or appropriate assumption or ideal than is the liberal vision of persons as rational, calculating and self-interested. This is not to say, of course, that self-interest is not a feature of human motivation; but it is at least to admit that self-interest, even when a dominant motivation, has need of social means and framework for both its development and effective pursuit to a greater extent than is often acknowledged in liberal theory.

It is often objected to the vision of genuinely participatory democracy and to the ideal of human beings as committed to community, that in the context of large, heterogeneous political societies, the former is impractical, the latter unrealistic. This is not the place for any full exploration of the effects of numbers on human attachment or alienation; suffice it to say that it does not seem appropriate to give up the ideal without exploring much more fully than do most objectors the possibility of overcoming this problem – as indeed several political theorists have begun to do.[8] The possibility of decentralised, participatory local government united by a federal or partially centralised state run on representative lines is just one of the more obvious options. Moreover, it seems on the face of it possible that, linking the two features, the experience of participation in community decision-making would actually foster and enhance the sense of community and social responsibility which I have argued is a natural corollary to human beings' primarily social nature.

Thus the notion of community which I shall be employing in developing a theory of punishment is that of a group of human beings, each participating directly, and also possibly indirectly by electing representatives, in the development of their group framework, policies and norms, bound by a sense of commitment to the maintenance of the community, through acknowledgment of its importance for themselves and others, and united thus by a second-level commitment to the values and goals adopted through the process of public decision on democratic principles. In such a community, members could maintain a sense of themselves, whilst acknowledging, creatively, their interdependence. This conception of community represents an idealised version of the notion of a group developed by Honoré[9] and discussed in chapter 4. Our discussion of legal obligation is also relevant here in that the fully committed adoption of an internal attitude envisaged by MacCormick and Finnis as the 'central case' does indeed turn out to exemplify the attitude towards the law which would represent the ideal in our vision of a just community: the argument comes into its own as part of prescriptive rather than analytical theory.[10] Moreover, as we shall see, the vision of the community conception with its emphasis on interdependence and mutual responsibility substantially modifies the liberal position on the issue of political obligation.

COMMUNITY AND CRIMINAL LAW

What function and place would a system of criminal law have within a community such as the one which I have described? If we conceive criminal law in terms of the conception developed in chapter 5, as a set of public norms generally backed up by the threat of punishment for breach, it follows from the conception of community that it would be employed primarily to preserve the framework of values perceived as necessary to the maintenance, stability and peaceful development of the community. In other words, the central commitment to community which I have described would inform a commitment to preserving the necessary framework of values in the most effective way possible (whilst accepting, of course, the possibility of changes in those values through political decision). And one important means of upholding framework values, I shall argue, would be through a system of criminal laws, instituted as a response to behaviour which directly violates socially acknowledged fundamental interests in such a way as to express rejection of or hostility to the values underlying those interests. By the same token, a limiting principle of urgency would also follow naturally from the conception of community, for, as we have seen, the concern with a framework of common values within which human beings can develop and flourish coheres with the idea of human diversity and a sense of freedom. Thus citizens within a community would probably be concerned to preserve the peculiarly coercive means of the criminal law to uphold standards seen as fundamentally necessary to the peaceful development of the community (such as the security of the state and the physical integrity of its citizens, where those standards are subjected to direct and serious attack) rather than to spread its net more broadly.

But would the criminal law be necessary in an ideal community? If we imagine ourselves into such a state, would it not follow that citizens would be generally motivated by common concern and good will to follow those norms central to the preservation of the community? Such speculations demand, of course, what amounts to an act of faith; but the thought experiment turns out, I think, to be unnecessary. For even though it might be the case that breaches of the law were rare in such a community, or that some symbolic admonition or formal response would be sufficient to underline the value of the norm breached and to prevent repetition, thus undermining any justification for sanctions of real severity, there would nonetheless remain good reasons for preserving institutions of the threat of punishment (which might, of course, include the formal or symbolic admonitions to which I have referred).[11] These ultimate reasons would, at least in part, be logically entailed by a commitment to the value of community, and related once again to our underlying conception of humans as essentially social beings. For if we accept the idea of the primacy of the social, and assume the existence of a community genuinely committed to the development of an environment in which human beings can flourish, developing their affective and productive capacities and achieving an adequate level of welfare, it seems appropriate also to acknowledge that the community, as a collective concept, is entitled to take such steps as are necessary to ensure its own continued existence and development. Naturally, the criminal law will represent only one small part of such a strategy, but it does have important practical and symbolic value. For it affirms the justifiability of the maintenance of standards aimed towards a common, if diffused, social good, which all citizens have reasons to uphold and to the formation of which all citizens have a real chance to contribute.

From this conception there also follows a particular conception of what we have referred to, with some reservations, as 'political obligation'.[12] For if human beings cannot survive alone, they will always have a good reason, in the context of a genuine community, to act so as to foster the common framework, even though on occasion the personal benefits of offending are tempting, and even though they may wish to engage in political action to modify the framework in certain respects. The relaxation of the rigid assumptions of liberal individualism renders the problem of political obligation less intractable; once 'individuals' are seen as social beings whose self-conception, development and welfare depend on their social environment and their relations with others, general reasons for them to uphold the framework values of their community are not hard to produce. In a community in which the general framework was conscientiously directed towards the autonomy and welfare of its citizens, both arguments from the bad consequences of disobedience, and arguments from responsibility and commitment to other citizens and to the community as a whole, enable a convincing picture of 'respect for law'[13] to be built up. Within this framework, then, we can construct a persuasive account of the reasons why the criminal law should generally be obeyed, whilst maintaining our earlier insistence on the primacy of reasons for obedience and the dubious validity of talk in terms of conclusive political obligation.

But it is necessary to clothe the bones of this conception with some flesh, and in particular to develop the ideas of welfare and autonomy in more detail, considering with more specificity the ends to which the criminal law might be directed in such a community. To fill out completely the concepts of welfare and autonomy would be to develop a whole political philosophy, which must remain beyond the scope of this book. But enough must be said to enable us fully to develop the functionalist conception of the criminal law in the context of the vision of community. Beginning with the concept of autonomy, how would this value, which has been closely associated with the liberal tradition,[14] be realised under the different assumptions underlying our alternative conception of community? I would argue that, despite our loosening of the assumptions of liberal individualism, an important and indeed central place in the moral and political thinking underlying this alternative conception has to be reserved for a revised conception of autonomy which, whilst acknowledging the influence of the social, the strong connections between people, their self-definition through relationships, and their interdependence, would also recognise the importance of their conceptions of themselves as actors in their personal lives, as in the social and political process. As Joseph Raz has argued,[15] the fulfillment of the conditions of autonomy is a matter of degree, having to do not only with the degree to which a person is free from subjection to the will of others, but also with the existence of an adequate range of options and in particular the lack of necessity to spend most of one's time struggling to attain the minimum standards necessary to a worthwhile life. Even relaxing the strong liberal assumptions of free will and responsibility, it seems that human beings would retain a sense of their own importance – of their special identity – even if they defined their identity to a greater extent through their relations with others and position in the community than is assumed by liberal theory. This idea may well proceed from the status of the community conception as an idealised extrapolation from the development of values implicit in current social arrangements, combined with a particular view of human nature, rather than an ultimate utopia. But the difficulty of surrendering completely some ideal of human freedom is reflected even in the most socially deterministic of theories such as Marxism.

Moreover, on this conception of autonomy we can see, once again, the falseness of the dilemma set up by traditional liberalism between personal autonomy and social good: because of the relationship between autonomy and a certain range and quality of possible lives, and because the value of the exercise of autonomy depends to some extent on the background social environment, any straightforward opposition between personal autonomy and welfare or social good can be seen to misrepresent the moral situation. Thus, I would argue, the value of autonomy would have to be respected by the criminal law of our idealised community of social beings: it would, in other words, constitute one of the fundamental political principles underpinning the framework values the maintenance and protection of which it is the primary function of the criminal law to secure. And this sense of empowerment and responsibility would, of course, be both recognised and fostered by the institution of participatory democracy. This is not to say, however, that the importance to be attached to autonomy is immutable, given that the experience of human life in the idealised community which I am contemplating might well lead to personal identification with and through social and community values to a much greater extent than we currently find it possible to envisage.

Turning to the concept of welfare, what I envisage is a register of welfare which is importantly 'objective' or 'ideal-regarding'[16] in the sense that it would be defined in terms of the level of fulfillment of certain fundamental needs and interests, acknowledged to be such within the community itself. Thus what count as fundamental needs and interests, as well as the threshold (which I would argue should be absolute rather than comparative) below which the failure to meet them is seen as a grave social wrong calling for an urgent political response, would be a function of social and political decision. Clearly, it will be constrained by material conditions such as economic and natural resources, and by facts about human physiology and psychology (which is not to say that these facts themselves cannot change over history – they, too, are subject to a certain degree of social modification[17]). It is hard to imagine a community in which shelter, nourishment and physical integrity and indeed a certain level of fulfillment along these dimensions would not count as basic needs within the social conception of welfare; but within this minimal framework, there exists room for choice and decision, not to mention modification and development through the democratic process. As I argued in chapter 5, in the context of criminal justice, we are concerned with the most fundamental or central components of welfare, towards the fostering of which the norms and sanctions of a criminal justice process have a real chance of contributing when the appropriate limiting principles are met. It is thus in the pursuit of welfare in this relatively minimal or framework sense, through the specification of certain particularly interest-threatening forms of behaviour as serious social wrongs, that the criminal law takes on its distinctive functionalist aspect. But in this plurality of values which informs the functions of the criminal law, we encounter the problem of commensurability and balancing two principal political values of welfare and autonomy. This issue has important implications for not only the question of the distribution of punishments but also for the whole design of the criminal law and the criminal process. I shall return to this issue after discussing in more detail the contributions to social and personal welfare which might be expected from the criminal justice process.

It seems, then, that we can conceive of the functions and place of the criminal law in a community in terms of a modified or extended version of the functionalist conception sketched in chapter 5. Given the relativity of basic needs and interests to particular societies (never to mention the different potential efficacy and therefore, indirectly, justifiability of the resort to penal measures in different kinds of societies) it will not be necessary or useful to go substantially beyond the specification of those needs outlined in the earlier chapter. But one important modification or change of emphasis must be stressed. Our conception of community, as we have seen, differs importantly from liberal society in terms of the importance attached to public goods and common values. It is likely, therefore, that norms pertaining to the preservation of at least those values most important to the framework of the community would occupy a fuller and more salient position in the criminal law than I envisaged in chapter 5, or indeed than they occupy in our society. To give some examples, actions which threatened common resources such as the environment, or safety on the roads or at work – in other words, actions which create social dangers rather than specifically causing individual losses and harms, will be likely to occupy a central place in the criminal law of our community. Moreover, although many of the 'individual' interests currently protected by the criminal law would also have a central place on the community conception, that conception would emphasise the social impact of the offence – the harm to the victim *as a member of the community* and thus, indiretly, to the community itself. Conversely, the occasion of an offence would, ideally, provide a setting in which the community would reassess the justice and reasonableness if its demands both on the particular offender and on all potential offenders against the law or laws in question. In addition, as anticipated by our discussion in chapter 5, the criminal law of such a community may, depending on the outcome of the political process, proscribe certain actions which would be protected within the liberal conception of moral harms or liberal hostility to paternalism, always within the limits set by our revised conception of autonomy.[18]

THE FUNCTIONS OF PUNISHMENT

We are now ready to turn to an exploration of what the salient aims of punishment would be in the community we have envisaged. We do not have to assume, of course, that the forms which punishment would take in such a society would necessarily be the same as those practised in our society: consistently with the definition from which we started out in the first chapter, we need only envisage a social response to breaches of the criminal law which imposes what are generally regarded as disadvantages within that society, in order for the problem of justification to arise. What reasons can be adduced, within the political values of community, for this disadvantaging social response: by what means can the prima facie wrong of punishment contribute to the welfare and autonomy of members of a community? By stating the problem in this way, it will be clear that by 'functions' I am comprehending not only goals in the sense of tangible effects to be sought, such as general deterrence, but also the values which the practice seeks to foster and promote – its legitimate purposes in a more general sense. Thus one aim of a punishment may be to deter a harmful form of behaviour, but it is also part of its function to underline and support the social judgment that that form of behaviour is indeed harmful and wrong – to reinforce, in other words, the 'moral analogy' which I have argued constitutes an important part of the social meaning of criminal as opposed to civil law. This breadth of perspective will in fact be crucial to the main thrust of my argument.

We have already considered the reasons which the members of a political community would have for setting up norms of criminal law. And, at the crudest level, the contemporaneous setting up of the threat of punishment (which seems, in the absence of unrealistic assumptions about the possibility of shams, to presuppose the actual infliction of punishments in the case of at least a significant number of detected offences[19]) is justified simply by its necessity as a means of making the standards of the criminal law *real*: as a way of stating that the meeting of those standards is a matter of duty or obligation, from community's legal point of view, rather than merely a matter of exhortation or aspiration.[20] From the point of view of the law of the community, as we saw in chapter 4, the standards of the criminal law become non-optional – and the very idea of non-optionality seems to presuppose some kind of consequence on breach. In some cases mere formal conviction may be sufficient to preserve the reality and efficacy of the standards of the criminal law; but, at the systemic level, it seems necessary to have in reserve some stronger marker of the reality of the law's prescription, and penal sanctions constitute the most obvious candidate for such a role. This is not a question of righting the wrong done in the compensatory sense of making good the loss to the particular victim (although this kind of response may also be called for). Nor is it exclusively a matter of deterrence, individual or general. It has principally to do with a collective need to underpin, recognise and maintain the internalised commitments of many members of society to the content of the standards of the criminal law and to acknowledge the importance of those commitments to the existence and identity of the community. If, in general, the norms of the system can be breached with impunity, why should any member of the community put her faith in and give her allegiance to the community as guardian of the framework of common values within which citizens can develop their lives?[21] If the criminal law is indeed one of the planks of survival of the community, yet can be broken at will, why should citizens continue to observe it themselves, or not attempt to form an alternative community in which framework values are taken seriously and enforced? If no social response enforcing central values is forthcoming, why have a community at all?

Flowing from this general argument from necessity at the systemic level is a cluster of specific aims and goods which can and should be fostered by the existence of institutions of punishment. Beginning with the most general factors, it seems likely that inflictions and threats of punishment, although not occasions for celebration, could in this context have beneficial side-effects in terms of restoring social cohesion which may be threatened or disturbed by certain sorts of offending which present clear threats to fundamental social values, and in reaffirming the social values endorsed by the political process and entrenched in the criminal law. By the same token, the public process of conviction affords an opportunity for reassessing the criminal law itself, and especially when a particular kind of offence becomes prevalent, or a conviction seems counter-intuitive, the process may prompt a rethinking of the substantive law, if the political structure is appropriately sensitive. Such possibilities can, of course, be allowed for by institutions such as the absolute discharge in English law,[22] which registers a technical conviction but acknowledges that it raises an unforeseen defect in the law by removing the normal consequences from that conviction, punishment included. These factors stress the importance of maintaining a practice of punishment which is, in so far as is possible, public and open. Linked to these general side-benefits is the educative function which a criminal process can have, through the affirmation of social values fostered by the denunciation of the behaviour involved in the offence, that denunciation being implicit and also often explicit in the process of conviction and sentence.

Moving on to a plane of greater specificity, we come to the

more familiar goals encompassed by the utilitarian theories of punishment, perhaps more directly apposite to the rationale of individual punishments than the general functions already mentioned. Hard though the attainment of such objectives may be (their assessment presents further problems of its own[23]) a certain level of general deterrence through the threat of punishment, and individual deterrence through its experience, might realistically be hoped for, although in the ideal community it might well be hoped that more 'internal' motivations having to do with the affirmation of the values embedded in the law, or at least recognition of their importance to others and to the community itself, would suffice for the great majority of the population.[24] Furthermore, there is the (albeit very modest) contribution which can be made to the level of social security by the practice of punishment, not only by way of deterrence, but also, in the case of some forms of punishment, through the incapacitation of the offender for a certain period of time. Related to social protection, but also closely linked to the need to demonstrate that the norms of the criminal law are 'for real', is the need to forestall, or at least to minimise, any resort to private vengeance or self-help, which might cause disproportionate suffering and indeed involve excessive costs, whilst undermining the stability of and respect for the community's legal system as a whole. Again linked to these aims is that of appeasing and satisfying the grievance-desires of victims, not only so as to reduce their suffering and forestall self-help, but also to demonstrate that the community takes seriously the harm done to the victim and takes upon itself the responsibility for upholding the standards breached, which it hopes to vindicate through the process of conviction and punishment. I leave until last, because I take it to be an indirect side-effect rather than a central aim of punishment, the opportunity which it may give to the offender to reflect and resolve to reform; in so far as this could be said to be a direct aim of punishment, it seems to be an aspect of the reaffirmation of collective values, in which it is possible for the offender to participate from a special point of view. The value attached to autonomy, however, is such as to dictate that this aim be pursued no further than in the giving of an opportunity: 'coerced cure' would be ruled out. I shall have more to say on this when considering the forms which punishment might take in the ideal community.

It is thus, I would argue, a combination of, and the interdependence between, the symbolic meaning of punishment, the values it seeks to enforce and uphold, and its practical effects which constitutes, in Hart's terms,[25] its general justifying aim. The concept of the functions of punishment which I have defended thus goes beyond his utilitarian conception in important respects. It is because of the meaning and significance which punishment would have for the citizens of a community that it can hope to have the practical consequences which we have explored. Conversely, without any hope of those real, countervailing benefits, punishment as a merely symbolic social response, without any practical enforcing aspect, would become the pointless, empty moral alchemy which I argued to be the implication of a pure retributivism. In a sense, this conception forges the retributive and utilitarian aspects of punishment, (although doubtless neither a utilitarian nor a retributivist would see it in quite that light!). For although at the core of my account is what I shall call the argument from necessity, that necessity itself flows to at least some extent from the potency of intuitions which are most obviously and centrally acknowledged in the traditional retributive theories. The idea of punishment as a significant and necessary symbol of the assertion of the community's own entitlement to enforce, to respond severely to breaches of its democratically determined central values, may be difficult to explicate purely in terms of rational judgments about how particular social goals may be pursued. It does, however, form a central part of our moral thinking. The community conception reflects, whilst it restrains in a morally acceptable way, the role of punishment in our emotional and affective lives. But I do not accept the retributivist claim that a *purely* symbolic system of punishments, an institution which had no beneficial effects, could be justified. It is the combination of its social meaning and its actual consequences which provides the strongest argument for preserving the threat of punishment at the centre of political life in the community.

But my solution, unlike Hart's mixed theory and weak retributivist arguments, is not dependent on the *separation* of distinct questons – although I acknowledge the special significance and complexity of distributive issues, which I shall deal with in the next section. The conception of punishment which I have described, like its counterpart conception of the criminal law, is neither backward-looking nor forward-looking in a purely instrumental sense: it is rather *functional*. In other words, my conception emphasises the significance which punishment has for the citizens of a community, the place which it occupies in the development and cohesion of the community, rather than simply tangible goals such as deterrence or a particular desirable endstate. By conceiving the functions of the criminal process in both direct and indirect, in both general and specific terms, and by broadening the conception of its aims beyond any utilitarian vision of goals in the sense of tangible states of affairs, I hope to have developed a conception of the nature of punishment which is sufficiently complex to generate the sorts of limitations on the practice which we generally think to be necessary from within the conception itself, rather than by appeal to any independent principles. Thus whilst my theory resembles the mixed theories both in its pluralism and in many common aims, it differs in terms of the structure of the argument which it employs. The significance of this difference will be explored in the course of the discussion of the distributive aspect of the community conception.

THE DISTRIBUTION OF PUNISHMENTS

On this conception of punishment, justified ultimately by its contribution to the welfare and autonomy of members of a community, principally through its necessity as a central plank in the maintenance of the community itself and the stability of the relations within it, the question naturally arises as to who should be punished, and this question in turn raises in a stark form the issue of the relationship between the two principal political values: autonomy and welfare. Are the dictates of autonomy, realised principally in the context of punishment as a requirement of responsibility, to act as absolute side constraints on the pursuit of the general justifying aims of punishment as they do in Hart's theory? Should we, conversely, merely accommodate autonomy as one aspect of human welfare? Or must we forge, as I suggested in the last section, a middle way through these extremes?

It is important to emphasise, at the outset, the place of the value of autonomy within our conception of the aims or functions of punishment, both directly, for example through its contribution to social protection and thus the autonomy of potential victims of crime, and indirectly, through its support of the community which is committed to maintaining and fostering the value of autonomy. Thus the question concerning the need for trade-offs which the issue of punishment raises do not relate only to trade-offs between the core values of welfare and autonomy, allowing the realm of each value to be confined within one particular question (welfare with general justifying aim, autonomy with distribution, in Hart's scheme). Because the two basic values relate to the questions *both* of the functions of punishment *and* of its proper distribution, the potential need to make trade-offs turns out to be much broader, the issue more fragmented: trade-offs will have to be made in order to answer the allegedly separate questions which Hart identifies, as well, of course, as in considering the relative and potentially conflicting claims to autonomy and welfare of different persons and groups of persons. For example, decisions about whether to include a particular form of behaviour within the ambit of the criminal law, and what function criminal regulation should fulfil, already require balancing judgments which proceed from a plurality of values. However, these problems are not acute in the way suggested by the traditional mixed theories because, as we have seen, the realisation of the two values is interdependent and not always a matter of opposition or competition. But it is crucial to see that these problems arise *not only* at the stage of distribution, but also in the specification of the aims and functions of punishment. It is not a question of punishment aiming to promote welfare but limited by a principle of autonomy in distribution: the pluralist picture emerges with respect to both function and distribution. Thus, as R.A. Duff has convincingly argued, we should expect to find *internal*, logical relations between the 'general justifying aim' of punishment and the principles on which it is to be distributed.[26] Although, as Hart has shown, the two questions can usefully be separated as an expositional device in bringing out different aspects of the problem of justification, the device can be misleading if used so as to suggest a discontinuity of justifying arguments – hence the difficulty adverted to in chapter 2 in relating the two parts of Hart's theory to one another.[27] Problems of both aim and distribution are equally a part, in a manner of speaking, of the meaning of punishment.

In the community which I have envisaged, which endorses a pluralist conception of political value, citizens would demand that their political practices acknowledge and accord a special weight to human autonomy over and above its direct or indirect contribution to welfare. This is not to say that they would never be prepared to make trade-offs between welfare and autonomy, nor to make the mistake of assuming that the demands of autonomy and welfare are always in competition or that autonomy is something which one either has or has not: there can clearly be degrees of autonomy and in the general run of things we value our remaining autonomy more as we suffer further encroachments upon it. I am not going to defend autonomy as a side constraint upon the pursuit of the aims of punishment, as a principle with a rigid lexicographical priority such as Rawls' principle of liberty.[28] It seems to me quite clear that the threshold at which human beings would be willing to trade off some measure of their sense of their own power, freedom or diversity for other goods will vary between people and will depend in an important way (as Rawls acknowledges to a limited extent[29]) on material social conditions and the nature of the other goods in question. Thus I do not suggest any fixed or precise solution to the ordering of the two general political principles in the context of criminal justice, but would refer again to the conception of a consistent pluralism[30] in which a conscientious effort is made to balance the pursuit of, and to recognise the discrete value of the goods in question, endorsing them consistently across different persons and spheres of political life whilst, of course, recognising relevant differences between the various spheres. Notwithstanding the attractions of a formal scheme of priorities or conflation of different values into a common currency, the determinacy which such devices offer simply seems to be inconsistent with a genuine commitment to a plurality of values and an adequate appreciation of the complexity of moral problems.

Bearing in mind this background structure of political value, and our conception of the legitimate functions of punishment, it is not difficult to see why punishment in a community would be restricted to those who had been judged to have actually perpetrated criminal acts – the 'actus reus' requirement of the criminal law. Any other solution would unjustifiably violate important aspects of the very values which the general functions seek to realise, not only because, for example, the preventive detention of a person who has not committed an offence would be likely to harm her welfare in a specially grave way, but also because it would directly violate, to the extent of denying, that person's autonomy by acting towards her for reasons which are irrelevant to and unsubstantiated by any unambiguous and interest-threatening expression of her own disposition towards the criminal law. Any practice of punishment which sanctioned such a victimisation would thereby sacrifice its claim to be acting in the interests of the welfare and autonomy of each member of the community by legitimating penal responses which evinced no respect for and accorded no weight to autonomy. This is not to say, of course, that it is never justifiable for the criminal law to step in before any tangible interest has been 'harmed'; it may do so when a citizen's behaviour produces a clear and immediate threat to fundamental interests (as in the case of inchoate offences such as attempt, incitement or conspiracy); but this must be a matter for political decision about the content of the substantive law, and not as an exercise of residual punitive power exercised without proper political safeguards. As I have argued, this conception of punishment must be taken to generate limitations not only on proper ends but also on the means to be employed in reaching them.

The proper meaning of punishment within a community, then, has to do with its response to actions which are hostile to and express rejection of fundamental community values in the sense explored in chapter 3: that is, actions which violate the fundamental interests upheld and protected by the criminal law. To punish those who have exhibited no such hostility would be to fly directly in the face of those values themselves, and to join the same moral category of wrongful action as offending against the criminal law. By emphasising the place of protection of autonomy within the functions of punishment, we can see how an adequate distributive principle can actually flow from, rather than merely act as a limit upon, the justifying aim itself. But this is only possible if we keep at the forefront of the argument the underlying general political values of the community and the place which punishment occupies in the structure of political value. It is also to acknowledge the existence of intrinsic values, or at least to modify one's conception of consequentialism so as to include such goals as securing or maintaining respect for values, thus arguably undermining the status of consequentialism as a distinctive form of moral reasoning.[31]

But we have not yet resolved the problem of distribution, for we have yet to confront the problem of responsibility: should punishment be limited beyond those who offend in the sense of causing or being otherwise closely involved in producing criminal actions, and be applied only to those who do so responsibly, in some sense? Can the mode of argument I have employed generate a commitment to the dispositional conception of responsibility developed in chapter 3? Again, the structure of the problem is a complex one: given the basic values underlying the criminal process – given its goals, its functions, and the values it seeks to promote – what conditions should be generally necessary for the imposition of criminal liability and hence punishment? We saw in chapter 3 that the attractive traditional answer is that only those who offend intentionally, recklessly or negligently – those who are capacity-responsible in the sense of having understood their actions and having had a genuine opportunity to do otherwise than they did, may fairly be punished. I argued that this conception was inadequate in several respects, notably in its failure to relate to the concerns of the general justifying aim, its strong assumptions about human freedom, and the unfeasibility of making genuine inquiries into individual capacities at this level of refinement. I argued that the alternative dispositional conception provided an attractive albeit not unproblematic challenge to the traditional capacity conception, principally in its coherence with the functional aspects of the criminal process. Can that conclusion be endorsed in the context of our community conception of punishment? Here too I would argue that its attractions are clear. In terms of pursuit of the goals and fulfillment of the functions of punishment as I have conceived them, it is apparent first and foremost that these tasks could be most efficiently carried out, and indeed that it would only be necessary to carry them out, by responding to those whose criminal acts genuinely express a hostility to the values of community which the law in question exists to protect and foster. And the test of whether or not a particular action manifests a relatively settled disposition to carry out such actions, as evidenced by all the circumstances including, significantly, whether it appears that the action was committed intentionally, recklessly or negligently, would seem a particularly appropriate test of such hostility. This, moreover, constitutes an internal relation between function and limitation: given the ultimate ends and functions of the criminal law, to serve the values of welfare and autonomy by specific means, the limitation of punishment to those who are dispositionally responsible for their offences is entailed both by the lack of need to punish others, whose offences are in some sense fortuitous, and by the different reactions we have to someone who does wrong as an aberration, and one who does so in a considered, characteristic way. In a community, it seems overwhelmingly likely that social cohesion, reaffirmation of common values, and denunciation would be best served in response to those whose actions exhibit a considered, settled rejection of community values or some aspect of them. Against other offenders, such a community can afford to (and therefore should, in accordance with the principle of urgency) adopt an attitude of toleration.

But does adherence to the dispositional conception of responsibility violate the very notion of autonomy, the very sense of freedom, empowerment and diversity, which we have argued to be a central political value? To answer this question, we must turn once again to the assumption of the primacy of the social, and the indirect but central function of punishment in supporting the community itself, its public culture and its framework values. For if humans are primarily social beings who must live in some form of community, it follows, as we have seen, that a just community has some entitlement to preserve at least its basic framework, so long as a certain degree of support and commitment survives. In order to do so, the community's institutions have to take its citizens, in a manner of speaking, as they find them; and if a certain number of them purposefully, heedlessly or negligently express themselves through hostility, opposition or indifference to the community's central values in the form of criminal behaviour, whether or not they can help the relevant aspects of their dispositions, whether they are capacity-responsible for those dispositions or not, the community must either effectively defend itself (in part through the practice of punishment), or allow itself to be undermined.

Another factor to be borne in mind in evaluating the implications of the principle of dispositional responsibility for human autonomy and political protest is the argument put forward in Chapter 5 that adoption of that principle should be tempered by adherence to the principle of residual autonomy[32] and, along the lines of the argument in chapter 6,[33] a certain toleration of both civil disobedience and, to a lesser extent, conscientious refusal. But if the community takes its own values seriously – including, of course, the possibility and indeed responsibility of political participation on the part of all citizens, who can thus contribute to the gradual transformation of their own societies – it must respond to those who fundamentally oppose or exhibit indifference to the importance of its basic framework. Conversely, and operating a principle of humane economy, it can afford to be tolerant towards those who offend against its norms through accident, mistake or other aberration, and who in their usual self-expression manifest a disposition to support and participate in the development and life of the community. Moreover, in assessing the strength of any apparent functional argument in favour of a victimisation in any particular case, we must bear in mind the fact that punishment is only one possible social response to offending, and one the importance of which it is all too easy to overestimate. The threat of punishment, which is justifiably made to all members of the community in the name of the values which the community fosters, may only be executed against those whose behaviour manifests a disposition to reject that framework, and whose continued treatment as fully participating members of the community thus presents a threat to or denial of the value of the welfare and autonomy of other citizens.

There is, however, another problem of distribution, already adverted to, and of great practical significance. I am referring to what I shall label the problem of uniformity of application; should each and every dispositionally responsible offender be detected, convicted and punished? This raises many questions, not all of which can be tackled here, and several of which could only be answered in a concrete political context. How many resources should be devoted to the detection of crime, and what proportion of suspected offenders should be arrested and prosecuted? What should the shape and nature of the trial process be; how high should we set the burden of proof, and how many resources should be devoted to the development of elaborate procedural safeguards?[34] It is often assumed in liberal (particularly retributive) theory that the actual incompleteness of application in most systems raises grave problems of injustice because of the principle that like cases must be treated alike. However, it seems that on the community conception of punishment, mere incompleteness of application does not raise an intractable problem of fairness, although unevenness in the sense of a skewed distribution of enforcement on irrelevant lines such as class, race or outward appearance certainly does so.[35] On the community conception, so long as the antecedent chances of detection and conviction are roughly equal for similar kinds of offenders, it is consistent with a concern to foster equally the welfare and autonomy of all that the community should determine a certain level of enforcement (at the points of detection, prosecution and procedural legislation) for certain bands of offences, as a conscientious political decision in the light of available resources, other social goals and priorities, respect for the autonomy and welfare of different groups, and judgments about the relative likelihood of efficacy of criminal enforcement as opposed to other social responses. There will generally be a threshold below which non-enforcement will risk a loss of credibility of that particular norm or even the system as a whole, but the threshold will depend on the type of offence. Particularly with some kinds of offence, it may be more efficacious to put social resources into the development of preventive devices such as environmental design than to spend them on the expensive business of criminal enforcement. There may also be occasions when resources within the system need to be specially diverted to particular offences or indeed particular localities, where the prevalence of a certain kind of offending is such that a public response to it has become a social priority, thus creating a relevant difference between that instance of the offence and its occurrence at a different place or time. Moreover, as well as such distributive decisions *within* the criminal process, important political decisions have to be made about the total resources to be devoted to criminal justice as opposed to other social concerns such as health and education. Once again, we witness the continuity of problems of distributive justice and efficacy in the community, and the impossibility of insulating criminal justice as a political issue. Once we locate punishment within its proper political context, we see that the issue of uniformity of application is not so intractable as it seems; each responsible offender of any particular type runs a certain risk of punishment: beyond this, the proper threshold of even-handed, non-universal application is a matter for social and political decision from the community's point of view. Within our political conception, although the impact of the *threat* of punishment must be equal or not disproportionately different for different offenders, the impact of *enforcement* may be unequal. For the offender, this is an instance of the inevitable influence of 'moral' luck.[36]

THE FORM OF PUNISHMENTS

It remains to make some relatively brief observations about what form punishment might take in such a community, given its central justifying functions and related principles of distribution. Perhaps the main point to be made here is that, on our conception of punishment, in which a central function is its reaffirmation of social values, punishments might well be expected to be, at least to a greater extent than is now the case, of a formal or symbolic nature. This would mean not only an emphasis on the symbolic or denunciatory element implicit in all punishments, but the use in some cases of a *purely* symbolic penalty in the form, for example, of a formal statement of conviction and denunciation handed down by the judge and perhaps publicised more systematically than is currently the practice. An element of denunciation and disapproval would be an important feature in such punishments, and it might often be the case that the disadvantages meted out could be both moderate and symbolic, supplemented by adequate practices of social compensation for the victims of crime. However, it may often be the case that, in order to fulfil its important function of fostering the central values of community and supporting the community itself, it will be necessary to punish more severely in order to satisfy strong grievance-desires on the part of victims, to prevent resort to self-help, to underline a social judgment of behaviour as especially injurious, or to emphasise a generally deterrent threat in the case of a particularly advantageous form of offending, which form an immediate aim of particular punishments.

What place would a principle of 'proportionality', supported by retributivists and acknowledged by several exponents of mixed theories, have in setting the scale of punishments? It is clear that proportionality to socially acknowledged gravity could serve a useful function in underlining community values, but the symbolic element in punishment will probably detract from the tendency towards a rigid hierarchy of punishments according to gravity of offences. And the central functions of punishment will dictate that the scale be modified in order to accommodate goals such as deterrence, incapacitation and prevention of resort to self-help. Indeed, it seems very likely, not least on the basis of the empirical evidence examined in chapter 2, that such goals could be pursued optimally by means of a penalty scale of much more moderate severity than those used in our current system, and in particular that, at least for first offenders, a system organised around the values I have defended would be willing to employ purely or principally symbolic measures. However, this conception would not rule out the use of severely incapacitating methods such as incarceration in secure but humane conditions for persistent and serious offenders who pose grave threats to the fundamental framework of the community or the most important interests of its members. Indeed, the logic of my argument might well suggest that the proper punishment for such offenders would be exclusion from the community, at least on certain conditions. Whether or not this constitutes a feasible and humane option will depend on many factors; in the present world, it is hard to envisage exile as a real moral possibility. If such conditions continue to prevail, internal incarceration in humane conditions seems the best alternative. Ultimately, the shape of and moral limitations upon the scale of punishments will be to a significant extent socially conditioned: what my conception of criminal justice dictates is that the scale must accord with a conscientious attempt to meet and balance the welfare and autonomy not only of victims and potential victims, but also of offenders and potential offenders. The principle of residual autonomy must be preserved, for no punishment must be so severe as to reflect a complete absence of respect for or denial of the offender's autonomy – or indeed for her welfare. Also implicit in this conception is a principle of humane economy; the commission of an offence does not deprive an offender of her civil rights. She, like other citizens, may be treated, within the limits of overriding political values, in a way which advances central community ends. She has behaved in such a way as to put herself in a relevantly different position from other citizens, which renders her liable to be punished according to the substantive argument which we have examined, for the good of the community of which she is a member – but the justification runs only to the extent that is absolutely necessary to the fulfillment of legitimate functions of the criminal law.

THE ACTUAL AND THE IDEAL

We have now constructed, in a fairly basic form, a set of arguments for punishment, based on a set of ideal assumptions about background social conditions, in the form of the existence of a community in which all citizens are fully participating members, and which exists to protect and promote, within a framework of common goals and values, the welfare and sense of autonomy (not only in terms of power and control of persons over their own lives, but also of their sense of responsibility for each other and for the development of the community) of all members of the community. Of what possible relevance are these arguments to actual societies such as our own, which fail in important respects to meet those background assumptions about social conditions? Can we really claim that the criminal justice system genuinely contributes to the welfare and autonomy of all citizens, for example, in the UK, given the uneven distribution of convictions across the population, skewed practices of incomplete enforcement, unequal impact of the threat of punishment, stringent and inhumane penal measures, apparent ineffectiveness of the threat of punishment in many areas, and the background inequalities and injustices, such as poverty and prejudice, which influence those injustices specific to the criminal process?[37] What should our attitude to criminal 'justice' be in an unjust society?

If anything at all is to be said in favour of the practice of punishment in our society along the lines of the ideal conception which I have sketched, it must, I think, come from one of two directions. In the first place, it could be argued that our society, whilst certainly not ideal, is at least not tyrannous in many respects, and that in certain spheres, governments are indeed motivated by a genuine concern for the social good and indeed often act in such a way as positively to contribute to the realisation of important socially acknowledged human interests and the fostering of basic social goods. By the same token, some aspects of the criminal law are, to varying degrees, punished with an appropriate degree of moderation, effective to prevent or mitigate the impact of grave harms, evenly if incompletely enforced, relatively equally difficult or easy for all to comply with (leaving aside, as I have argued we must, the influence of practically immutable dispositional traits), and so on. In these cases, similar arguments to those put forward on the ideal conception will apply with varying degrees of closeness of analogy. But the further we depart from the conditions underlying the ideal conception, the harder it will become to apply by analogy its arguments for punishment. Is there anything positive which we can say about punishment for breach of the criminal law which in at least one important respect violates the conditions of the community conception? I think that there is, but that the arguments are both indirect and negative. They would take the form of the claim that a practice of punishment is ultimately necessary in order to support the core of any legal order. The legal order is in some important senses unjust, but the political alternatives at the moment seem likely to be worse rather than better. There is therefore at least some indirect, non-ideal reason to support the practice of punishment in this society. Moreover, a failure to punish might lead directly to certain kinds of harm and disorder – a growth in a particular form of offending, private vengeance, public resentment and so on. Thus, *given* the limited extent to which present society is committed to the equal pursuit of the welfare and autonomy of all its citizens, the best option may nonetheless be to support (at least some of) its practices of punishment, in the absence of any realistic prospect of getting anything better in the near future.

This 'second-best' theory of punishment is a pale reflection of the community conception described above. What it aims to capture is a conviction which is important to my argument, in that it helps to explain the relationship between ideal and second-best theory, and indeed the utility of engaging in ideal thinking in a patently non-ideal world. This conviction is that it is misleading to speak in terms of (totally) justified and (totally) unjustified punishments; it is more illuminating to think in terms of what can be said for and against punishment, bearing in mind the existence of different points of view and different social conditions. Indeed, as we saw from chapter 6, there may sometimes be good reason for a citizen to resist the prescriptions of the criminal law despite a conscientious public commitment to punishment. The situation is further complicated by the interaction of, yet distinction between questions of the justice and stability of the system as a whole and that of individual or groups of laws within it. But by attempting to construct a second-best theory of punishment, and by implying that there could also be 3rd, 4th, . . . nth -best theories, according to the degree to and ways in which a society or particular laws within it violated the values of community, I do not mean to remove the cutting edge from the argument. In other words, I *do* suppose that we can reach a threshold where the arguments for punishment have become too pale a reflection of the ideal conception to provide a justification, or indeed where they have run out altogether, and where punishing and even threatening to punish becomes straightforwardly morally wrong.

The fact that I am assuming a continuum between fair, humane and effective punishments at one extreme and unfair, cruel or inefficacious ones at the other of course poses the difficulty of drawing lines, as well as those of determining whose responsibility such line-drawing should be and when citizens themselves are entitled to protest and resist the practice of state punishment. These seem to me to be moral dilemmas which cannot be avoided on any decently complex approach to punishment. Where the social background has become so tyrannous or otherwise cruel or unjust that its maintenance ceases to have any value, the decision to resist may be relatively easy to make, although hard to execute. In most circumstances the context will not be so clear. In our present society, I would argue, it is the question rather of resistance to certain salient laws which materially and avoidably entrench background inequality and injustice or which fail to respect fundamental interests or social values which poses the uppermost practical moral dilemma for reflective citizens, raising as it does not only questions of personal sacrifice, but also complex educated guesswork about the impact of disobedience and the existence of alternative political strategies. It is certainly true, then, that at a general level something can be said for punishment, although it is often hard to assess the strength of the available arguments. Because we are so used to living with a system of punishment, and doubtless also because punitive responses are a salient feature of our emotional lives (this, of course, might change), the idea of being without a penal system, or even with one far less extensive than is our current one, tends to throw us into a state of alarm and anxiety. This in turn feeds into the arguments for punishment. But we should not duck the difficult issue of how to go about changing social attitudes which act as barriers to changes towards a more acceptable criminal process, and in particular the question of the (eminently manipulable and often manipulated) level of social alarm, which crucially affects the form and severity of punishments in our society.

CONCLUSION

We have now come to the end of the journey mapped out in Chapter 1, and it will be useful to conclude with a concise statement of the principal claims which I have tried to substantiate and defend during the course of this book. First and foremost, it has been my contention that, in order to produce the most convincing possible set of arguments for the practice of punishment as defined in Chapter 1, it is necessary to develop an *integrated* account. In other words, one must acknowledge fairly and squarely the place of punishment within political philosophy; the interaction between the question of punishment and that of the nature of a just society;[38] and, most specifically, its relationship with questions such as political and legal obligation and the nature and functions of the criminal law. Without this placing in context, we fail to appreciate the complexity of the problem of punishment, and thus fail to say the best that can be said for it.

Secondly, and related to this principal point, I have argued that the strongest possible arguments for punishment can be developed within a communitarian conception which envisages a society genuinely committed to pursuing with equal concern the welfare and autonomy of each of its citizens, and of creating an environment in which human beings may flourish and develop, whilst acknowledging the role of the community in constructing the values and human interests which it seeks to defend. In constructing this 'community conception' of punishment, I have argued that it is of central importance to loosen certain strong assumptions made by liberal theory about the nature of human individuality and the implications of that individuality for the role of the state. This is because some of the strongest arguments in favour of punishment lie in its contribution to diffused social good, yet the moral boundaries between persons set up by liberalism prevent it from accommodating these arguments and thus from giving an account of those strong points. This relaxing of liberal assumptions has introduced a modest element of modern social theory's insight into the construction of human nature to our picture. It has also suggested an explanation for the continuing puzzle of punishment, through its identification of most modern thought about punishment within the liberal tradition.

Finally, the conception of punishment which I have defended is pluralistic, like the mixed theories considered in chapter 2, in that it identifies punishment as pursuing and respecting a set of different values which cannot necessarily be reduced to each other, or into some overriding common currency such as general utility. But there is an important difference between my pluralist conception and that espoused by the mixed theories. In the first place, whilst maintaining the pluralist vision, I have resisted a rigid prioritisation of the values involved, or a specification of one as a side constraint on the other(s). This has made for a somewhat less neat conception than that offered by the traditional theories, and one which gives an important place to the power, status and legitimacy of conscientious, reflective political decision in particular social, historical and material contexts, about which it is not useful or appropriate to theorise or specify 'objective' standards in advance. My aim has been not so much to produce a blueprint for an ideal criminal justice system as to examine critically the assumptions which underlie much normative thought about punishment and to suggest the principal moral and political concerns which should inform political practice. Doubtless many philosophers will feel that this conception gives too great a place to the mediation of intuition in the balancing and accommodation of the values which I have argued must be fundamental to a morally acceptable practice of criminal justice, or that it gives too much away to cultural relativism in its degree of willingness to defer to differing political decisions which may be made within the general framework in different social contexts. My argument remains, however, that the appropriate enterprise here *is* the construction of a framework, rather than the working through of detail, which can only be futile when attempted in a social vacuum.

Secondly, my pluralist conception differs from the mixed theories in that, whilst acknowledging the need to attend to the distributive as well as the functional aspects of the question of justification, it attempts to incorporate adequate principles of distribution within what is akin in my argument to the 'general justifying aim' of Hart's theory. In other words, it is not that one needs a distinctive, limiting principle which in a sense opposes itself to a general justifying aim; it is that, when properly understood in the context of general political principles, the justifying aims or functions of punishment themselves incorporate certain limitations on their own pursuit or fulfillment. Thus, in Duff's terms,[39] there is an internal relation between aim and limitation; once one abandons the idea of a purely utilitarian aim and includes non-utilitarian values in the justifying functions themselves, there is no need to add on an additional principle. This is not to say, as we have seen, that the relations between the different parts of the pluralist justifying functions are simple or easy to resolve, but it does, I think, pose a more straightforward and intuitively plausible account than does the total separation of the general aim and the question of distribution.

What we have ended up with, then, is a conception of punishment as a social practice within a community, geared towards the pursuit of (which entails respect for) a plurality of the community's central goals and values, moderate in its severity, and with an importantly symbolic aspect. It has both particular (preventive, deterrent and so on) and general (support of the community and its framework values) functions. In terms of importance, especially in understanding the continuity of political problems and the place of punishment within them, and resolving problems of partial injustice, its general functions might well be described as primary, and principally related to the *institution* of punishment, whilst some of its particular functions are principally related to *individual acts* of punishment. In applying a particular sanction, the idea of some specific function will probably be uppermost; taking the system as a whole, the general function can be seen to occupy a place of primary importance. Punishment, on this conception, is also characterised by a distinctive combination of conservative and dynamic aspects, perhaps corresponding to the insights represented by the retributive and utilitarian traditions respectively. On the one hand, it supports the status quo by enforcing pre-existing power relations, reacting to any upsetting of the existing distribution of goods; conversely, it can also be used to further important social goals and to develop the social environment, in particular the sense of social responsibility, commitment and vindication on the part of citizens. Punishment, then, is a Janus-faced concept: both backward- and forward-looking at once.

In constructing the community conception of punishment, despite our relaxation of certain important liberal assumptions and our rejection of some central liberal values, we have been able to preserve and utilise important aspects of the arguments about legal and political obligation and the nature of the criminal law set out in the earlier chapters which integrated the question of punishment in its proper political context. Those sections drew in important respects on arguments closely associated with the liberal tradition, albeit modified in certain ways. By this method, I hope to have succeeded in preserving the main strengths of liberalism, including, of course, its commitment to tackling the issue of justification at a philosophical level. Doubtless this method will draw criticism from liberals and the critics of liberalism alike. I should perhaps underline the fact that I do not regard labels as being of ultimate importance, and I do not wish the acceptability of my arguments to hang on the question of whether the conception of punishment which I have defended counts as a liberal conception or (as I myself would maintain) otherwise.

Ultimately, then, I am offering a set of arguments in favour of the practice of state punishment, the strength of those arguments being subject to modification in the light of, because continuous with, arguments about background conditions of political justice. In the time-honoured tradition of such work, I have undoubtedly raised more questions than I could answer, even setting limitations of space or time aside. The best that I can hope for my arguments is that they will prompt reaction and further development, in a constructively critical spirit.

NOTES

CHAPTER 1 PRELIMINARIES

1 For recent and contrasting contributions to the debate, see T. Honderich, *Punishment: The Supposed Justifications*, Harmondsworth, Penguin, 1984, pp. 143–83, and Postscript, pp. 212–44; R.A. Duff, *Trials and Punishments*, Trowbridge, Cambridge University Press, 1986, pp. 233–77; W. Sadurski, *Giving Desert Its Due*, Dordrecht, Reidel, 1985, pp. 221–58.

2 See A.K. Sen, 'Well-being, agency and freedom', *Journal of Philosophy*, vol. 82, 1985, p. 214.

3 See Honderich, op. cit., pp. 51–65.

4 For an illuminating discussion of authority, see J. Raz, *The Morality of Freedom*, Oxford University Press, 1986, pp. 23–105.

5 J. Floud and W. Young, *Dangerousness and Criminal Justice*, London, Heinemann, 1981, pp. 38 ff..

6 Perhaps most notably that of H. Kelsen, *General Theory of Law and State*, trans. A. Wedberg, Twentieth Century Legal Philosophy Series, New York, 1961, pp. 18–20, 50–64.

7 J. Rawls, *A Theory of Justice*, Oxford University Press, 1971, pp. 20 ff., 48–51.

8 A.M. Quinton, 'On punishment', *Analysis*, vol. 14, 1954, p. 133.

9 H.L.A. Hart, 'Definition and theory in jurisprudence', *Law Quarterly Review*, vol. 70, 1954, reprinted in Hart, *Essays in Jurisprudence and Philosophy*, Oxford University Press, 1983, p. 21.

10 Quinton, op. cit..

11 H.L.A. Hart, *The Concept of Law*, Oxford University Press, 1961, pp. 13–17, 121–32.

12 J. Finnis, *Natural Law and Natural Rights*, Oxford University Press, 1980, p. 11; see generally his discussion of the central case technique and the selection of viewpoint, pp. 6–18. The criteria of significance which I have used are discussed during the course of the section on definition.

13 Quinton, op. cit..

14 Honderich, op. cit., pp. 18–19.

15 For a general discussion of the conceptual framework of the English criminal law, see G. Williams, *Textbook of Criminal Law*, 2nd edition, London, Sweet and Maxwell, 1983, Chapters 1, 3–7.

16 For the purposes of this argument I am assuming a simple model of adjudication which, whilst lacking the sophistication necessary to a

convincing theory of judicial decision, serves to highlight the discrete problem of victimisation.

17 J. Griffin, *Well-Being*, Oxford University Press, 1986, Ch. XII.
18 See below, Chapter 5, pp. 98–108.
19 M. Lessnoff, 'Two justifications of punishment', 1971, *Philosophical Quarterly*, vol. 21, p. 141.
20 J.L. Mackie, 'Can there be a right-based moral theory?', *Midwest Studies in Philosophy*, vol. III, 1978, reprinted in J. Waldron, ed., *Theories of Rights*, Oxford University Press, 1984, p. 168.
21 J.S. Mill, *On Liberty*, Harmondsworth, Penguin, 1974.

CHAPTER 2 THE TRADITIONAL JUSTIFICATIONS

1 Examples of such theories are to be found in I. Kant, *The Philosophy of Law*, transl. W. Hastie, Edinburgh, 1887; J.D. Mabbott, 'Punishment', *Mind*, vol. 48, 1939, p. 152.
2 See T. Honderich, *Punishment; The Supposed Justifications*, Harmondsworth, Penguin, 1984, pp. 22–33, p. 210.
3 See H. Gross, *A Theory of Criminal Justice*, New York, Oxford University Press, 1979, pp. 74–88; Honderich, op. cit., pp. 26–33; A. Von Hirsch, *Doing Justice*, Hill & Wang, New York, 1976, pp. 45–55, 66–94.
4 See Chapter 3, pp. 73–8; Chapter 8, pp. 186–9.
5 J.S. Mill, *On Liberty*, Penguin, Harmondsworth, 1974; H.L.A. Hart, *Law, Liberty and Morality*, Oxford University Press, 1963.
6 H.L.A. Hart, *The Concept of Law*, Oxford University Press, 1961, chs 8 and 9; 'Positivism and the separation of law and morals', *Harvard Law Review*, 71, 1958, p. 593.
7 See A. Von Hirsch, *Past or Future Crimes*, Manchester University Press, 1985, pp. 31–7; D.J. Galligan, 'The return to retribution in penal theory', in *Crime, Proof and Punishment*, ed. C. Tapper, Butterworths, London, 1981, p. 144, pp. 163–71.
8 A.H. Goldman, 'The paradox of punishment', *Philosophy and Public Affairs*, vol. 9, 1979, p. 42; Honderich, op. cit., pp. 216–18.
9 C.S. Nino, 'A consensual theory of punishment', *Philosophy and Public Affairs*, vol. 12, 1983, p. 289; R.A. Duff, *Trials and Punishments*, Cambridge University Press, 1986, pp. 217–28; Honderich, op. cit., pp. 48, 219–24.
10 Galligan, op. cit., pp. 152–63; H. Morris, 'Persons and punishment', *The Monist*, vol. 52, 1968, p. 475; J.G. Murphy, 'Marxism and retribution', *Philosophy and Public Affairs*, vol. 2, 1973, p. 217; Finnis, 'The restoration of retribution', *Analysis*, vol. 32, 1972, p. 131.
11 Kant, op. cit., pp. 195–8.
12 See G.W. Hegel, *The Philosophy of Right*, transl. T.M. Knox, Oxford University Press, 1942, pp. 69–70, discussed by Honderich, op. cit., pp. 45–47.
13 I. Kant, *The Metaphysical Elements of Justice*, 1797, transl. J. Ladd, Indianapolis, 1965, pp. 55 ff.; for a modern descendant of social

contractarian theories, see, J. Rawls, *A Theory of Justice*, Oxford University Press, 1971, Ch. 3.

14 See Chapter 6, pp. 123–6, Chapter 7, pp. 144–5.

15 Hart, *The Concept of Law*, op. cit., pp. 153–63.

16 H.L.A. Hart, *Punishment and Responsibility*, Oxford University Press, 1968, pp. 13–27.

17 J. Bentham, *Introduction to the Principles of Morals and Legislation*, ed. J.H. Burns and H.L.A. Hart, London, Methuen, 1982, pp. 70, 145, 165, 166, 186, and Ch. 13 generally.

18 W. Quinn, 'The right to threaten and the right to punish', *Philosophy and Public Affairs*, vol. 14, 1985, p. 327.

19 For modern discussion and modification of classical utilitarianism, see J.J.C. Smart, 'An outline of a system of utilitarian ethics', in J.J.C. Smart and B. Williams, *Utilitarianism: For and Against*, Cambridge University Press, 1973, pp. 3–74; D.H. Hodgson, *Consequences of Utilitarianism*, Oxford University Press, 1967, Ch. 1; D. Lyons, *Forms and Limits of Utilitarianism*, Oxford University Press, 1965.

20 Bentham, op. cit., pp. 147, 171, ch. 5.

21 See J. Andenaes, 'The preventive effects of punishment', *University of Pennsylvania Law Review*, vol. 114, 1966, p. 949; D. Beyleveld, 'Identifying, explaining and predicting deterrence', *British Journal of Criminology*, 1979, p. 205; G.S. Becker, 'Crime and Punishment: An economic approach', *Journal of Political Economy*, vol. 76, 1968, p. 169; R. Hood and R. Sparks, *Key Issues in Criminology*, Weidenfeld & Nicolson, London, 1970, chs 6 and 8; Panel on Research on Deterrent and Incapacitative Effects, Report in A. Blumstein, J. Cohen and D. Nagin (ed.), *Deterrence and Incapacitation: Estimating the Effects of Criminal Sanctions on Crime Rates*, US National Academy of Sciences, 1978, pp. 19–63.

22 H.L.A. Hart, *Punishment and Responsibility*, op. cit., pp. 4–6.

23 D.H. Hodgson, *Consequences of Utilitarianism*, op. cit., pp. 38–62; but see D. Regan, *Utilitarianism and Co-operation*, Oxford University Press, 1980, pp. 54–82.

24 Hood and Sparks, op. cit., chs 6–8; R. Martinson, 'What works? – Questions and answers about prison reform', *The Public Interest*, vol. 35, 1974, pp. 22–54; S. Brody, *The Effectiveness of Sentencing*, Home Office Research Study no. 35, HMSO, 1976, pp. 1–48, 50–9.

25 J. Gunn, *et al.*, *Psychiatric Aspects of Imprisonment*, London, Academic Press, 1978.

26 Duff, op. cit., pp. 242–66.

27 See M. Foucault, *Discipline and Punish*, trans. A. Sheridan, Harmondsworth, Penguin, 1979; D. Garland, *Punishment and Welfare*, Aldershot, Gower, 1985.

28 Hood and Sparks, op. cit., chs 6 and 8: Brody, op. cit., pp. 1–48; A. Ashworth, *Sentencing and Penal Policy*, London, Weidenfeld & Nicolson, 1983, pp. 25–31; N.D. Walker, D.P. Farrington and G. Tucker, 'Reconviction rates of adult males after different sentences', *British Journal of Criminology*, 1981, p. 357.

29   Ashworth, op. cit., pp. 320, 382–5; Hood and Sparks, op. cit., ch. 6.
30   Hood and Sparks, op. cit., p. 180; G.J.O. Phillpotts and L.B. Lancucki, 'Previous convictions, sentence and reconviction', *Home Office Research Study Number 53*, London, HMSO, 1979, pp. 16–17; Home Office, *The Sentence of the Court*, London, HMSO, 1969, pp. 66–7.
31   Ashworth, op. cit., pp. 31–3; S. Brody and R. Tarling, *Taking Offenders out of Circulation*, Home Office Research Study no. 64, HMSO, 1975; N. Shorer, *Aging Criminals*, Beverley Hills, Sage Publications, 1985.
32   In 1985, the average monetary cost of keeping an offender in prison in England and Wales was £256.00 per week, i.e. £13,312.00 per year: the psychological costs are, of course, incalculable.
33   Honderich, op. cit., pp. 33–45, 231–7.
34   E. Durkheim, *The Division of Labour in Society*, 1893, Glencoe, Free Press, 1960, vol. 1, ch. 2.
35   See, for example, D. Cameron and E. Fraser, *The Lust to Kill*, Polity Press, 1987, on the role of the British press in constructing the social meaning of sexual murder.
36   G. Fletcher, 'Punishment and compensation', *Creighton Law Review*, vol. 14, p. 691, 1981.
37   See J. Raz, *The Morality of Freedom*, Oxford University Press, 1986, pp. 145–8.
38   R. Nozick, *Anarchy, State and Utopia*, Oxford, Basil Blackwell, 1974, ch. 3.; C. Taylor, 'Atomism', in *Philosophy and the Human Sciences*, Cambridge University Press, 1985, p. 187.
39   J. Rawls, op. cit., pp. 22–7; see also Raz's critique, Raz, op. cit., pp. 271–3.
40   I am grateful to Gerry Maher for pointing out that the question of punishment of the innocent arises not only at the point of applying the rules of a system but also of framing those rules: burdens and standards of proof and other rules of evidence in effect entrench an institutionally accepted level of risk of victimisation.
41   A.M. Quinton, 'On punishment', *Analysis*, vol. 14, 1954, p. 133.
42   See Chapter 1, pp. 4–10.
43   Bentham, op. cit., pp. 158–64.
44   Bentham, op. cit., pp. 182–4.
45   Bentham, op. cit., p. 183.
46   Hart, *Punishment and Responsibility*, op. cit., pp. 17–21.
47   Archdeacon Paley, *The Principles of Moral and Political Philosophy*, 1809, pp. 310–11; discussed in W.L. Twining, *Theories of Evidence*, London, Weidenfeld & Nicolson, 1985, pp. 95–100.
48   J. Floud and W. Young, *Dangerousness and Criminal Justice*, London, Heinemann, 1981, pp. 38 ff.
49   Hart, *Punishment and Responsibility*, op. cit., pp. 13–53.
50   Fletcher, op. cit.
51   Mill, op. cit.

52 T. Honderich, '*On Liberty* and morality-dependent harms', *Political Studies*, vol. 30, 1982, p. 504.

53 Duff, op. cit., pp. 151–64.

54 See, for example, J.C. Smith and B. Hogan, *Criminal Law*, 5th edition, London, Butterworths, 1983, p. 47–80, 87–92.

55 Hart, *Punishment and Responsibility*, op. cit., p. 12.

56 For important modern criticisms of utilitarianism see Rawls, op. cit., pp. 22–7; B. Williams, 'A critique of utilitarianism', in Smart and Williams, op. cit.; Nozick, op. cit., pp. 39–41, 153–5.

57 For examples of modern theorists who retain a consequentialist element, see Rawls, op. cit., chs 1–3; R.M. Dworkin, *Taking Rights Seriously*, chs 4–9, 12–13.

58 Indeed, even H.L.A. Hart identifies the 'general justifying aim' of punishment as being basically utilitarian; *Punishment and Responsibility*, op. cit., pp. 8–10, 14.

59 Hart, *Punishment and Responsibility*, op. cit., pp. 5–6.

60 Nino, op. cit.

61 S.I. Benn, 'An approach to the problems of punishment', *Philosophy*, vol. 33, 1958, p. 325.

62 For an illuminating discussion of the differences between Hart's and other mixed theories, see M. Lessnoff, 'Two justifications of punishment', *Philosophical Quarterly*, vol. 21, 1971, p. 141.

63 J. Rawls, 'Two concepts of rules', *Philosophical Review*, vol. 64, 1955, p. 3.

64 See D. Lyons, *Forms and Limits of Utilitarianism*, op. cit., chs 2–4; for a critique of this position, see D.H. Hodgson, op. cit., ch. 3.

65 Quinton, op. cit., and see Chapter 2, pp. 4–10.

66 Lyons, op. cit..

67 This is not to say, of course, that each of the mixed theories encounters these objections in just the same way or indeed to the same extent; see Lessnoff, op. cit..

68 Goldman, op. cit.

69 Hart, *Essays on Bentham*, op. cit., ch. 4.

70 Goldman, op. cit.

CHAPTER 3 THE RELEVANCE OF RESPONSIBILITY

1 J. Glover, *Responsibility*, London, Routledge & Kegan Paul, 1970, pp. 62–84; T. Honderich, *Punishment; The Supposed Justifications*, Harmondsworth, Penguin, 1984, pp. 105–41; J.L. Mackie, *Ethics*, Harmondsworth, Penguin, 1977, pp. 220–6.

2 P. Foot, 'Freewill as involving determinism', in her *Virtues and Vices*, Oxford, Blackwell, 1978, pp. 62–73; Glover, op. cit., pp. 21–48; Mackie, op. cit., pp. 203–26; P.F. Strawson, 'Freedom and resentment', *Proceedings of the British Academy*, 1962, p. 127.

3 H.L.A. Hart, *Punishment and Responsibility*, Oxford University Press, 1968, Ch. 1; see chapter 2, pp. 47–9.

4 B. Wootton, *Crime and the Criminal Law*, London, Stevens, 1963; second edition, 1981.

5 Honderich, op. cit., pp. 132–41; Strawson, op. cit..

6 Hart, op. cit., pp. 12, 22–3, 222–30.
7 See chapter 5, pp. 100–19.
8 See chapter 1, pp. 11–12.
9 Hart, op. cit., chs 1 and 9.
10 Hart, op. cit., ch. 1; see chapter 2, pp. 47–9.
11 M. Bayles, 'Character, purpose and criminal responsibility', *Law and Philosophy*, vol. 1, 1982, pp. 5–8.
12 For legal discussion of the mens rea doctrine, see J. Smith and B. Hogan, *Criminal Law*, 5th edition, London, Butterworths 1983, pp. 47–80; Cross and Jones, *Introduction to Criminal Law*, ed. R. Card, 10th edition, London, Butterworths, 1984, pp. 28–55, 89–127.
13 See Smith and Hogan, op. cit., ch. 5; *Elliot v C* (1983) 2 All England Law Reports p. 1005; *R v Stone and Dobinson* (1977) 2 A.E.R. p. 341.
14 Hart, op. cit., ch. 6.
15 R.A. Duff, 'Recklessness', *Criminal Law Review*, 1980, p. 282; '*Caldwell* and *Lawrence*: the retreat from subjectivism', *Oxford Journal of Legal Studies*, vol. 3, 1983, p. 77.
16 Hart, op. cit., p. 140.
17 See Smith and Hogan, op. cit., pp. 161–221.
18 Bayles, op. cit., pp. 5–20.
19 Smith and Hogan, op. cit., pp. 164–81; Cross and Jones, op. cit., pp. 90–9.
20 See chapter 5, pp. 100–8.
21 Chapter 5, *passim*.
22 Smith and Hogan, op. cit., pp. 222–69.
23 T. Nagel, 'Moral luck', in his *Mortal Questions*, Cambridge University Press, 1979, pp. 24–38.
24 See chapter 2, pp. 47–56; M. Lessnoff, 'Two justifications of punishment', *Philosophical Quarterly*, vol. 21, 1971, p. 141.
25 R.A. Duff, 'Mental disorder and criminal responsibility', in Duff and N.E. Simmonds (ed.), *Philosophy and the Criminal Law*, ARSP Beiheft 19, 1984, p. 31; Duff, *Trials and Punishments*, Cambridge University Press, 1986, pp. 14–38.
26 Chapter 2, pp. 48–9.
27 M. Kelman, 'Interpretive construction in the substantive criminal law', *Stanford Law Review*, vol. 33, 181, p. 591.
28 Wootton, op. cit.; American Friends Service Committee, *Struggle for Justice*, New York, Hill & Wang, 1971, pp. 34–47, 83–144.

CHAPTER 4 THE QUESTION OF LEGAL OBLIGATION

1 J. Finnis, *Natural Law and Natural Rights*, Oxford University Press, 1980, pp. 354 ff.
2 See P. Hacker, 'Sanction theories of duty', *Oxford Essays in Jurisprudence*, Second Series, ed. A.W.B. Simpson, Oxford University Press, 1973, p. 131.
3 H.L.A. Hart, *The Concept of Law*, Oxford University Press, 1961, pp. 79–88.

4 Hart, op. cit., pp. 55–60.
5 Hart, op. cit., pp. 84–5.
6 Routledge & Kegan Paul, London, 1983, ch. 4.
7 Cf. Hart's views expressed in his *Essays on Bentham*, Oxford University Press, 1982, p. 160.
8 A.M. Honoré, 'Groups, laws and obedience', in *Oxford Essays in Jurisprudence*, ed. Simpson, op. cit., p. 1.
9 Honoré, op. cit., p. 10.
10 Hart, *The Concept of Law*, op. cit., pp. 55–6.
11 J. Raz, *Practical Reason and Norms*, Hutchinson, London, 1975, pp. 170–7.
12 Hart, *Essays on Bentham*, op. cit., pp. 154–5.
13 See J. Raz, *The Concept of a Legal System*, Oxford University Press, 1970, p. 47.
14 R.M. Dworkin, *Taking Rights Seriously*, Duckworth, London, 1977, Ch. 3.
15 Raz, *Practical Reason and Norms*, op. cit., p. 171.
16 Hart, *Essays on Bentham*, op. cit., p. 157–61: Hart objects to Raz's analysis of legal obligation in terms of reasons for action, and prefers to proceed on the basis of a non-cognitive theory of duty in which the statements asserting that an individual has a duty refer to actions due from him 'in the sense that they may properly be extracted from him according to legal rules or principles' (p. 160). This corresponds to the idea of the law's *claiming* obedience for itself, discussed below, a characteristic of law which will naturally be of no practical significance if there are no agents who adopt the legal point of view themselves.
17 D.N. MacCormick, *Legal Reasoning and Legal Theory*, Oxford University Press, 1978, pp. 285–92.
18 Finnis, op. cit., pp. 11–18.
19 See Chapter 1, pp. 6, 9–10; Hart, *The Concept of Law*, op. cit., pp. 13–17, 121–32, 233.
20 Finnis, op. cit., pp. 354, 357–9.
21 Honoré, op. cit., pp. 1–2, 19–21.
22 Honoré, op. cit., pp. 6–7.
23 Chapter 8, pp. 173–6.
24 Finnis, op. cit., pp. 363–6.
25 For persuasive arguments, see M.B.E. Smith, 'Is there a prima facie obligation to obey the law?', *Yale Law Journal*, vol. 82, 1973, p. 950.
26 See J.W. Harris, *Law and Legal Science*, Oxford University Press, 1979, pp. 34–43, 81–4.
27 See also Honoré, 'Real laws', in *Law, Morality and Society*, ed. P. Hacker and J. Raz, Oxford University Press, 1977, p. 99, at p. 104.
28 E. Durkheim, *The Division of Labour in Society*, 1893, Glencoe, Free Press, 1960, vol. 1, Ch. 2.
29 H. Kelsen, *General Theory of Law and State*, trans. A. Wedberg, Twentieth Century Legal Philosophy Series, New York, 1961; see also Harris, op. cit., ch. 4.

30 Honoré, 'Groups, laws and obedience', op. cit..

31 Campbell, op. cit., chs 6 and 7.

32 J. Rawls, 'Two concepts of rules', *Philosophical Review*, vol. 64, 1955, p. 3.

CHAPTER 5 THE NATURE AND LIMITS OF THE CRIMINAL LAW

1 See chapter 8, pp. 178–81.

2 A. Jaggar, *Feminist Politics and Human Nature*, Brighton, Harvester Press, 1983, pp. 18–21, 27–48, 125–33; C. Taylor, *Philosophy and the Human Sciences*, Cambridge University Press, 1985, pp. 187–210.

3 The issue will be taken up again in chapter 7.

4 See H.L.A. Hart, *The Concept of Law*, Oxford University Press, 1961, pp. 189–95.

5 See J. Rawls, *A Theory of Justice*, Oxford University Press, 1971, pp. 118–92; discussed by T. Nagel, 'Rawls on justice', and R. Dworkin, 'The original position', in N. Daniels (ed.), *Reading Rawls*, Oxford, Blackwell, 1978, pp. 1 and 16. It is not clear, however, that Rawls would now attach fundamental importance to this aspect of his theory: see his 'Justice as fairness: Political not metaphysical', *Philosophy and Public Affairs*, vol. 14, 1985, p. 223.

6 J.-J. Rousseau, *The Social Contract* (1762), trans. G.D.H. Cole, London, Dent, 1973; J. Locke, *Two Treatises of Civil Government* (1690), trans. W.S. Carpenter, London, Dent Everyman, 1924; T. Hobbes, *Leviathan*, ed. J. Plamenatz, London, Fontana, 1962, chs 26 and 30.

7 A similar kind of argument is developed in J. Rawls' 'Justice as fairness: Political not metaphysical', op. cit.; as a basis for the development of general principles of justice this idea seems problematic given the heterogeneous nature of many societies; it should be noted that I am using the method in a more limited sphere, i.e. that of general principles governing criminal regulation.

8 P. Devlin, *The Enforcement of Morals*, Oxford University Press, 1965, pp. 1–25.

9 See Devlin, op. cit.; H.L.A. Hart, *Law, Liberty and Morality*, Oxford University Press, 1963; B. Mitchell, *Law, Morality and Religion in a Secular Society*, Oxford University Press, 1967; *Report of the Committee on Homosexual Offences and Prostitution* (The Wolfenden Report), Cmnd. 247, 1957.

10 Cf. A. Sen, 'Well-being, agency and freedom; The Dewey Lectures 1984', *Journal of Philosophy*, vol. 82, 1985, pp. 208–12.

11 B. Barry, *Political Argument*, London, Routledge & Kegan Paul, 1965, pp. 38–43, 173–86.

12 Cf. J. Raz, *The Morality of Freedom*, Oxford University Press, 1986, pp. 288–320.

13 See, for example, F. Heidensohn, *Women and Crime*, London, MacMillan, 1985, pp. 31–58; C. Smart, *Women, Crime and Criminology*, London, Routledge & Kegan Paul, 1976, pp. 77–107; S. Edwards (ed.), *Gender, Sex and Law*, London, Croom Helm, 1985, essays by Edwards, 'Gender "justice"?', p. 129; L. Luckhaus,

'A plea for PMT In the criminal law', p. 159; Edwards, 'Male violence against women', p. 183; S. Edwards, *Women on Trial*, Manchester University Press, 1984, pp. 25–118.

14 J. Smith and B. Hogan, *Criminal Law*, 5th edition, London, Butterworths, 1983, pp. 273–403, 450–9.

15 Smith and Hogan, op. cit., pp. 87–108, 450–9; S. Box, *Power, Crime and Mystification*, London, Tavistock, 1983, pp. 16–79.

16 Smith and Hogan, op. cit., pp. 81–6: see chapter 3, pp. 63–5.

17 Theft Act 1968; Theft Act 1978; see Smith and Hogan, op. cit., pp. 460–599.

18 See Theft Act 1968, ss. 1 & 2; Criminal Damage Act 1971, s. 5(2); G. Williams, *Textbook of Criminal Law*, 2nd edition, London, Stevens, 1983, pp. 549–93.

19 Smith and Hogan, op. cit., pp. 404–49.

20 See C. MacKinnon, 'Feminism, marxism, method and the state: Toward feminist jurisprudence', *Signs*, vol. 8, 1983, p. 653; C. Wells, 'Law reform, rape and ideology', *Journal of Law and Society*, vol. 12, 1985, p. 63.

21 Sexual Offences Act 1956, ss. 14 & 15; see now Sexual Offences Act 1986.

22 Smith and Hogan, op. cit., pp. 415–16, p. 443; Sexual Offences Act 1956, s. 6; Sexual Offences Act 1967, s. 1.

23 Smith and Hogan, op. cit., pp. 405–7; Wells, op. cit..

24 See M. Walzer, *Spheres of Justice*, Oxford, Blackwell, 1983, especially pp. 3–30.

25 J.S. Mill, *On Liberty*, 1859, Harmondsworth, Penguin, 1974.

26 See e.g., T. Honderich, '*On Liberty* and morality-dependent harms', *Political Studies*, vol. 30, 1982, p. 504; C.L. Ten, *Mill on Liberty*, Oxford University Press, 1980; R. Wollheim, 'John Stuart Mill and the limits of state action', *Social Research*, vol. 40, 1973, p. 1.

27 H.L.A. Hart, *Law, Liberty and Morality*, op. cit., pp. 30–2, 69–83; R. Dworkin, *Taking Rights Seriously*, London, Duckworth, 1977, pp. 240–58.

28 J. Feinberg, *Rights, Justice and the Bounds of Liberty*, Princeton University Press, 1980, pp. 45–68, 110–29; G. Dworkin, 'Paternalism', in R. Wasserstrom (ed.), *Morality and the Law*, Belmont, California, Wadsworth Publishing Co. 1971, pp. 107–26.

29 *Report of the Committee on Obscenity and Film Censorship*, (Chair, B. Williams), Cmnd. 7772, 1979; R. Dworkin, 'Do we have a right to pornography?', in his *A Matter of Principle*, London, Harvard University Press, pp. 335–72.

30 See C. Mackinnon, op. cit.; A. Dworkin, *Pornography: Men Possessing Women*, London, Women's Press, 1981.

31 See chapters 7 and 8.

32 For examples of such injustice in the practice of English criminal justice, see C. Wells, 'Restatement or reform?', *Criminal Law Review*, 1986, p. 314; Box, *Power, Crime and Mystification*, op. cit.

33 On which, see chapter 8 on selective enforcement, pp. 192–3.

34 S. Atkins and B. Hoggett, *Women and the Law*, Oxford, Blackwell, 1984, pp. 124–46; K. McCann, 'Battered women and the law: the limits of the legislation', in C. Smart and J. Brophy, ed., *Women in Law*, p. 71; R. Dobash and R. Dobash, *Violence Against Wives*, London, Open Books, 1980; see also Metropolitan Police Report into domestic violence, reported in the *Observer*, 9 November 1986, and the *Guardian*, 10 November 1986.

35 See Box, op. cit.

36 The Home Office publishes Criminal Statistics annually, but these are not broken down in any very sophisticated way. For useful information and comment, see, for example, J. Braithwaite, *Inequality, Crime and Public Policy*, London, Routledge & Kegan Paul, 1979; R. Quinney, *Class, State and Crime*, 2nd edition, New York, Longman, 1980; M. Rutter and H. Giller, *Juvenile Delinquency – Trends and Perspectives*, Harmondsworth, Penguin, 1983, pp. 120–62.

37 See chapter 3, pp. 68–78.

38 T. Nagel, 'Moral luck', in his *Moral Questions*, Cambridge University press, 1979, p. 24.

39 B. Barry, *Political Argument*, op. cit., pp. 4–8, 35–38, 94–96, 286–91.

40 Supra, note 21.

41 J. Bentham, *Introduction to the Principles of Morals and Legislation*, London, Methuen, 1982, ed. J. Burns and H.L.A. Hart, pp. 156–64.

42 See chapter 3, pp. 59–61.

CHAPTER 6 POLITICAL OBLIGATION

1 J. Finnis, *Natural Law and Natural Rights*, Oxford University Press, 1980, pp. 352–62.

2 See the debate between Hart and Fuller: H.L.A. Hart, 'Positivism and the separation of law and morals'; L. Fuller, 'Positivism and fidelity to law – A reply to Professor Hart', *Harvard Law Review*, vol. 71, 1958, pp. 593, 630.

3 J. Raz, *The Authority of Law*, Oxford University Press, 1979, pp. 250–62; Raz, *The Morality of Freedom*, Oxford University Press, 1986, pp. 94–9.

4 J. Raz, *Practical Reason and Norms*, London, Hutchinson, 1975, pp. 35–84; Raz, 'Promises and obligations', in *Law, Morality and Society*, ed. P. Hacker and J. Raz, Oxford University Press, 1977, p. 210.

5 D.N. MacCormick, 'Law, obligation and consent: Reflections on Stair and Locke', in his *Legal Right and Social Democracy*, Oxford University Press, 1982, p. 60; J. Rawls, *A Theory of Justice*, Oxford University Press, 1971, pp. 333–62.

6 J.-J. Rousseau, *The Social Contract* (1762), trans. G.D.H. Cole, London, Dent, 1973; J. Locke, *Two Treatises of Civil Government* (1690), trans. W.S. Carpenter, London, Dent Everyman, 1924; T. Hobbes, *Leviathan*, ed. J. Plamenatz, London, Fontana, 1962, chs 26 and 30.

7   See H.L.A. Hart, 'Are there any natural rights?', *Philosophical Review*, vol. 64, 1964, p. 175; Hart's position is criticised by Robert Nozick in his *Anarchy, State and Utopia*, Oxford, Basil Blackwell, 1974, pp. 90–5.

8   See chapter 2, pp. 22–5; H. Morris, 'Persons and punishment', *The Monist*, vol. 52, 1968, p. 475.

9   See R. Dworkin, 'The original position'; T. Nagel, 'Rawls on justice', pp. 16, 1, in N. Daniels (ed.), *Reading Rawls*, Blackwell, Oxford, 1975; T. Honderich, *Violence for Equality*, Harmondsworth, Penguin, 1980, pp. 101–44, 173–9; M. Sandel, *Liberalism and the Limits of Justice*, Cambridge University Press, 1982, pp. 24–40, 104–32.

10 J. Rawls, 'Two concepts of rules', *Philosophical Review*, vol. 64, 1955, p. 3.

11 See chapter 2, pp. 49–53.

12 See Hart and Fuller, op. cit., note 2.

13 J. Raz, *The Authority of Law*, pp. 233–49; M.B.E. Smith, 'Is there a prima facie obligation to obey the law?', *Yale Law Journal*, vol. 82, 1973, p. 950.

14 E. Durkheim, *The Division of Labour in Society*, Glencoe, Free Press, 1960, ch. 2; D. Garland, 'Durkheim's theory of punishment: a critique', in Garland and P. Young, ed., *The Power to Punish*, London, Heinemann, 1983, p. 37.

15 See chapter 5, pp. 103–5; chapter 8, pp. 178–81.

16 J. Rawls, *A Theory of Justice*, op. cit., pp. 363–91, and his 'Justice as fairness: Political not metaphysical', *Philosophy and Public Affairs*, vol. 14, 1985, p. 223; see also R. Dworkin, *Taking Rights Seriously*, London, Duckworth, 1977, p. 206–22; *Law's Empire*, London, Fontana, 1986, pp. 190–224.

17 S. Box, *Power, Crime and Mystification*, London, Tavistock, 1983, pp. 1–15, 165–223; J. Braithwaite, *Inequality, Crime and Public Policy*, London, Routledge & Kegan Paul, 1979; *Police and Criminal Evidence Act 1984* section 25; A.K. Bottomley, *Decisions in the Penal Process*, Oxford, Martin Robertson, 1973, pp. 2–21, 37–73, 84–124.

18 Rawls, *A Theory of Justice*, op. cit., pp. 368–71, 377–82.

19 Raz, *Practical Reason and Norms*, op. cit., pp. 170–77; *The Morality of Freedom*, op. cit., pp. 94–9.

20 See N. Walker, *Sentencing: Theory, Law and Practice*, London, Butterworths, 1985, pp. 250–5.

21 See, for example, *Commission of the European Communities v United Kingdom* (1984) vol. 1, All England Law Reports, p. 353.

22 On the problems of controlling public power through judicial review, see C. Harlow and R. Rawlings, *Law and Administration*, London, Weidenfeld & Nicolson, 1984, chs. 1, 2 and 9.

CHAPTER 7 PUNISHMENT AND THE LIBERAL WORLD

1   See, for example, R. Dworkin, 'Liberalism', in S. Hampshire (ed.), *Public and Private Morality*, Cambridge University press, 1978,

p. 113; J. Raz, *The Morality of Freedom*, Oxford University Press, 1986, pp. 1–3, 16–19, 107–33 and passim; M. Sandel, *Liberalism and the Limits of Justice*, Cambridge University, 1982, pp. 1–28, 66–72, 113–22.

2 For example, R. Dworkin, 'Liberalism', op. cit., *Taking Rights Seriously*, London, Duckworth, 1977, and *Law's Empire*, London, Fontana, 1986; J. Rawls, *A Theory of Justice*, Oxford University Press, 1971; R. Nozick, *Anarchy, State and Utopia*, Oxford, Blackwell, 1974; B. Ackerman, *Social Justice in the Liberal State*, New Haven, Yale University Press, 1980.

3 I. Kant, *Foundations of the Metaphysic of Morals* in *Kant's Critique of Practical Reason and Other Works on the Theory of Ethics*, trans. T.K. Abbott, London, Longmans, 1873, 6th edition, 1909, pp. 46–64; R. Walker, *Kant*, London, Routledge & Kegan Paul, 1978, pp. 151–9; see J. Raz, op. cit., pp. 145–8.

4 R. Dworkin, 'Liberalism', op. cit.; *Taking Rights Seriously*, op. cit., pp. 180–3, 272–8.

5 H.L.A. Hart, *Punishment and Responsibility*, Oxford University Press, 1968, pp. 11–13, 21–4.

6 J. Bentham, *Introduction to the Principles of Morals and Legislation*, ed. J. Burns and H.L.A. Hart, London, Methuen, 1982, pp. 11–16, 38–41.

7 P. Singer, *Practical Ethics*, Cambridge University Press, 1979, pp. 14–47.

8 J. Locke, *Two Treatises of Government*, ed. P. Laslett, New York, Cambridge University Press, 1967; R. Nozick, *Anarchy, State and Utopia*, Oxford, Blakcwell, 1974, pp. 3–25.

9 For critical discussion, see A. Jaggar, *Feminist Politics and Human Nature*, Brighton, Harvester Press, 1983, pp. 27–48; M. Sandel, op. cit., pp. 1–65, 104–32; C. Taylor, *Philosophy and the Human Sciences*, Cambridge University Press, 1985, pp. 187–210.

10 See A. Jaggar, op. cit.; C. Taylor, op. cit., pp. 134–51.

11 R. Dworkin, *Law's Empire*, op. cit., pp. 151–224.

12 J. Rawls, op. cit., pp. 3–53, 118–92; see Raz, op. cit., pp. 110–33.

13 R. Dworkin, *Law's Empire*, op. cit., pp. 271–5.

14 J. Rawls, op. cit., pp. 118–92.

15 R. Dworkin, 'What is equality; Part 2: Equality of resources', *Philosophy and Public Affairs*, vol. 10, 1981, p. 283.

16 C. Taylor, op. cit., pp. 134–51.

17 See J.S. Mill, *On Liberty* (1859), Harmondsworth, Penguin, 1974; I. Berlin, *Four Essays on Liberty*, Oxford University Press, 1969; J. Raz, op. cit., pp. 1–19.

18 I. Berlin, 'Two concepts of liberty', in his *Four Essays on Liberty*, op. cit., pp. 118–72; see C. Taylor, op. cit., pp. 211–29.

19 J.S. Mill, op. cit., chs 1 and 3–5.

20 R. Dworkin, 'Liberalism', op. cit.

21 B. Ackerman, op. cit., pp. 10–30, 43–5, 327–48, 356–71.

22 J. Bentham, op. cit., pp. 38–51; his views on pushpin and poetry are

expounded in *The Works of Jeremy Bentham*, ed. J. Bowring, Edinburgh, W. Tait, 1843, volume 2, pp. 253–4.

23 See, for example, V. Haksar, *Equality, Liberty and Perfectionism*, Oxford University press, 1979; J. Raz, op. cit., pp. 110–62.

24 J. Raz, op. cit., pp. 111–33; J. Finnis, *Natural Law and Natural Rights*, Oxford University Press, 1980, pp. 221–6.

25 A. Jaggar, op. cit., pp. 34–5, 143–8.

26 See, for example, B. Ackerman, op. cit.; R. Dworkin, op. cit.; R. Nozick, op. cit.; J. Rawls, op. cit..

27 J.S. Mill, *Utilitarianism*, 1861, London, Collins, 1962, pp. 296–321; see A. Ryan, *The Philosophy of John Stuart Mill*, London, MacMillan, 1970, pp. 213–32; J. Gray, *Mill On Liberty – A Defence*, London, Routledge & Kegan Paul, 1983, pp. 25–8, 63–9.

28 H. Collins, *Marxism and Law*, Oxford University Press, 1982, pp. 47–52, 124–46.

29 R. Dworkin, *Taking Rights Seriously*, op. cit., pp. 81–130, 150–205, 266–79; R. Nozick, op. cit., pp. 26–53.

30 J. Bentham, *Anarchical Fallacies*, in *The Works of Jeremy Bentham*, vol. 2, ed. J. Bowring, Edinburgh, 1838, p. 491; see H.L.A. Hart, *Essays on Bentham*, Oxford University Press, 1982, pp. 79–104.

31 See R. Nozick, op. cit., pp. 26–53; J. Locke, op. cit.; R. Dworkin, *Taking Rights Seriously*, op. cit., pp. 266–78; C. Taylor, op. cit., pp. 187–210.

32 R. Dworkin, *Taking Rights Seriously*, op. cit., pp. 234–8, 275–8; see H.L.A. Hart, 'Between utility and rights', and R. Sartorius, 'Dworkin on rights and utilitarianism', in M. Cohen (ed.), *Ronald Dworkin and Contemporary Jurisprudence*, London, Duckworth, 1984, pp. 214, 205; see also Dworkin's reply, pp. 281–91.

33 R. Dworkin, 'Liberalism', op. cit.; see J. Raz, op. cit., pp. 217–44.

34 R. Dworkin, *Taking Rights Seriously*, op. cit., pp. 180–3, 272–8.

35 P. Singer, op. cit., pp. 14–47.

36 R. Dworkin, 'What is equality? Part 1: Equality of welfare', *Philosophy and Public Affairs*, vol. 10, 1981, p. 185; A. Sen, 'Utilitarianism and welfarism', *Journal of Philosophy*, vol. 76, 1979, p. 463.

37 Supra, note 6.

38 R. Dworkin, 'What is equality? Part 2: Equality of resources', op. cit., p. 283.

39 B. Williams, 'The idea of equality', in P. Laslett and W. Runciman (ed.), *Philosophy, Politics and Society*, Second Series, Oxford, Blackwell, 1972, p. 110.

40 P. Singer, op. cit., pp. 34–40; J. Rawls, op. cit., pp. 83–90.

41 J. Raz, op. cit., pp. 217–44.

42 A. Jaggar, op. cit., pp. 40–8, 186–98; H. Collins, op. cit., pp. 128–46.

43 H.L.A. Hart, *The Concept of Law*, Oxford University Press, 1961, pp. 151–63, 195–207.

44 See J. Finnis, op. cit., p. 270–90; L. Fuller, 'Positivism and fidelity to law: a reply to Professor Hart', vol. 71, *Harvard Law Review*,

1958, p. 630; J. Raz, *The Authority of Law*, Oxford University Press, 1979, pp. 210–29.

45　See R. Dworkin, 'What is equality? Part 1: equality of welfare', op. cit.; A. Sen, 'Utilitarianism and welfarism', op. cit.; J.J.C. Smart, 'An outline of a system of utilitarian ethics', in Smart and B. Williams, *Utilitarianism: For and Against*, Cambridge University press, 1973, pp. 3–30.

46　J. Rawls, op. cit., pp. 60–90.

47　R. Dworkin, *Taking Rights Seriously*, op. cit., pp. 150–240, 266–78.

48　J. Bentham, op. cit., pp. 282–3; see P. Singer, op. cit., pp. 48–71.

49　*Report of the Committee on Homosexual Offences and Prostitution*, Cmnd. 247, 1957, p. 24.

50　A. Jaggar, op. cit., pp. 34–5, 143–8.

51　S. Atkins and B. Hoggett, *Women and the Law*, Oxford, Blackwell, 1984, pp. 124–46; R. Dobash and R. Dobash, *Violence Against Wives*, London, Open Books, 1980.

52　M. Walzer, *Spheres of Justice*, Oxford, Blackwell, 1983, especially chapters 5, 6, 8–11.

53　See, for example, J. Finnis, op. cit., pp. 134–60.

54　See J. Raz, *The Morality of Freedom*, op. cit., pp. 267–87.

55　R. Dworkin, *Taking Rights Seriously*, op. cit.

56　H.L.A. Hart, *Punishment and Responsibility*, Oxford University Press, 1968, Ch. 1.

57　J. Raz, *The Morality of Freedom*, op. cit., pp. 321–68.

58　See J. Rawls, op. cit., pp. 40–46, 60–75.

59　H.L.A. Hart, *Punishment and Responsibility*, op. cit., pp. 11–13, 17–24; R. Nozick, *Anarchy, State and Utopia*, pp. 26–53.

60　See J. Rawls, op. cit., pp. 34–40, 315–32.

61　B. Barry, *Political Argument*, London, Routledge & Kegan Paul, 1965, pp. 4–8, 35–8, 94–6, 286–91.

62　J. Finnis, op. cit., pp. 260–6, 291; see also his 'The restoration of retribution', *Analysis*, vol. 32, 1972, p. 131.

63　J. Murphy, 'Marxism and retribution', vol. 2, *Philosophy and Public Affairs*, 1973, p. 217.

64　See chapter 2, pp. 18–27 and chapter 6.

65　See chapter 2, pp. 16–25, and T. Honderich, *Punishment: The Supposed Justifications*, revised edition, Harmondsworth, Penguin, 1984, pp. 212–41.

66　R.A. Duff, *Trials and Punishments*, Cambridge University Press, 1986, pp. 233–66.

67　For example, A. Von Hirsch, *Doing Justice*, New York, Hill & Wang, 1976.

68　See T. Honderich, op. cit., pp. 35–6, 177–81, 202–6, 238–41.

69　T. Honderich, op. cit., pp. 28–9, 231–41.

70　See, for example, A. Goldman, 'The paradox of punishment', *Philosophy and Public Affairs*, vol. 9, 1979, p. 42.

71　J. Rawls, op. cit., pp. 22–7; see also Raz's discussion in *The Morality of Freedom*, op. cit., pp. 271–87.

72　See chapter 2, pp. 37–41.

73   J. Bentham, *Introduction to the Principles of Morals and Legislation*, op. cit., p. 11.
74   See H.L.A. Hart, *Punishment and Responsibility*, op. cit., pp. 18–21, 40–50; J. Bentham, op. cit., pp. 161–2.
75   See J. Andenaes, *Punishment and Deterrence*, Ann Arbor, University of Michigan Press, 1974, pp. 3–84, 183–9; D. Beyleveld, *A Bibliography of General Deterrence Research*, Farnborough, Saxon House, 1980, pp. xv–xliii, 131–43; R. Hood and R. Sparks, *Key Issues in Criminology*, London, Weidenfeld & Nicolson, 1970, pp. 172–5.
76   J.S. Mill, *On Liberty*, op. cit.
77   J. Bentham, supra, note 22; J.S. Mill, *On Liberty*, op. cit., ch. 4.
78   J.S. Mill, *On Liberty*, ch. 2; J.J.C. Smart, op. cit., pp. 12–42; D. Lyons, *Forms and Limits of Utilitarianism*, Oxford University Press, 1965, pp. 8–17, 173–7; D. Hodgson, *Consequences of Utilitarianism*, Oxford University Press, 1967, pp. 32–7, 166–81.
79   D. Lyons, op. cit., pp. 119–60; chapter 2, pp. 49–53.
80   T. Honderich, '*On Liberty* and morality-dependent harms', *Political Studies*, vol. 30, 1982, p. 502.
81   'Between utility and rights', vol. 79, *Columbia Law Review*, 1979, p. 828; reprinted in Hart's *Essays in Jurisprudence and Philosophy*, Oxford University Press, 1983, p. 198.
82   See, for example,. M. Sandel, op. cit.; M. Walzer, op. cit..
83   See G. A. Cohen, 'Robert Nozick and Wilt Chamberlain – how patterns preserve liberty', *Erkenntnis*, vol. 11, 1977, pp. 5–23.
84   See A. Jaggar, op. cit., pp. 353–89; S. Harding and M. Hintikka (ed.), *Discovering Reality*, Dordrecht, Reidel, 1983.
85   See P. McAuslan and J. McEldowney (ed.) *Law, Legitimacy and the Constitution*, London, Sweet & Maxwell, 1985; I. Harden and N. Lewis, *The Noble Lie: The British Constitution and the Rule of Law*, London, Hutchinson, 1986, pp. 223–60.
86   M. Walzer, op. cit.; J. Raz, *The Morality of Freedom*, op. cit.; R. Dworkin, *Law's Empire*, op. cit., pp. 151–224.
87   See generally J. Paul (ed.), *Reading Nozick*, Oxford, Blackwell, 1982, Part IV, pp. 305–411.
88   See P. McAuslan, 'Administrative law, collective consumption and judicial policy,' *Modern Law Review*, vol. 46, 1983, p. 1; T. Prosser, 'Towards a critical public law', *Journal of Law and Society*, vol. 9, 1982, p. 1.
89   K. O'Donovan, *Sexual Divisions in Law*, London, Weidenfeld & Nicolson, 1985.
90   H.L.A. Hart, *Punishment and Responsibility*, op. cit., pp. 21–4.
91   R.A. Duff, op. cit., pp. 99–150.
92   See chapter 8, pp. 192–3.
93   T. Nagel, *Mortal Questions*, Cambridge University Press, 1979, p. 24–38.
94   See R.A. Duff, op. cit., pp. 233–46; J. Feinberg, 'The expressive function of punishment', in his *Doing and Deserving*, Princeton University Press, 1970, p. 95.

CHAPTER 8 PUNISHMENT AND COMMUNITY

1   J. Rawls, *A Theory of Justice*, Oxford University Press, 1972, pp. 245–8.

2   R. Bernstein, *Beyond Objectivism and Relativism*, Oxford, Blackwell, 1983, pp. 1–49.

3   Psychopathy is defined, in the *Shorter Oxford English Dictionary*, Supplement, Volume 3, ed. R.W. Burchfield, Oxford University Press, 1982, at p. 887: 'In modern use, a personality disorder . . . characterised by markedly impulsive, egocentric behaviour, and an inability to form normal relationships with others'.

4   For recent discussions of the notion of community in the context of political philosophy, see M. Sandel, *Liberalism and the Limits of Justice*, Cambridge University Press, 1982, pp. 59–65, 96–103, 147–83; M. Walzer, *Spheres of Justice*, Oxford, Blackwell, 1983, pp. 31–94, 227–42; R. Dworkin, *Law's Empire*, London, Fontana, 1986, pp. 164–71, 206–24, 400–10.

5   J. Raz, *The Morality of Freedom*, chs 10, 14, 15.

6   The nature of this process is clearly both complicated and not unproblematic; if we take a view which emphasises the deterministic element in both history and the (historical) social construction of human nature, we need an account of how, at some moments, human experience encompasses a vision beyond present social frameworks and facilitates an active struggle for social change, and in particular we need some account of the interplay between theory and practice. This issue has perhaps received most attention within the Marxist tradition: see H. Collins, *Marxism and Law*, Oxford University Press, 1982, pp. 4–7, 17–61.

7   See B. Barber, *Strong Democracy*, University of California Press, Berkeley and Los Angeles, 1984, pp. 117–311.

8   Barber, op. cit..

9   A.M. Honoré, 'Groups, laws and obedience', in A.W.B. Simpson (ed.), *Oxford Essays in Jurisprudence*, 2nd series, Oxford University Press, 1973, p. 1.

10 See J. Finnis, *Natural Law and Natural Rights*, Oxford University Press, 1980, pp. 11–18; D.N. MacCormick, *Legal Reasoning and Legal Theory*, Oxford University Press, 1978, pp. 285–92; see chapter 4, pp. 85–8.

11 W. Quinn, 'The right to threaten and the right to punish', *Philosophy and Public Affairs*, vol. 14, 1985, p. 327.

12 See chapter 6.

13 J. Raz, op. cit., pp. 94–9; Raz, *The Authority of Law*, Oxford University Press, 1979, pp. 250–61.

14 See, for example, Raz, *The Morality of Freedom*, op. cit.; J.S. Mill, *On Liberty*, 1859, Harmondsworth, Pelican, 1974; H.L.A. Hart, *Law, Liberty and Morality*, Oxford University Press, 1963; A. Sen, 'Well-being, agency and freedom: the Dewey Lectures, 1984', *Journal of Philosophy*, vol. 82, 1985, p. 169.

15 Raz, *The Morality of Freedom*, op. cit., pp. 154–7; 373–8.

16 B. Barry, *Political Argument*, London, Routledge & Kegan Paul,

1965, pp. 38–43; 173–90; R. Dworkin, 'What is equality?; Part 1: Equality of welfare', *Philosophy and Public Affairs*, vol. 10, 1981, p. 185; A. Sen, op. cit., pp. 183–203; Raz, *The Morality of Freedom*, op. cit., pp. 288–320.

17 A. Jaggar, *Feminist Politics and Human Nature*, Brighton, Harvester Press, 1983, pp. 15–21, 27–35, 39–48.

18 See chapter 5, pp. 109–11.

19 Quinn, op. cit.

20 Cf. H. Gross, *A Theory of Criminal Justice*, New York, Oxford University Press, 1979, pp. 375–412.

21 Cf. J. Finnis, op. cit., pp. 260–64; see also his 'The restoration of retribution', *Analysis*, vol. 32, 1972, p. 132.

22 A. Ashworth, *Sentencing and Penal Policy*, London, Weidenfeld & Nicolson, 1983, pp. 379–80.

23 See chapter 2, pp. 28–36, R. Hood and R. Sparks, *Key Issues in Criminology*, London, Weidenfeld & Nicolson, 1970, pp. 171–92.

24 See R.A. Duff, *Trials and Punishments*, Cambridge University Press, 1986, ch. 9.

25 H.L.A. Hart, *Punishment and Responsibility*, Oxford University Press, 1968, pp 8–11.

26 Duff, op. cit., pp. 151–64, 233–5.

27 Hart, op. cit., ch. 1; see chapter 2, pp. 49–53.

28 Rawls, op. cit., pp. 40–5, 243–51, 541–8.

29 Rawls, op. cit., pp. 152, 247–8, 542–3; see also H.L.A. Hart, 'Rawls on liberty and its priority', in N. Daniels (ed.), *Reading Rawls*, Blackwell, Oxford, 1975, p. 230.

30 See chapter 5, pp. 117–18; B. Barry, op. cit., pp. 4–8, 35–8, 94–96, 286–91.

31 Raz, *The Morality of Freedom*, op. cit., pp. 267–71.

32 See chapter 5, p. 119.

33 See chapter 6, pp. 131–41.

34 For an illuminating discussion of the significance of procedural safeguards, see Duff, op. cit., chs 1 and 4.

35 See chapter 5, pp. 113–17.

36 T. Nagel, 'Moral luck', in his *Moral Questions*, Cambridge University Press, 1979, p. 24; B. Williams, *Moral Luck*, Cambridge University Press, 1981, p. 20–39.

37 See S. Box, *Power, Crime and Mystification*, London, Tavistock, 1983; C. Wells, 'Restatement or reform?', *Criminal Law Review*, 1986, p. 314.

38 For a similar view, see T. Honderich, *Punishment, the Supposed Justifications*, Harmondsworth, Penguin, 1984, pp. 237–41.

39 See Duff, op. cit., pp. 151–64.

INDEX